Theory of the Artificial

Virtual Replications and the Revenge of Reality*

Massimo Negrotti

intellect™

Exeter, England

*including 'Artistic communication and the artificial' by Danila Bertasio

First Published in 1999 by
Intellect Books
School of Art and Design, Earl Richards Road North, Exeter EX2 6AS

Consulting Editor:	Masoud Yazdani
Copy Editor:	Wendi Momen
Cover Design:	Sam Robinson
Production:	Julie Strudwick
	Anne Rösler

A catalogue record for this book is available from the British Library

ISBN 1-871516-55-2

Acknowledgements

I wish to express my appreciation to the many colleagues and friends listed below who read and criticized parts of the manuscripts or related papers. Each provided expert advice that greatly enhanced the final product: Denis Baggi, Parthasarathi Banerjiee, Danila Bertasio, Federico Braga, Aldo Celeschi, Roberto Cordeschi, Domenico Donnanno, Hubert L. Dreyfus, Michele Federico, Karamjit and Satinder Gill, Willem Kolff, Giuseppe Longo, Lars Qvortrup, Giorgio Marchetti, Vittorio Marchis, Giovanni Messori, Sabrina Moretti, Ephraim Nissan, Giuseppe Padovani, Mario Pascocci, Michela Pereira, Giorgio Sacchi, Fumihiko Satofuka, John R. Searle, Marco Somalvico, Franco Zambelloni, Romano Zanni.

The following journals have my sincere thanks for having published various versions of the theory of the artificial: Prometeo, Cybernetics & Human Knowing, Scienza & Vita, Sistemi e Impresa, Prometheus, AI & Society, Lo Spettacolo, Nuova Civiltá delle Macchine, Sapere, Technology Review.

Several parts of the research were financially supported by the Italian Ministry for the Scientific and Technological Research (MURST) and by the University of Urbino.

Printed and bound in Great Britain by Cromwell Press, Wiltshire

Contents

Introduction

1. The instinct to reproduce the world

Though it will be defined and explained more deeply in the next pages, the concept of artificial, as adopted in this book, needs some starting specification. In our approach, artificial does not mean something purely man-made or, even less, something unnatural. In our use, the term artificial will refer to any object, process or machine which aims to reproduce some pre-existing natural object or process by means of different materials and procedures.

Actually, this meaning is not an arbitrary one: much of the historical use of the term artificial is consistent with our own. Examples range from the artificial perspective introduced in the Renaissance painting to current artificial heart technology; from the artificial rainbow imagined by Bacon to today's artificial life projects. In fact, in all these instances – and in the several others which adopt the term in this sense – the artificial object is surely designed and built by man, but it is also conceptually and functionally very close to nature as a reality which man tries to imitate rather than simply to control or to modify.

Where the latter case is concerned, other classes of objects, processes or machines have to be considered in the technological tradition, that is to say, all the ones which do not aim at reproducing natural instances, and which, therefore, come merely from 'technological reason', or the ability of man to invent something which is new and unexperienced.

On the other hand, the concept of artificial (objects, processes or machines), once it is carefully theorized, will reveal itself as one of the many possible ways of describing the relationship between man and the world. At a general level, it plays the same role as the concept of knowledge plays in philosophical research or within a critical study of science. The difference between these concepts lies in their conception of man. The concept of the artificial involves an account of man as an agent who acts upon the real in order to reproduce it, whereas the concept of knowledge involves an account of man as a knowing entity.

We are here not simply renewing the idea of man as a generic Homo faber. Rather, by considering the broad range of human activity, we seek to investigate the whole of cultural and logical features which aim at reproducing the reality in which man is involved. Although the dispositions to know and to change the world by means of technology are highly important issues, we should not forget that the disposition to imitate, to mimic, to copy, to simulate, in a word to reproduce the world, is also a human disposition which is not as widely studied as the former two.

It is easy to understand that to know, to produce and to reproduce are intrinsically different activities which denote different attitudes towards the real world. For instance, it is possible to know, or try to know, the reality without having any intention of changing it, as for example, in the case of the Greek speculative tradition. On the other hand, it is quite possible to change the reality whilst ignoring its nature or having little knowledge of it. This presumably was the case for primitive man and it is the case again today, evident when we try to modify something based on a naïve understanding. But a further and different issue is the attempt to reproduce existing things or events, although this seems to require both some knowledge (about the object we want to reproduce) and an attitude and ability to change the reality.

For this reason, the artificial is arguably related to technology in the same way as Icarus, or rather his wings, are related to his father, Daedalus: the art of constructing, or the ability to modify, nature becomes the art of reproducing it or, rather, the attempt to reproduce it.

This would seem to elevate the field of the artificial to a stage higher than that of the knowing and producing activities, which are conceived as those stages which provide the basis for reproducing reality. However, what actually occurs differs from this as, even here, a number of cases demonstrate that man's disposition to reproduce reality is too strong and permanent to allow for an ordered, cumulative, step-by-step strategy. In other words, the disposition to the 'artificial' is a strong one and often, as in Icarus's case, man tries to achieve artificial projects without any well-founded knowledge or well-tested technology.

This presumably means, as we have maintained above, that the disposition to reproduce is a key one and that its function is not limited to achieving historically well-known technological attempts. Perhaps, the human need to reproduce reality, the world's external or internal nature, is man's way of confirming to himself his own identity and his own consciousness, and perhaps is an extension of his instinct to self-reproduce.

Considered in these terms, the issue of the disposition towards the artificial becomes a crucial theme, not only from an anthropological point of view, but also from an epistemological one. In dealing with the relationship between man and reality, we cannot avoid declaring the sense in which we shall consider this relationship and its features, as we shall now proceed to do.

2. The 'reality of the world' as a problem

This work is based on a general epistemological understanding in which reality can be conceived as being both objective and relative. Reality is objective in the sense that our interactions with it, both in terms of information or perception inputs and energy outputs, openly demonstrate that there is something in the world which exists independently of our mind, with a life of its own. The external world, in this sense, does not suffer a lesser dignity compared to our mind. In other words, to say that nature is objective means that it lives according to its own models and not according to ours. Consequently, the problem for us is how to understand nature and the limits within which understanding is possible.

This does not imply taking a position which rejects the creative contribution of the human mind in depicting the world. On the contrary, as we shall see, we are persuaded that the only means we have at our disposal for knowing reality are our own mental categories. Nevertheless, the mental 'constructions', the means by which we relate to reality, could not survive if they were completely arbitrary images. When this seems to be the case, as in numerous human beliefs or in non-rational attitudes, this is made possible by the replacement of nature by culture: what does not exist in nature is often given legitimacy for its existence by our cultural models and in this way it can survive. On the other hand, beliefs and non-rational attitudes often decline because the scientific successes attained by relating to reality exhibit a more powerful compatibility with reality itself.

Reality is also relative because every effort we make to understand it will result in a selection of observation levels per unit of time and, hence, in a loss of richness which prevents us from capturing it as a whole. Our knowledge of nature is always related to some observation level – or system – but, at the same time, it can also be considered to be objective since the assumed observation level is not necessarily beyond reality: it is inside the reality, although it is a reduced form of it.

The selected observation level is not a 'part' of reality: it is the reality which is 'visible' at that level, interacting with us through the kind and the amount of sensitivity of our sensors. Since we cannot imagine a human being lacking some kind of sensors, we have to accept the idea that what we observe is the result of something that exists in the external world and is transduced into some image in order to be compatible with our physical capacities.

Questions such as 'what is reality in and of itself' have no meaning in the context of this work. The reality we refer to is the reality we can potentially or actually perceive, and not its ontology. We refer, in other words, to the reality about which we are able to make some shared judgements, based upon some shared empirical criteria. In this sense, the concept of objectivity does not necessarily overlap with that of truth: while the former fully depends on the observation levels available to our physiological structure, the latter belongs to the world of ontology rather than to science.

We also have to take into account a different discussion about reality, namely the 'construction of reality', which is fashionable today, particularly in the human and social sciences, following the classic study by Berger and Luckmann (1966). The core of this school of thought can be summarised as follows:

> social constructionist theories. . . argue that people categorize the world the way they do because they have participated in social practices, institutions and other forms of symbolic action. . . that presuppose or in some way make salient those categories.
>
> (Shweder, 1991)

We cannot deny that, in certain kinds of circumstances, the concepts we use do not derive from empirical evidence but, rather, from a shared cultural normativity whose acceptance is intrinsic to our social involvement. Our conception of reality as objective, and at the same time relative to some system we belong to, may be understood as a case of social or cultural construction. This, however, would be true, by definition, for any epistemology, including the constructivist one.

This point is well-known in the sociological analysis of science: according to Merton (1981), sociologists should be aware that, when they deal with science as a social construction process, they are doing science. Thus, it is a very obscure matter to understand how or what gives the sociologists of science the capacity to do their own science with a larger knowledge power than the scientists they study. In these terms, the question of social construction of science becomes a true and useless *petitio principii*. This argument also applies to the so-called social construction of technology (Woolgar, 1991) which, since the Eighties, has grown beside the established social construction of science.

Since no human being is able to live without *Weltanschauungen*, a 'view-about-the-word' will accompany every society in every historical period. Scientists also base their work on some *Weltanschauung* in which they trust, not because they are scientists but because they live in a certain culture: in a sense, we could speak of pre-paradigms when we refer to the cultural premises of the normal scientific paradigms. To be effective, a study of these pre-paradigms cannot be undertaken by applying the same scientific criteria involved in ordinary paradigms: this strategy would clearly be self-referential.

Though these problems are very interesting in their own right, they are beyond the aims of this book. Within our frame, we think that the human mind re-elaborates, or reconstructs, reality according to some psychological or cultural rules, attributing to it features that it does not always have. On the other hand, the attribution of human features to reality, though it is a quite frequent and perhaps 'natural' activity, does not prevent nature from imposing, gradually or suddenly, its own existence and its own rules. As far as the problem of the objectivity of science is concerned, I shall limit myself to arguing that the social construction of reality is a fact, like its objectivity (in the sense outlined above), according to different circumstances and situations: that is, according to a *continuum* of situations. The crucial point is that the concept of objectivity does not always overlap that of truth and, in the same manner, the concept of construction does not overlap that of falsehood.

An objective observation can be false, for instance, because of the intrinsic and unknown unreliability of the instrument of measure or due to some shared but wrong survey criterion, just as a socially constructed belief could be true when, for instance, human beings unconsciously perceive the physical dimensions which, for example, induce them to fear some real recurrent phenomena and to refer to them by means of some constructed image.

The *continuum* which lies between the two ideal extremes of truth and falsehood, in a non-formal understanding, is wider than that linking objectivity and subjectivity, or objectivity and social construction.

Thus, the main topic of this book, namely the artificial, will be treated as if the above sketched problems and solutions were correct. In other words, we study the behaviour of man, both as an entity interacting with the world having the possibility to observe something real, and as an entity which constructs what he will see in his own mind. The spectrum of these possibilities ranges between two new ideal extremes: on the one side reality as a quite real and objective substance and, on the other, reality as a total construction, either individual or social.

This is a key point in dealing with the artificial, because the first premise of our theory is as follows: the artificialist, that is every man, makes artificial things by taking something which exists in nature as an *exemplar*: that something which man perceives or thinks as reality. In other words, we are not so much interested in a discussion of what happens in our mind, and in our cultures, *prior* to our forming some representation of the real world: rather, we are concerned with what happens *after* this, when man tries to reproduce the reality he has modelled in his own mind.

To summarise, the fact that sometimes human representations appear to be compatible with the real world and sometimes reveal, *a posteriori*, their constructed nature, is only relevant as an epistemological constraint to human efforts to observe the world as it is, and not to human attempts to reproduce the world according to those representations.

As it happens in science, the failure of an artificial enterprise will consist in a discrepancy between what we expect from the artificial device as compared to what we get from the natural object that the artificial claims to reproduce. If we are persuaded that a natural phenomenon behaves in a certain way and we get from the artificial device just that behaviour, then we could conclude that we were successful in reproducing that phenomenon.

This could be a trap, since we could have reproduced a reality which only exists in our mind. But this is an unavoidable risk: we have no possibility, following in some way Gödel's theorem, to justify beforehand the results of our research or the outcomes of our attempts to reproduce reality, that is to say, to make the artificial. We can only swing between the external reality and the categories of our mind, making decisions on the world and performing concrete actions. In so doing, it happens sometimes that any new achievements, perhaps for their intrinsic greater compatibility with the world, change our cultural models and, therefore, the way we evaluate future achievements.

3. The reality of the artificial

The problem we have before us is mainly to define a class of actions within which human beings seem to be oriented to take the reality of the world as given and try to re-build it in the same terms by which they observe and describe it, but following different strategies as compared to those nature follows.

The concept of the artificial needs to be studied both as a class of empirical objects and as an analytical category. However, we need first to define, in a sufficiently shared way, the criteria or means by which we establish when, and under which conditions, something is 'authentically artificial'.

Man's technological activity does not constitute a unique and indistinct whole. Some areas of technology, from the primitive to the present, show a strong propensity towards the reproduction of natural entities while others seem to develop according to original lines, true 'creations' of technological reason.

If this is plausible, then we must, necessarily, find some dimension, underlying technology, that we could call anthropological, in which the technological motivations assume different meanings from each other.

We can imagine this dimension as being characterised, at one extreme, by the disposition to invent *ex novo*, to use Tarde's phrase (French sociologist Gabriel Tarde, cfr. 1890) and, at the other extreme, by the disposition to imitate something that already exists.

Neither of these dispositions induce only technological behaviours. In fact, the disposition to invent is related to all activities that generate originality (for example, theories, ideas and several classes of machines). The disposition to imitate aims at reproducing existing entities, not only natural objects, but also psychic and social objects (representations, repertoires of action and also some classes of machines). Both dispositions play a role that, as for every material culture (see Mukerji, 1994) is economic: slight in the first case and significant in the second. However, both dispositions are manifestations of 'human nature'. They seem to characterise our species, in any bio-cultural sense: invariants or evolutionary universals, or anything else.

The theoretical proposals contained in this work deal, in particular, with the latter attitude, which we will term 'artificialistic', but the disposition to invent plays more than a purely residual role. It weaves constantly with artificialism for the simple fact that the artificial, throughout man's technological and non-technological spectrum, has only been achieved through the invention of some expedient – technique, material or language – whose nature is always heterogeneous as compared to the object to be reproduced.

On the contrary, when man can exploit the same 'matter' and follow the same procedures that characterise the object to be reproduced, we can no longer speak of the artificial but, rather, of imitation or, at the highest level, of replication.

Artificialism, then, exhibits a paradoxical character that, presumably, is consistent with the paradox implicit in our human condition: when man tries to reproduce something which exists in nature, he is constrained to transfigure the object of reproduction through the unavoidable contribution of his own reason, selections, inventions and also of the materials he uses.

Within this perspective it is possible to locate not only many types of technologies but science and art. The latter is treated in the last chapter of this book, with richly persuasive references of a theoretical and empirical nature, by Danila Bertasio.

The inexorable destiny of the artificial places it in a necessary oscillation between the inseparable wholeness of reality and the selective and inventive attitude of human reason. We would like to demonstrate that the ambition to replicate reality as it is or, sometimes, as we believe it is, i.e. objects, systems, images, ideas or feelings, is a process that, if satisfied, would simultaneously destroy the artificial, communication as we know it, as well as art and science.

Instead of having abilities to replicate, only available to human beings in some particular cases, man is given a reproductive intentionality: a disposition which is unavoidable and constitutive of his nature, of his technology, of his art and of his communication, activities that are, just for this reason, very rich in ambiguity and, therefore, in cultural variety.

Communication, for example, is obtained through a transduction process which is made possible by some shared semiological or symbolic system. Such a system is clearly artificial since it refers to something different from itself, as underlined in the philosophical tradition which traces its origins, at least, to Hegel and Cassirer.

In turn, art perhaps is able to further transform the object of reproduction, thereby adding a higher level of heterogeneity, i.e. some rules of style, or poetics, to the usual transfiguration involved in every process of communication.

On the other hand, the use of languages, machines, expedients, materials, which in this book are called 'conventional technology', which are invented and heterogeneous compared to the objects to be reproduced, always makes the artificial somewhat unpredictable yet characterised by a status of its own. It has a sort of 'life' whose complexity appears, in principle, to be neither lower nor greater compared to the object to be reproduced and is at times not reducible. After all, the artificial object is something real and reality does not consist in regions which are more or less dense in potential observation levels. This means that even if the artificial object is built simply to reduce the complexity of something real, it embodies all the features of the 'matter' it is made of or with which it interacts. Our hope to reproduce 'what is essentially relevant' in the existing reality, whether outside or inside us, is always weakened by our choices and our technology: just as in science, when our hypotheses are 'bets' upon a reality which remains a whole in itself, despite our attempt to grasp what is essential.

At the end, the 'nature of the artificial', as every other reality built by human reason, is something intrinsically rich, at least, as much as the object of reproduction: this is true of technology and of communication, music, theatre and painting.

Thus, we think that there is enough reason for considering the field of the artificial a very promising one. It has been reinvigorated by some recent achievements in advanced technologies, ranging from artificial intelligence to virtual reality, which promise to clarify those dimensions of man that are only partly explained by human sciences and almost neglected by technologists, communication experts and artists who see themselves in narrow areas, often making it impossible to capture the aspects common to different phenomenologies.

1. The place of the artificial

1. Drawing exemplars from the world

Let us consider the following possible experiment. In a classroom, 20 children have been given some plastic material along with some suitable tools for manipulating it. The teacher invites them, to 'build an object of your choice' without any further explanation. Furthermore, let us suppose that in the room, in addition to benches, chairs and a blackboard, there are also some flowering plants, and, on the desk, some other objects such as a hammer, a skull, some potatoes and apples. Through the window the children can see mountains, houses, the sun and a lot of trees.

After two hours, what kind of objects might we observe on the children's benches? We can predict that about 90 per cent of the children (the 'reproducers') will have tried to reproduce some of the objects they have seen around them, while the other 10 per cent (the 'inventors') will have produced something unrecognizable, using their imagination. A more accurate analysis, will reveal:

1. The objects built by the 'reproducers' involve many 'novelties' compared to the original objects (it is well-known that children often give interesting explanations, often incomprehensible to adults, when questioned on the meaning of their free constructions);
2. The objects built by the 'inventors' involve partial aspects or components from the environment around the children, although these are intentionally highly transfigured.

A second version of the experiment could be set up in the same way as the previous one, except that now the room is empty, apart from the children themselves, of course. The results will differ very little: 90 per cent of the children will build recognizable objects, drawing their form and appearance from their memory of the common experience, while the other 10 per cent will produce imaginary objects.

The main thesis of this book is that, as an anthropological rule, human beings possess both the above dispositions, namely that which aims to reproduce the world, reproducing exemplars drawn from the world, and that which aims to invent something new, i.e. something which has no known exemplar. Nevertheless, the former disposition, based on a general tendency to imitate, is more commonly found, both in terms of daily life or life cycle and of cultural evolution.

It is clear from the introduction above and the pages that follow, that certain concepts play a key role: reproduction, invention, representation and the concept of observation, which underlies everything.

These four concepts constitute the core of a significant part of an ancient epistemological and scientific debate, as well as of the most recent controversy in human sciences. I support the thesis that the term 'artificial' and a theory of it could help us to understand, from a unified point of view, the relationship among these concepts in the same moment in which we understand more accurately the intrinsic differences we can find inside the process to design and then to build physical objects and machines.

2. Representing the world

In a sense, everything we do depends on how we represent the world around us, including the conceptual separation of body from mind, and how our actions cause changes in the world. This is why we can conceive a representation based process as a process of building objects. Generally speaking, every object we plan to make is a reproduction of the representation of it in our mind and of the steps we think are necessary to accomplish our task. However, the concrete process of constructing it may, and usually does, introduce several changes in the original idea. The representational system adopted by the subject gives meaning to his action and this meaning may evolve during the problem solving process (cfr. Leiser, Cellèrier and Ducret, 1976).

The representation process implies that the subject conceives and perceives the external world as a separate reality, although he may easily understand that this is simply a useful convention.

Since Aristotle philosophers have viewed representations as having an intermediate role between sensation and conceptualisation. According to Aristotle, a representation not only describes the thing that it refers to, but is also an intentional act which allows us to make present the things that are the absent.

Whereas in the Middle Ages philosophy reduced representation to a sign, the lively debate on the concept was sparked by Descartes. For the first time he introduced a property, according to which a representation is a mental fact which at the same time refers to the reality of the thing represented.

This sort of dualism, as we have maintained above, is somewhat unavoidable if one is to speak of representation. It actually was given a deeper foundation by Hegel, who gave it the character of being both an intermediate function between sensation and conceptualisation and having the possibility to be actively generated by the mind. This point of view was emphasised by phenomenologists, who maintained that the representational process is the only way we have at our disposal to 'give sense' to things.

In any case, no philosopher would deny that a natural world exists: the philosophical debate concentrates on how the human mind interacts with it. On the one hand, the empiricist or the positivist would underline the capacity of natural objects to impose their own presence and features upon the human mind, through the process of observation. On the other hand, the idealist and, to a greater degree, the phenomenologist, would claim that the sensation of natural objects is less important than the creative capacity of the mind. In both cases the world is viewed as a reality in itself but, in positivism, it is possible to understand the world simply by observing its features: this is a false problem for the phenomenologist, since sensation within the world depends on our mind. The fact is that assigning supremacy either to the world or to the mind is a false problem. Kant tried to demonstrate, on philosophical grounds, that experience and intellect have a distinct but equal power in the formation of representations and in the process of knowledge.

The Kantian revolution gave the mind a power of its own and to the world a dignity of its own. If we accept the idea that the 'substance' of things is beyond the power of the human mind, and that the human mind has its own tools to understand the things at a phenomenal level, then we should conclude that representations play this intermediate role in knowing whatever stuff, structure and dynamics they are made of. In other words, a solution to dualism does not require the supremacy of either pole.

Such a solution is necessarily the foundation of a methodological bridge which allows human beings to grasp the world at levels compatible with their own mental tools. Compatibility does not guarantee the objectivity of our knowledge, which would require that the essence or substance of objects be captured. The compatibility between the mind and the world will only allow a variable degree of agreement among human beings on the state of affairs in the world at the observation levels consistent with their nature.

Of course, within our mental tools there exists a fundamental human disposition – symbolism – which is also deeply related to the representational process. At a cultural level, it is quite apparent that our knowledge systems have developed in a symbolic form and not within a growing 'intelligence', *stricto sensu*, of the substance of the world.

At the cultural level, as Cassirer maintained, the symbols which human beings generate set up systems whose development goes beyond the natural data and tend to live their own life. This is true, for example, of mathematical and logical systems, the theoretical sciences and even of musical systems. If the complexity and the heterogeneity of our contemporary symbolic systems enable a more effective control of natural phenomena, as in science, the methodology we found for solving or, better to say, for bridging the dualism in which we are involved, is a good one but only and always at the levels and with the constraints of our own mental configuration, on the one side, and depending on the 'nature of nature' on the other.

Psychology deals with representations, both in terms of their empirically verifiable features and at a theoretical level. The psychologist's concept of representation, at the theoretical level, is similar to the classical philosophical one. For instance, Denis (1989) defines representations as the production of

> symbols having as characteristics that of holding for other entities. Human beings are producers of symbols. They create representations, materials objects which function like other objects. Even the human mind supports representations of psychological stuff, cognitive products which reflect what the individual holds of his interactions with the world.
>
> (Denis, 1989)

Generally speaking, representations are seen to lie at the heart of thinking activity, or, in other words, of the generation and explanation of cognition and its status, without requiring a relevant relationship between symbols and the external world. Fodor (1987) introduced the representational theory of mind (RTM) saying that:

> Mental processes are causal sequences of occurrences of mental representations. . . A thought sequence, for example, is a causal sequence of occurrences of mental representations, that express the propositions, that are the objects of the thought.
>
> (Fodor, 1987, see also Silvers, 1989)

In making representations the basic objects of thought, the activity of thinking is reduced to causal syntax between propositions which bear the representations. Representation may acquire too central a role in thought and it apparently is unable to account for a large class of mental processes, such as invention or creativity. On the other hand, far from being simply a weakness of the concept of representation in itself, it is the cognitive psychology that is unable to describe and to explain the several aspects of being human. We could say that it is the 'central ring' in a chain which links us to the world and the best that we can do is to accept this in an heuristic way: i. e. without making unreasonable demands in trying to unravel it.

3. Constructing the world

Within the tradition of psychology and 'philosophy of mind', representation is a central idea, as both of these fields try to avoid a metaphysics of sensations and concepts. Nevertheless, in saying that representations are an important mental function, we would not want to say that the life of the mind totally revolves around representations; rather, without representations, or something similar, we could not relate to the world: we could not, in fact, act basing our actions solely on immediate sensations or on abstract concepts.

In the case of sensations, we would act according to a stimulus / reaction model which is more suitable for depicting the behaviour of animal or plants and, in the case of abstract concepts, we would act according to a solipsistic model, which would imply a total closing to the world.

In fact, we can have representations of whatever we want, including, of course, sensations and concepts, but their main feature is to fix the world's events in our minds in a non-abstract way, including that of our mind itself. Concepts, meanwhile, generalise the events by a process of abstraction.

It has rightly been remarked that even with regard to the problem of meaning,

> Beyond the various interpretations given to the representations and to the concepts, we may consider with Vergnaud the meaning as the concept and the significant as the representation of the concept itself.
>
> (Braga, 1996)

The idea that representations play a key role in relating the human mind to the world does not imply that the mind radically 'constructs' the world. Rather, if we take the dualism between the world and the mind as a human condition, and see representations as a sort of mental interface between them, then we could allow the world to enter the mind just at the moment that the mind enters the world. Representations, in other words, are structures and processes that are marked by this dualism: they unavoidably bear the nature of the world and of the mind and are the result of a natural methodology which is able to match, in order to adapt, the man to his environment.

The world's events enter the mind through channels which are compatible with it and, in the same way, the mind processes the events in the world in ways that derive from its nature and from its individual and species history, including the cultural.

As far as the whole problem of knowledge is concerned, we cannot assign any particular role to representations, as they have no theoretical power, although they hold the 'material' of both the internal and external experience, waiting, sometimes, to be processed at a higher level.

This position does not match the views of constructivism, according to which the human mind does not observe the world at all: rather, it constructs the world according to subjective or cultural rules. As a consequence, representation, either as a process or a structure, becomes nothing more than an active construction of the mind, whose reference to the world is quite illusory:

> As an experiencing organism, I have no doubt that I am contained in a world; but that my experience is 'of' that world is not something I can be sure of. The only world I know is the world I am patching together from bits of experience. I am in no position to say anything about that 'outer' world, because my concepts and the words I use to talk about them are all derived from my experience. Whatever is the 'object of experience', i.e., its cause (if there is such a thing), can obviously not be described in terms that invariably refer to its effect.
>
> (von Glaserfeld, 1993)

Constructivism places too great an emphasis on the concept of cybernetic loop and loses, in the end, any capacity to explain what happens both in the world and in our mind. On the one hand, it correctly describes the epistemological constraints which characterise the process of knowing as largely reflexive, since it is clear that the world is not an entity that is fully separated from our mind and vice versa. But it gives a paradoxical power to the mind in constructing the world just at the moment that the mind itself is viewed being able only to describe the world by means of the experiences coming from it. In the same time, this position destroys the solipsism and the objectivism, without at all saying what remains.

On the one hand, this kind of constructivism neglects both the capacity of the human mind and the external world to break the loop, thereby giving power back to the concept of cause. For instance, in some circumstances the human mind and the world act as if they could 'take the initiative', cutting their reciprocal linkage or the continuity that includes them. Such circumstances are to be found in the process of abstraction within the mental system, which enables creative imaginings, visions and acts, as happens in mathematical, logical or even musical thought and in several aspects of theoretical scientific thinking.

On the other hand, a symmetric process occurs when nature acts upon us with such strength, that is to say with such a pressure on one of our senses, that it forces our mind to pay attention only to the experiences involved, whatever our constructive attitude might be and whatever words we might adopt for describing it.

In a sense, constructivism seems to be more fated to a metaphysical outcome than the positivism it fights: actually, according to the constructivist point of view, the world exists but we cannot know it since we cannot stand outside of it. Thus, the world is a reality destined to remain ontologically separated from us just at the moment we recognise our link to it.

By setting the intrinsic target of the knowing process in such ontological terms constructivists can easily demonstrate the impossibility of knowledge being objective.

We might also remember that, in the systemic tradition, the reality of the world is often totally denied. Take Bateson, who maintains that the importance of the reality

> must be denied not only to the sound of the tree which falls unheard in the forest but also to the chair that I can see and on which I may sit.
>
> (Bateson, 1972)

As is well known, this position claims a communication based understanding of the world, whereby the only reality is our ideas which become messages that we believe as if they were a true description of the world. At the end, all of these positions seem either to be afraid of reality and its hard ontology, or else are excited by the power of the human mind and its close self-reference.

We cannot decide if and what happens in the forest but, in principle, if we were to be equipped with a much more powerful and large spectrum of sensory organs, we might notice many more events in all forests and elsewhere: actually, if this power were infinite, we would be totally immersed in the reality and, in a sense, we would coincide with it without having any possibility to describe it. But there is no reason to think that, having to deal with a finite, limited and filtering sensory power, reality should disappear from our horizon. Rather, paraphrasing Niklas Luhmann's thought, it is likely that, thanks to the limitations and the selectivity of our sense organs, we can really know something of the world. Furthermore, the human mind has its own tools, namely deduction and induction abilities, to 'hear' nature even in the absence of sensory stimulus. For instance when, standing on a hill, we observe a car in the valley below, we cannot hear the noise of its engine but we know that is very likely to be making some.

4. Interacting with the world

Within this work, we hold that the concept of knowing does not aim at capturing the whole reality nor at defining knowledge as an *a priori* construction of the mind.

Rather, we define the process of knowing as an interaction through which the mind generates representations that are more or less creative images of those contours of the world which are compatible with our sensory capacities, that is to say at different, selected observation levels per unit of time. In other words, representations are mental constructs whose consistency with the world depends, according to different psychological or social circumstances, on the strength of our subjectivity, or cultural models, or the world.

For instance, we cannot say that the peaceful appearance of a silent and clean room is an objective reality: in fact, it is only possible to adopt a human-based observation level, because at another level the room could be described as a stormy one, owing to the clash of billions of ions, the invasion of electromagnetic flows and so on. But, at the same time, to consider the room as being peaceful 'works fine', not only in a pragmatic sense but also as an accurate description of the contour of the reality we can grasp.

Sometimes biologists define the environment as being that set of the world's dimensions to which an organism can be sensitive. This is a very clear definition of reality, for any species, and of what is meant by the concept of observation levels. The existence of many alternative observation levels, according to any species and their variable selections, does not mean that we cannot know the reality in itself. Rather, reality includes, that is to say, it has in itself, all the features observable by all the species, along with infinite others which cannot be observed by any species and which are sometimes revealed through investigations using scientific instruments.

As we shall see later, what we can grasp is not 'a part' of reality: it is the reality compatible with our perception tools, and its representations depend upon both our mental categories and on the world phenomena.

Furthermore, we should not forget that, while our perceptual abilities are limited in their range, the effects that the world has on us come – thanks to a sort of principle of inheritance, which we shall define in the following chapters – from a much wider spectrum. Thus, a system which is unable to detect radioactivity is not un-harmed by it.

In its turn, social constructivism claims that even the growth of scientific concepts and theories is supposed to be socially constructed: by means of negotiations and other bargaining acts among scientists rather than through a pure intellectual process based on empirical evidence, as the traditional conception of science would maintain. Latour and Woolgar (1979) seem to be its most radical proponents, when they emphasize that scientific knowledge is socially conditioned and its development is, from the very beginning, built upon the basis of microsocial processes. As it has been remarked,

> The password of radical constructivism seems to be: nothing precedes the process of social negotiation.
>
> (Ancarani, 1996)

Apart from the evident purpose of this kind of study to 'demystify', the social determination of science implies a further step compared to mental constructivism. While the latter means to over amplify the capacity of the human mind to depict the reality or the inputs coming from it, the former absorbs even the autonomous role of the mind in a social context of reciprocal and undefined causation in which, nobody really seems to be responsible for anything.

Such views are mistaken in a way that can be viewed as a strong realistic or empiricist view when it seems to maintain that a representation is a sort of imprint of the world. Piaget has prudently underlined that:

> knowledge cannot be conceived as pre-determined nor by internal structures of the subject – since they result from an actual and continuous construction – nor by the pre-existing features of the object, since they aren't known but thanks the necessary mediation of those structures, enrich them framing them.
>
> (Piaget, 1972)

5. The world and the mind: representation as interface

For the aims of this book, representations will be defined as original objects that human beings consciuously have in their mind when they relate to the world, that is, at each moment of their life. In other words, the world lives in our mind in representations and the mind then builds up models of the world based on these, waiting for any changes owing to feedback from the reality and from new theoretical criteria.

In this sense, because of the mind's active role in building up representations and because of the complexity of the world itself, the configuration of a particular representation in a particular mind at a particular moment is a quite personal or subjective reality. This means, in turn, that studying the representations themselves is an almost impossible task and we can only hope to infer them from human actions, including the processes of communication.

To do so, it is neither necessary nor useful to give an epistemological supremacy to either the mind or to the world: rather, we need to understand the nature of the relationship between the intentionality of the subject and the concrete productions he often generates.

The fact that cultures embed and transport some kind of representations, for instance that of God or the universe, of the State or of the phlogist, only means that some issues, which are very relevant for human beings, become standardised enough to be a common way of representing the world.

The concept of the artificial, in this work, denotes the final product of a human being's action to reproduce his own representations of the world, whether it is external or internal to him. In this regard, it does not matter what the world is in itself, since the only ways we have at our disposal to describe the world are our representations of it. It is not necessary that something exists in order to reproduce it: it is sufficient that people be persuaded that it exists and have a shared description of its features, that is to say, a model of it. In this regard, the subjective representation constitutes the lower limit in terms of sharing, while the dominant cultural models constitute the upper limit of it.

All the kinds of models we adopt, both in daily and scientific life, are to be understood in just this way. Hence, we are able to 'recognise' the image of the devil depicted in paintings of the Middle Ages, or recognise the orbits of electrons around the nucleus in a contemporary drawing.

We assume, in our representations of the world, that they are the original entities, as if the world were imprinted in them: in our mind, there is nothing prior to them but pure 'methodological dispositions' or categories along with previously generated representations, including those acquired during inculturation.

Furthermore, it is useful to clearly distinguish between the kinds of representations we have discussed so far: the mental entities from the concrete ones, the latter being the final, actual result of the human attempt to reproduce the former. Thus, by 'concrete representations' we mean everything generated by man in order to reproduce his own representations of the external or the internal world: from symbols to concrete machines, from communication acts to paintings.

In this way, we arrive at the concept of social representations: systems of socially shared symbols, symbolic systems or models which allow people to understand each other on an operative or practical level.

We could say that, in a sense, everything man makes is a reproduction, or at least develops on the basis of a reproduction, that is, of what he has in his own mind. This includes the representations or the images of the external world and, therefore, of the exemplars belonging to it. Thus, a representation could be defined as something meta-artificial through which we relate in a dynamic crosstalk between active feed-forward and feed-back mental acts, to the world, and to a large extent, even the internal one.

Nevertheless, what we actually mean by the term artificial is something different and needs to be more precisely defined.

6. From representations to the artificial

Whatever action man is involved in he acts on the basis of his representation of the world, but the teleology of his action, particularly when he is involved in setting up actions, may be very different. Whilst an innovative machine is the result of a process which starts with the designer's representation of it and of the context in which it has to operate, a machine properly belongs to the realm of the artificial when it reproduces an object that is already present in the world, even in the internal one, *before* it is represented in the designer's mind.

The difference is not an irrelevant one. Building an object or a machine by not taking an exemplar from the external world means, potentially, to place that object in a cultural vacuum because of the lack of any shared representations (or models) of it. This is what happens when scientists set up new concepts or develop new theories, when mathematicians or philosophers produce innovative abstracts or theoretical works, when artists propose a new language or even, generally, when people mentally construct something which they feel, or fear, has never been experienced before and which, therefore, does not belong to any system of socially shared symbols.

In these cases, after the meta-artificial process, from representation to actual achievement, the final result will be a really new object or machine in which only unpredictable parts or aspects will be recognisable by people.

All this applies, as we said, also to the internal world since within it subjectivity is nothing but the personal meaning which we attribute to reality. It is actually impossible for a human being to relate to the world without such a personal representation, whose richness exceeds that of socially shared symbols. Thus, beyond the simplest and widely shared psycho-biological sphere, when we can rely upon representations which are operatively effective, it is not possible to reproduce this kind of representation using the established communication tools or languages. This explains why man often tries to introduce new communication tools or languages as a continuous evolution of the basic linguistic 'technology' (Leroi-Gourhan, 1964).

As we know, the history of science, of art and of cultures shows how often innovators have come across major difficulties in introducing their new proposals. Nevertheless, a history of solipsistic innovations is impossible by definition.

On the contrary, the attempt to reproduce an exemplar belonging to the external world (including that large class of standard psycho-biological events which human beings perceive as common and natural, like hunger or pain, being cold or sleepy), will place the resulting object or machine within a context of potentially shared representations concerning the original object and, therefore, it will be evaluated, that is understood or refused, according to culturally established criteria.

This is what happens when a technologist produces a machine which emulates some biological function; when a painter, staying within some established figurative tradition, reproduces someone's face; or when a graphic designer with a practical aim tries to generate a simple, highly informative ideogram. It also happens in daily life when people try to communicate the information content of their practical needs or plans, by adopting a language which they know is shared by the interlocutors. On a daily level, human beings often express themselves without involving the deepest issues which they feel in their personal context, within which the exchanged information assumes meaning, for them, understandable.

In fact, personal meanings, or, on a different level, tacit or personal knowledge (Polanyi, 1966) are the original objects that belong to the subjective context and, therefore, can be reproduced in a sharable way only if their bearer succeeds in making them visible as if they were, so to say, objects of the external world. This explains the frequent, though often illusory, use of the analogy by which someone who does not know the object at the centre of someone else's discourse tries to build a reliable representation of the matter.

The aim of this book is to put forward a theory of what it means to build an artificial object or machine when human beings are not intentionally looking for radically new realities but are, on the contrary, trying to reproduce something which potentially everybody sees, or something they perceive in their own internal 'landscape', which they wish to share with other people.

As we shall see, this very ancient ambition of re-building the external natural world

Mental level	**A, meta-artificial** generation of representations based on the shared external or internal world (e.g. the solar system, expecting a warm day, the Haway)	**B, personal world** generation of self-based non-shared representations (e.g. new concepts, subjective meanings, fantasy entities)
Social level	**artificial** reproduction, by means of symbols or machines, of the shared external or internal world, based on **A** (e.g. artificial kidney, maps, figurative arts)	**creativity** production of new realities, objects or machines, based on **B** (e.g. innovating machines, foundation of new concepts, non-figurative arts)

Table 1. The role of representations in setting up new realities and in building the artificial.

on the one hand, and replicating our own ego on the other, implies very complex processes.

We shall conclude, for a number of reasons, that, in principle, it is an impossible aim and that in trying to produce the artificial, human beings unavoidably and paradoxically set up new realities, even against their will or dispositions. We shall see that this is not only due to general epistemological reasons, although relevant in themselves, but the logical and empirical constraints in our actions, implied by the attempt to reproduce any object.

If they succeed in becoming culturally established, the products of the creative level become candidates for the meta-artificial level and, then, of the artificial one. On the contrary, the representations from the personal world have to be defined as original objects and do not necessarily lead to actual or concrete achievements.

The case of the non-figurative arts (e.g. abstract painting or even all music) is particularly interesting since they could be defined as processes of reproduction which generate artificials which only the author can recognise within his own personal world. Although the above condition involves most deep, non-operative communication, it characterises several other kinds of human circumstances or activities, such as personal memos, children's games or some autistic pathologies.

7. Scope of the Theory of the Artificial (TA)

We would emphasise at this point that our proposal to introduce a theory of the artificial is limited to a portion of human activity, namely that of reproducing something natural, using different materials and procedures. In other words, the theory does not purport to account for all aspects of human technology. Rather, the theory will help in distinguishing a conventional technology from that of the artificial, where the former is conceived as the creative invention of new realities and the latter as the effort to reproduce existing natural objects by using current technology. We conclude this section with two remarks with regard to this.

First of all, we should take into account that human invention often generates realities that, unknown to the designer, are already present in the world, although the designer has not taken reality as an exemplar. Somenzi rightly remarks (1996) that man often invents something 'new' which has alrady been anticipated by nature. This seems to have been the case, for instance, with the nuclear fission reactor, activated in Chicago's Stagg Field by Fermi and his group in 1942 which was conceived, of course, as a pure invention of human technological reason. According to subsequent discoveries reported by Cowan (see Somenzi, 1996), the remains of a natural reactor of this kind was found in a uranium mine in Gabon.

The same situation frequently occurs in pharmacology when natural molecules of a given kind are found in natural substance or systems after they have been invented by man. Furthermore, on a social level, it is a well-known fact that many inventors, simultaneously or with some time delay, create the same new objects or machines without knowledge of each other.

These facts only serve to demonstrate that we live in a closed system and that, within it, despite its almost infinite variety, identical processes may randomly arise, based on the same or similar materials, procedures and hints to the human mind. One could come to think that, in the end, everything that happens in the world is natural, since we cannot attribute some extra-world features to what we do: this would include, of course, all the phenomenologies belonging to science, technology and culture. Nevertheless, this would be quite a useless premise if one understood the world in a non-metaphysical way.

The second remark is that our position implicitly requires that we think that what is going to be reproduced exists before we attempt to reproduce it. It is an unavoidable constraint from a logical point of view, though it does not imply a univocal causal relationship between the original object and the final achievement. In fact, what actually happens is that the original object to be reproduced is quickly abandoned to advantageous unpredictable new targets which may arise from the subsequent stages of the reproduction attempt. The new targets, in turn, may be again of a reproductive kind or not, giving room to innovations according to a great variety of circumstances.

It is a matter of a kind of serendipity that involves, as we should expect, not only the generation of artificials in their 'hardware' form but also the ones which come from 'soft' reproduction attempts. This is just what happens in the communication process where what we often try to reproduce changes just at the moment we express it or, as a consequence of the feed-back coming from our interlocutor.

8. The concept of the artificial: cultural backgrounds

A first conclusion from the above considerations is that all artificial devices are, generally speaking, machines but not all machines are to be conceived as artificial devices. This simple consideration marks the starting point for the proposal for the theory of the artificial.

On the one hand we have conventional technology which aims at helping man to survive by giving him control of the natural world; on the other we have a technology oriented to reproducing any existing natural reality: we will call this the technology of the artificial.

While natural objects and those of conventional technology possess, or however it could be scientifically thought to possess, an autonomous 'status of existence', since they exist or are made as self-defined items, the artificial would not have meaning without reference to something that man assumes to be an exemplar to reproduce.

The conceptual connection between the natural and artificial, through the interface of mental and cultural representations or both, is more narrow and constitutive than is commonly held to be the case.

The need for a theory results from both a scientific interest and a practical one. According to the former, we have an interest in discriminating the artificial from pure technology to create order in a subject of increasing complexity and also to try to understand the anthropological roots and the psychological motivations that differentiate these two ancient forms of human activity. The necessity for practical order refers to the different intellectual, perceptive and operational requisites, and in the different expectations that the user and the culture should on the one side guarantee and on the other accept in the adoption of the two different technologies.

Intrinsic differences among apparently close relations and practices like imitation, replication and reproduction also become particularly important.

Both conventional and artificial technologies legitimate an attempt at theorising not only in speculative terms but also in terms of social and cultural utility. In fact, as we have anticipated in the previous section, the disposition to give birth to the artificial concerns not only man's concrete technological activity but also other reproduction-oriented phenomena such as communication, art and many aspects of daily life.

This implies that what we mean by 'technology' in this book is not only the techniques, materials and necessary rules for building objects or machines, at every stage of cultural evolution, but a larger whole of knowledge systems adopted for reproducing the external or the internal world.

Therefore, we shall speak of technology not only with reference to the classical activity of building objects or machines but also as the technology of language, painting or music. All of these activities might be seen as being closer to the concept of technique: however, we prefer the term 'technology'. This denotes a more direct involvement of the rules or skills required to produce something, along with the materials and their influence on the design.

For our theoretical goals, the issue of the materials, or of the stuff of the objects or machines built by men when they try to reproduce something, is a very crucial one, both in the cases in which concrete materials (in the sense of empirical entities) are concerned and when the materials are of a non-concrete kind (in the sense of information or symbolic entities).

The main proposal that arises from the TA is, thus, a new way of conceiving the relation between artificial and natural in comparison to common sense. In common sense terms, the artificial is characterised as anything, phenomenon or machine, which is purely 'non-natural'.

Surprisingly, even Herbert Simon (prominant in the field of AI), in his very popular book (Simon, 1969), accepts this definition. When discussing the 'sciences of the artificial', he includes all man-made objects:

> unfortunately, the term 'artificial' brings a depreciatory meaning of which we should free ourselves. . . I use the term 'artificial' in the most neutral meaning: to me, it means only man-made, in opposition to natural.
>
> (Simon, 1969)

Instead of giving to the artificial its own relevance, Simon reduces it to being whatever man builds, making the crucial difference between an artificial heart and a cathode tube disappear.

Actually, Simon was one of the leading founders of a research tradition at the end of the sixties that took the name of 'artificial intelligence'. This was one of the greatest human efforts in this century to rebuild natural systems by using the advanced technology that was available. Unfortunately, and despite a few references at the beginning of his book, Simon did not realise that the discussion on the feasibility of the artificial intelligence project had to be preceded by a discussion on what is meant by 'artificial'.

Simon's analysis of the artificial, expeditiously defined in common sense terms which, though very important for understanding the strategies of the technological design in general, does not clarify the peculiar nature of a technology which is oriented to reproducing the world as compared to that only aimed at controlling it by means of invented machines, on the basis of scientific findings. Nevertheless, Simon himself touches on the problem when he recognizes that

> certain artificial objects are imitations of things existing in the nature. . . the artificial objects may imitate the appearances of the natural things but, under many aspects, don't possess the reality of them.
>
> (Simon, op. cit. pp.19-20)

Our aim is to investigate in depth the extent to which the 'appearances' of a natural thing could be approximated by human technology: which are the necessary methodological steps, what are the general constraints, what makes up for the unavoidable diversity that an artificial object exhibits compared to a natural one and in which sense can it advance? In doing so, we shall discover that the design of a truly artificial object or machine shows and involves differences with a generically defined technology that are remarkable enough to deserve specific research.

In a more subtle way but preserving the same implicit definition, Jacques Monod tried to find out what differentiates natural things from artificial ones when he referred to the materialised intention embedded in the objects or machines built up by man compared to natural objects that embed no intentions or projects.

Furthermore, in order for something to be truly artificial, the intentions or the projects have to be conceived as external forces with regard to the object. In this sense, Monod's position is very near to Kant's when he emphasises that something is natural if it includes what is needed for its own development, whilst something is artificial when it depends on external projects. In other words, adopting current terminology, something is natural when it is autopoietic while it is artificial when it is heteropoietic (see Qvortrup, 1995).

But, for our aims, the most interesting aspect of Monod's position is that, according to his thought, if a space shuttle were to land on Mars or Venus searching for signs of intelligent beings, it would be induced to look for geometrically ordered and repetitive objects:

> Because of the complete ignorance on the inhabitants, on their nature and on the projects that they could have conceived, the program [of an ideal computer] should use only very general criteria, based exclusively on the structure and on the form of the considered objects.
>
> (Monod, 1972)

The deductions we could draw from our own position would be very different from this, since, if it is clear that the problem posed by Monod is a true one, it is also clear that, at least ideally, an artificial object or machine as we are defining it could be recognised with a difficulty proportional to the quality or the effectiveness of its realisation. In fact, a good artificial object or machine should be made in such a way that it could be taken, at least at some observation level, as a natural one and not as something heterogeneous with nature and its forms, structures and so on.

The difficulty in introducing the idea of artificial objects or machines as entities different from the ones made by conventional technology is due to this generic use of the concept of artificial as being whatever is made by an intelligent agent. Rather, we should understand that among the objects made by such intelligent agents the class of the artificials is a peculiar one, since they are objects or machines whose deliberate intention is to mimic, copy, duplicate, simulate, cheat nature: in a word, to reproduce it.

We have nothing to oppose the distinctions introduced by Monod, provided the fact of being man-made, that is by an external system, is only conceived of as the necessary condition for the artificial (it is not an autopoietical object): the sufficient condition being the fact that it intends to reproduce something which exists in nature.

9. Production and reproduction

In anthropology, artifacts are characterised as being anything produced, generated, man-made, whose sum constitutes the culture. However, a deeper evaluation could not neglect, at least, the presence or the absence of intentionality at the base of that production (Posner, 1989). Within the class of artefacts, redefined as deliberate products, the TA aims at proposing a differentiation depending upon a sort of double orientation of the intentionality.

On the one hand we have conventional intentionality which characterises all the objects or machines built up by the conventional technology. Man builds objects or machines (artefacts, tools, instruments) with some purpose in mind, i.e. representing in his own mind both the real context and the design: the final product is generally destined to exhibit some utility function or to pursue some useful finality. We could define this as a genuine production process. Production, therefore, has a causal component (the entity E causes P) and a teleological one (the entity E causes P in order to achieve F).

To sum up, the process of production implies that some entity, for example man, sets itself as a generating cause and this process, in these terms, will also be valid for reproduction since it is also obviously a productive process.

On the other side, the process which leads to the artificial, that is to say reproduction – which implies that of production – shows instead a kind of double conscious teleology, since, in this case, some entity generates a product which is oriented to something existing and then, possibly, pursues some further purpose. Formally, we could state that we have a reproduction when an entity E causes P on the basis of the model P1 for achieving F, where P1 and F constitute two finalities which have to be compatible to each other. They could even show a relationship such that one can describe F as depending, in a more or less exclusive way, upon P1.

The reproduction of a natural context in a miniaturised plastic model, having in mind some architectural purpose, seems a cogent example: the existence of a natural context is assumed, at a scientific and technological level, as a fact and it, or, better to say, its mental representation will work as a 'controlling variable' for the design process.

In other words, bearing in mind, in some measure, Archimedes' proposed definition of technology, when building up an object or a machine, the designer tries to find the expedients to exploit the natural phenomena or to simply adapt itself to it. Nature, then, acts in a controlling sense only in terms of something which allows, or does not allow, the success of a designer's inventions according to the degree of his capacity to understand the natural world. On the contrary, the designer of artificial objects or machines, in addition to the above constraint, intentionally respects at least some of the main features, which we shall term the *essential performance*, of the natural object or system to be reproduced. This means that while conventional technology can be described as the attempt to adapt human beings to the environment, that of the artificial can be defined as an attempt to achieve an ultra-adaptation. In fact, it does not only look to exploit nature, but really to reproduce it, although accepting or looking for the challenge of adopting different materials and procedures.

The discussion on the concepts of production and reproduction reveals the necessity to avoid making the logical supposition that every activity of generating anything should be defined as a generation of the artificial.

As we shall see further below, there are plenty of reasons for making a distinction between what is artificial and what is not, although below certain thresholds of analysis, a kind of methodological decision is necessary to prevent the disappearance of the conceptual borders. Bearing in mind the necessary and sufficient conditions described above, the TA needs, through a process of simplification, to make two very different classes of human products visible.

10. Conceptualizing a new field of research

In a certain way theories always face this need for simplification. Just as the theory of suicide by Durkheim does not depict the single psychological dynamics of the subjects or just as Ohm's law does not depict the behaviour of the electrons within a circuit, the TA only proposes that the analysis be carried out at a level which can be maintained as fecund. This means to accept the risk that the concept of the artificial might be taken in too rigid a way.

Nevertheless, what we have to firmly hold onto is not the problem of placing an object or a machine within the class of artificial objects or machines or in a conventional one; rather, the aim of our taxonomy is to make a reliable set of deductions possible, in terms of configuration, power, limits and dynamics, on something that can be reasonably defined as truly artificial. As Wiener rightly wrote, scientists should not always pose themselves the question

> "How can I solve this problem?"

but, rather,

> "Now, having arrived at a final result, what problems have I solved?"
>
> (Wiener, 1993)

Thus, the above danger seems fairly remote to us if we assume a direction of work that we could characterize as functional whereby having defined the concept of artificial with sufficient plausibility, we ask why man shows a strong 'artificialistic' activity, of what does it consist and with what kind of consequences. It is our belief that the ability to describe the general features of the artificial *in se* would imply an ability to predict several facts that this growing technology will involve, even when it concerns, for an analogy, human and cultural reproductive behaviours like communication or art.

The conceptual distinction between production and reproduction is, in this sense, a central one and, since the latter implies the existence of something that we want to reproduce, the former immediately evokes a definition wherein something is set up as an original entity, at least in the sense that it was not deliberately generated from another which was assumed as an exemplar for it.

For instance, the curiosity that pushes an explorer to move from one point to another within a certain territory does not involve, as such, any reproductive finality but only that of getting information about a some natural context. On the other hand, when the same explorer, after having accomplished his own enterprise, designs a map of the territory he has visited, he will produce a chart which exhibits an evidently reproductive finality: that of fixing, in material and informational terms, his representation of the territory he visited. In fact, he will reproduce by means of certain codes, what he found to be the essential performance of that territory according to his own interests.

Likewise, the invention and the evolution of the microscope did not have, as such, any reproductive finality until the seventeenth century, when in order to enhance its power, the convex spheric shape of a water drop was assumed as an exemplar, just as it seems to have happened without any development in the ancient times, when, in order to magnify objects, bottles full of water were used.

11. The artificial as a class of empirical objects

What is in play in the distinction between production and reproduction is the possibility of distinguishing the innovative and original character of the former compared to the emulative character of the latter. By means of this critical tool it will be legitimate to establish the presence of two classes in the range of human dispositions: one which is able to trigger original mental events or representations and induce man to cause events and processes which are oriented towards the new; the other is the ability to regenerate mental events, already experienced, and to induce man towards those activities which are aimed at reproducing events, objects and processes, starting from their representations.

The first class will consist of activities or original events like thought, non-imitative ideation, intuition and, at a psycho-biological level, sensations and feelings; the second class will consist of all those activities that incline towards imitation, iteration, externalisation of internal representations and communication. In the context of the present work we could group them within the concept of artificialistic dispositions.

The first class includes all those activities that, although certainly caused by some other underlying activity, do not appear to be oriented towards reproducing anything but rather innovatively cause some kind of events.

The intuition involved in solving problems often does not reproduce anything and, likewise, the invention of a musical scale does not have any emulative finality. Rather, these activities indicate some adaptive function which aims at controlling the context within which man has to act: the invention of a measuring scale or the generation of new timbres of sound, for instance, should submit to precise constraints in terms of their operability and audibility.

The second class includes all activities that appear to be conservatively oriented towards the re-proposition of some kinds of internal or external events. As we said, these activities, then, tend to exhibit functions that we could characterise as ultra-adaptive, since they aim at generating what is already familiar, recognisable and tested, though by means of different materials and procedures. A good sociological example is that of the recurrent habit of immigrant people in many countries around the world to reconstruct various material aspects of the countries they come from, along with a series of related symbolisms.

At a physical level, and therefore not at a 'deliberate' level, cellular regeneration or cloning (biological replication) is an example of this ultra-adaptive though not artificial activity, just as, at a psychological level, is the deliberate and truly artificial attempt to communicate embedding feelings or ideas by means of any type of language, or to represent a face or a landscape upon a cloth, or, at a technological level, the effort to make an artificial heart or sensors to check the temperature.

Within this framework we will consider the artificial, or the artificials in plural form, as objects of the empirical world, as real systems which we can isolate in a space and time way and that embed an intentionality which differentiates them from other classes of objects produced by man. Such a disposition – call it 'naturalistic' or positive – seems to us to be quite legitimate as it was for the foundation of social, psychological or ecological dimensions: profiles of the world that cannot be seen before one isolates and constructs them, thereby showing the scientific usefulness of such a methodological operation.

Furthermore, man's attitude is adequate to the exploratory phase that the search for the artificial proposes after centuries of practice, from alchemy to the 'imitative arts', throught to automata, based on assumed implicit definitions, ambitions and claims. All these elements, which gave rise to the concept of artificial, ended by being reduced to that of the technological level, putting in the shade what, in our view, is the deep, ancient and enduring alternative disposition of human nature and culture.

12. The two souls of technology

The history of technology indicates that man's disposition to technology has been rooted, as it is today, in very different motivations and finalities.

The Western tradition assigns to technology – thereby to the artificial in the common sense meaning of the term – the role to set up new realities compared to the natural ones, to such an extent that

> The linear ideal of today is also often associated with the image of the artificial.
>
> (Karlqvist et. al., 1993)

But in other cultures the technological object

> takes already existing natural forms into account more smoothly and adaptively, but also integrates other types of influences, which within a rationalistic mentality are seen to be very strange.
>
> (Karlqvist et. al., 1993, ibid.)

The innovative character of conventional technology (the production of original artifacts) and the conservative character of the technology of the artificial (the reproduction of existing realities) do not, of course, implies that genuine productive activities could not be oriented towards further conservative finalities and that genuine reproductive activities could not be oriented towards further innovative finalities. The distinction is useful only for pointing out two alternative characteristics, because they are intrinsically divergent in their motivations and depict different behaviours and therefore need special analyses.

It is plausible to maintain that there are overlapping or alternate distributions, for units of time, of the two classes in considering the history of technology, culture and even of individuals themselves.

Nevertheless, it is likewise reasonable to maintain that at different time intervals, different distributions could be valid and that man's disposition to the artificial prevails or succumbs in relation to the productive dispositions, or vice versa, and thereby contributes to characterise the aggregative sense of a cultural phase as well as of the phase of an individual life.

In fact, daily life itself shows a permanent succession of imitative and innovative behaviours or, if we prefer, between actions dominated by commonly accepted models, shared representations, stereotyped techniques, and attempts to 'break the rules', that is to say, to explore other and new kinds of possible behaviours, values frameworks or technical models.

Moreover, a key point we should underline is that the overlap and the collaboration between conventional technology and artificial technology is ineluctable since, as we shall see, if the reproductive activities are often useful for the productive ones, the former is almost always intrinsically indispensable for the latter, although it is enslaved to artificial finalities.

In other words, a true technology of the artificial, at least within the domain of machines in the material sense, does not exist as an autonomous body of knowledge and tools: it is nothing more than the result, scientifically isolable in a class of observable phenomena (the artificials), of the deliberate orientation of the conventional technology toward reproductive targets. This applies to all technology of the artificial which, with its reproduction aims, cannot but exploit the current techniques available within conventional technology: from mechanics to electronics, chemical or metal engineering and so on.

This does not mean, of course, that collaborative work between, for instance, engineers and biologists cannot lead to highly specialised disciplines such as bioengineering in all its ramifications: ranging from the engineering of cells or tissue, to the technology of artificial hearts, livers and so on. The above considerations underline a matter of principle, i.e. the fact that, in order to make substitutes of natural exemplars, for instance 'biomaterials', the artificialists need materials and procedures which, intrinsically, have nothing to do with the stuff of natural objects. At the start, the materials and the technologies which are usually adopted for a given artificialistic enterprise are taken from the conventional technologies, as they are in their own area. We refer to the enthusiasm of Jacques Vaucanson, who was involved, in the eighteenth century in a project to reproduce the digestion process of a duck. When he heard of the new rubber materials coming from India, he said

> The life-saving heart surgery, often relies on a polymer originally developed for women's fashions or a plastic meant for insulating electrical wires.
>
> (The Whitaker Foundation, 1995)

The search for application-specific improvements of the materials which have been originally taken from other applications soon becomes a central concern for meeting the increasing pursuit of essential performances. In this way, new specialisations emerge, gathering knowledge from engineering and biology and, during this growth, it becomes more and more difficult to establish which of the two areas involved will re-design itself on the basis of the other. In these cases, it would be quite reasonable, on a daily common sense basis, to speak of artificial technology. But it is also clear that what it really consists of is a series of research and design strategies and techniques oriented to adapt the available materials and procedures to reproductive aims of technology and not a sort of Third Estate technology.

In other words, the knowledge of nature and the knowledge will increasingly collaborate in the future, but the result will not be a replication of nature by means of alternative materials since this would be absurd in itself. Rather, we shall witness a growth in the global variety of our world, because of the consequences of the intrinsic heterogeneity which comes and will come from the artificial at the very moment it succeeds in reproducing natural phenomena.

13. The artificiality of communication and of the arts

In a less material field, such as that of oral communication, things could be different, and a deeper analogy could be needed. In fact, assuming the artificial nature of communication, defined as such since it is a reproduction of subjective exemplars, it is difficult to assign to language the physiognomy of a conventional autonomous technology which is simply oriented to reproductive finalities: what is language useful for if not to communicate and, then, to reproduce mental, subjective exemplars like images, feelings, impressions or memories? In a sense, oral language seems to be the only instance of a truly artificial technology, although it quickly develops, during cultural evolution, towards conventionality by means of syntax and grammar, which have nothing, in themselves, to do with any reproductive finality.

In fact, any typology of language could be reduced to the application of some conventional technology, in the wider meaning adopted here, which is oriented to reproduction: postural language or that of dance, for example, uses articulation and the postures of the human body as communicative finalities, and then artificialistic finalities, although their origin and their main functions differ in nature.

This is even more evident in the postural languages adopted for communication amongst the deaf. Here, a complete symbolic codification, designed *ad hoc*, has been placed upon the articulations of the hands, such that they possess a low probability of belonging to the vast set of the articulations of a tool (the hand) whose functions are not intrinsically oriented to communication.

In addition, in the case of the figurative arts, if we assume that communication is often, although not exclusively, their artificialistic function, the tools are closely connected and functional to language, but such tools come from elsewhere. In this case one can not easily speak in terms of an autonomous technology of the artificial. The figurative arts in fact apply to the existing technologies, orienting them to their own reproductive finalities: it suffices to think of the sculptor's chisel and marble, or the painter's brush and canvas.

In contrast to prose and poetry, which adopt oral language and inherit the properties of this form of communication, musical instruments, at least the historic ones, do not seem to have any other possible function than a musical one. The vocal chords, for instance, seem to exhibit an inherent and exclusive function of a communicative nature based on the articulation of sound.

Maybe the issue is more complex when one thinks on the one hand of the strong convergence of conventional technology in the construction of ancient orchestral instruments and, on the other hand, of the most recent tendencies of experimental music. Among these, a fairly common denominator seems to be the adoption of technological tools that utter sound or noise but which were not originally projected for expressing finalities of musical order, such as tape-recorders, oscillators and computers.

We could sum up this aspect of our analysis in the following way. In all the cases above we deal with processes of communication and the exemplars are always constituted by mental states that we carefully try to reproduce like artificial entities in the mind of the receiving people.

In the case of oral communication, the exemplar and its essential performance are entrusted to a technology, namely language, which exists solely for this purpose. Here, we can properly speak of the application of a technology of the artificial.

Expressing a state of mind to a friend implicates adopting some linguistic tools available for reproductive purposes, although the involved linguistic technology has grown so much along with the cultural development that we cannot prescribe, for each state of mind, the correspondent, necessary linguistic rule to be adopted. Actually, the historically linguistic technology has to be conceived as a technology which has shifted from having a directly artificial nature to a conventional one.

The same considerations apply, of course, to those arts that coincide with the use of the word. In the case of non-verbal communication the exemplar is entrusted, instead, to a technology which is not oriented, *in se*, to communication. The expression of the same state of mind described above by means of gestures, implicates a translation *ad hoc* that will be affected by the power and limits of a specific technology: that of bodily articulations which basically exist for other finalities. The same considerations are true for the arts, such as dance, which use the body for expressive purposes.

In the case of artistic communication of a figurative nature, particularly music, the exemplar and its essential performance are only reproduced through partially specific technologies.

All of the painter's tools, as a rule, have many possible applications, both expressive or communicative; similarly, if it is difficult to imagine the use of a piano for finalities which are different from that of musical communication, it is, in any case, necessary to take into account that this tool does not have, in turn, any exemplar in the natural world. Hence it is considered as a product of conventional technology despite the fact that it coincides with the artificialistic finalities of music.

The use of painting and musical techniques literally constitutes a process which is similar to the shift from oral to written communication and is thereby necessarily learned and conventionally complex. In fact, in each case we shift from the pure and simple use of, say, basic technologies of the artificial (emission of onomatopeisms or simple words in the cases of oral communication and of primitive songs and simple arrangements of objects or elementary 'signs' in the case of the primordial painting) to technologies of a higher order. These more developed technologies, through the various composite, instrumental, semantic, syntactic and stylistic rules, transform the same technologies of the artificial from which they derive, into conventional technologies which, as is usual for the artificial, further transfigure the characteristics of the exemplar, either amplifying or reducing it.

14. Conventionality vs artificiality

What has become clear, in the above, is that to generate the artificial through an existing technology designed with just this aim in mind is one thing, but it is a different matter to do so by using a technology which already exists and was originally destined for other finalities. Since the latter case seems to be the most diffuse, or typical, circumstance, including the case of the learned use of language, the unavoidable statement that a true technology of the artificial does not exist becomes a plausible likelihood.

On the other hand, this highlights a paradox: one of the strongest and most ancient abilities of man – to reproduce exemplars and to give birth to the artificial – is culturally, and perhaps intrinsically, barred from the conventional nature of the technology that he must inexorably adopt. The more articulate technology, the more powerful and delicate it is, the more likely is the artificial product to be the sign of that technology rather than an approximation of the exemplar and of its essential performances.

With regard to the domain of reproducing the world by machines, we are all familiar with the efforts of mechanics to build machines in the eighteenth century, which often would mimic some living system. This was invaluable for giving pleasure, entertainment: consider the automatons of Erone (1st century AD) which imitated some natural human event, assumed as essential performance, such as a dance or the act of writing.

In the case of Vaucanson's machine also, the target of reproduction at that time was a living system. In a similar vein, we can refer back to the ancient dreams of authors like Homer of the *Iliad*, where the Efesto god creates a woman from clay, or of Plato who speaks of the self-moving statues of Daedalus, of the Argonauts and their artificial watch dog, through to Faust and to *R.U.R.* (*Rezon's Universal Robot*) of Capek. Human imagination has often generated images of automatons (Ceserani, 1969; Faenza, 1985; Losano, 1990) examples of which are present even in the Bible.

Nevertheless, the concept of the artificial appears only episodically as a possible object of direct or indirect study: for example in the *Perspectiva artificialis* of Leon Battista

Alberti and Piero della Francesca, in the modern distinction between the natural and the artificial by David Hume or in the discussions triggered by the mechanicism of Descartes and carried on, amongst the others, by Lamettrie and Diderot. Even Francis Bacon predicted the artificial bow in his famous technological forecasts.

In Eastern world, the term 'artificiality' appears among the six attributes of a great Sung-dynasty Chinese garden: antiquity, artificiality, broad views, seclusion, spaciousness and water. This tradition seems to be the basis of the current Japanese building art, of the so-called 'domes'. These are large, architecturally closed, highly engineered sites which reproduce landscapes and physical situations, such as climate, flora and fauna, based on various famous places around the world, and created purely for leisure.

Finally, the unshakable disposition to reproduce nature often leads to achievements in which imitational and truly artificialistic aspects will converge. Thus, for instance, for a century, the attitude of 'realism' in painting has been a sort of institutionalized aim, whose functions is to move in several directions: the perceptive enlargement of human spaces, for instance, rooms, halls and so on, by means of fictional landscapes, lights, people; the effort to set up a continuum between human presence on the Earth with Earth itself; the desire to re-create arbitrarily, or to overcome the physical constraints, aspects or environments which would be impossible in nature.

The illusory character of all these efforts is at times very clear, but it often performs an additional function: that of reinforcing some aspects of a situation or of a message, for example, the image of a dog will enhance the obligation to respect some restricted area. Mixed with intentional and elaborated reproduction techniques, the above function may generate some quite interesting and often unpredictable feelings and behaviours. Thus, for example, Pliny the Elder reports,

> . . . in the match between Zeusi and Parrasio, Zeusi draws grapes which deceive the sparrows. . . Parrasio draws a drapery which simulates so carefully a breadth of cloth, spread to cover a painting, that he cheated his competitor.
>
> (Anceschi, 1988)

Similarly, Negroponte reports that the addition of realism to an artificial system can sometimes have a strong effect on human beings. In the seventies, when one of the first tele-conferencing systems was designed for improving government emergency procedures, a mechanism was added to it in order to reinforce the realism of the message: the plastic head moved, thereby reproducing the speaker, for instance the president. The result was that the

> video recordings generated in this way provided so realistic a reproduction of the reality, that an admiral said to me that the 'speaking heads' gave him nightmares.
>
> (Negroponte, 1995)

Conventional technology has obtained through the centuries a clear supremacy over that of the artificial because of both the fantastic and visionary characters shown by the latter for a long time. Ever since the seventeenth century experimental science and the

Often the artificial plays an intentional role of cheating the observer, as many trompe l'oeil *demonstrate, but for a long time the attitude of 'realism' in painting has been a sort of institutionalized aim whose functions can be found to move in several directions: the perceptive enlargement of human spaces, for instance, rooms, halls and so on, by means of fictional landscapes, lights, people. Source: photograph by the author of a palace in Valle Camonica, Italy.*

development of abstract representational systems by Descartes have given a huge support to conventional technology. As Wiener rightly underlined,

> The sixteenth century symbolises therefore one of the most surprising marriages between a new form of thought and a new technology. In that period a philosopher like Spinoza could reinforce his own autonomy of thinking thanks to the economic independency given to him by his activity as a lenses grinder. Both the philosopher and the lense grinder could individually mark such a period as a great era of discoveries and inventions; but their union started a new period within which the technical advancement was no longer sporadic and integrated itself in our civilization.
>
> (Wiener, op. cit., p. 67)

The collaboration between these two extraordinary intellectual strategies allowed for an enormous leap, in terms of effectiveness, to the human need first to know and then to control nature, reducing in some measure the strain towards reproducting it. Thus, that most ancient of human ambitions, which perhaps constitutes also a desire for immortality, was confined within a cultural region characterised as being purely fantastic. This partially explains why, increasingly, the term artificial itself has assumed such a widely negative connotation that today it is again synonymous with 'not true', 'false', 'mere imitation', 'counterfeit' or 'expedient'.

These are the same terms with which Archimedes conceived of his own technological inventions, as secondary applications of geometry. Nevertheless, it is meaningful that our inclination to characterise some artificial products as being a 'fiction' originates from far away, and from the Latin verb *fingere* which meant to carve, to forge, but also to imagine, to depict, to represent and to reproduce something by means of the hands, i.e. by the fingers, that is to say by means of the most ancient tools for manipulating the reality and then adopting these also for communication purposes.

15. A new Renaissance of the artificial

A renewed closely scientific interest in the field of the artificial will be found later. But we are now fully into twentieth century, with cybernetics and information theory started by authors like Wiener, Bigelow, Ashby and Shannon. In fact they gave rise to a tradition of research intentionally destined to transfer the knowledge acquired from living systems into machines able to reproduce some of the performances, in particular, self-regulating processes. The fundamental purpose of cybernetic technology (a true bridge between the classical way to do conventional technology and the renewed orientation towards the artificial) is that of building adaptive machines which reproduce the structures or the processes that are necessary for generating systems capable of fitting the surrounding environment. Adaptation, as a distinctive disposition of the living systems, however, is only an example of what we call the essential performance attributed to an object or to a system, assumed by the designer as the exemplar of his own attempt at reproduction.

The attribution of an essential performance is always a process in which empirical reality and the autonomy of the mind overlap. The attribution of a certain performance to a ductless gland may be due to the way of life is perceived proposed by some established theory, to the premises of a religion, or to other subjective preferences of the researcher.

The conception of man himself is, of course, also based, in any culture, upon a multiple inclusion of essential performances. Philosophical research, regardless of the particular school of thought, is proof of the permanent effort to discover the essence of man.

Especially evident is the inclusion of selections, or of attributions, in the following Hindu axiomatics contained in the Chandogya Upanisad, in which one can find the

> various steps that mark the subsequent materialisation of the world: the saman is the **essence** of the poetical metre, the metre is the **essence** of the language, the language is the **essence** of the man, the man is the **essence** of the trees, the trees are the **essence** of the water and the water is the **essence** of the earth.
>
> (Schneider, 1960, emphasis added)

Once again, in the area of biology, perhaps botanics has shown that, through history, a strong disposition to generate attributions of changing essential performances is often dominated by extra-rational visions. We can see this phenomenon in *Malva silvestris*, which, according to its classification by Limneus, has been used since antiquity for its medical properties, and which, according to the Pitagoreans, also included the capacity to save human beings from the slavery of the passions, and later, from the eighteenth century, was appreciated for its alimentary virtues; another example is *Cheiranthus cheiri*, which, again according to its classification by Limneus, was used by the Greeks and the Arabs as a cleaning substance and whose cardiotonic properties were only later discovered in the twentieth century.

It is useless, of course, to remember that all human and social sciences have taken a similar attitude towards defining what a given reality 'essentially' is: it concerns all their major concepts, mind, intelligence, aggressiveness, social structure, social institutions, language, communication, and the concepts of cultural models and scientific paradigms themselves.

The scientific method, of course, gave a great impulse to the search for objectivity in this direction. Nevertheless, the scientific advancement of our knowledge, indicates that our selections, our hypotheses, are permanently provisional, and sometimes truly subjective, although they look for public consent.

On the other hand, if we think of the multiplicity of reality as an independent fact, we shall have to deal with selections of features or of performances from among the endless characteristics of reality, to be conceived as unavoidable steps for any scientific or technological enterprise. To give an example from the field of cybernetics, or rather proto-cybernetics, in the twenties Hull and Baerstein (Cordeschi, 1991) had already designed one of the first electric devices able to reproduce the reflex process in a logically identical way to those that we observe in living systems. These authors identified their own research target in

> non-living systems – maybe even of inorganic materials – able of exhibiting the **essential** functions of the phenomenon that we call 'reflex'
>
> (Hull & Baernstein, 1929, emphasis added)

The awareness about the difficulty of going beyond a certain threshold of accuracy in reproducing the exemplar and its essential performance, when they seem to represent a true problem of scientific reliability and not only a matter of exterior resemblance, was already realised by Vaucanson in the eighteenth century, when he said, whilst speaking on the digestion process of his artificial duck:

> I don't pretend that this should be a perfect digestion, able to generate bloody and nutritional particles in order to allow the survival of the animal. I only pretend to imitate the mechanics of this action in three points: in the swallowing of the wheat; in soaking, cooking or dissolving it; in allowing its going out forcing it to visibly change its stuff.
>
> (Vaucanson, 1738, quoted in Losano, 1990)

Conventional technology has not developed by assuming exemplars from nature but by building machines on the basis of the knowledge acquired about nature, that is to say on what we could call 'technological reason'. It constitutes an abstract and autonomous world that characterises and generates original objects and machines on whose basis, in their turn, new machines are generated. It is a matter of an abstract activity, not, of course, in a philosophical sense but in the sense that, given a reliable set of descriptions of the natural world, technological reason tries to build up systems by combining and recombining components and sub-systems whose *raison d'etre* and consistency depends only on the design itself and not on the structure of the world.

For this reason, history periodically exhibits more or less justified social oppositions to conventional technology: in fact, it does not aim, intrinsically, to preserve or reproduce the natural world as it is, or as it is thought to be, but to exploit it for some human need. In the end, the idea of a sustainable technology, just claims to be taking greater care of the intrinsic nature of nature on the one hand and of the nature of technology on the other.

Almost always, the objects, the machines of conventional technology, are designed by human beings to maximize their usability, but they do not have any vocation or finalization to reproduce exemplars of the natural world.

The artificialistic work, on the contrary, has tried, and has been trying again with renewed vigour for a few decades, to increasingly integrate man with his own environment through the design of devices that reproduce the reality itself, rather than of heterogeneous tools for adapting to it. Thus, even if the anthropological roots and the motivations for building the artificial are perhaps very deep and implicate mythical or magical dimensions, its real results could be interpreted as forming a kind of strategy of ultra-adaptation. In fact, the history of the artificialism fluctuates between two extreme models or syndromes.

On the one side there is the syndrome of Narcissus, that depicts man's ambition to reproduce images, feelings, ideas, that reside in our mind. On the other side there is the syndrome of Icarus, that depicts man's ambition to overcome his own limits for reproducing and even re-designing, nature and natural systems, his own included, in order to become a part of it and thereby increase his own freedom or his own will. Both these syndromes are, at the same time, ambitions and needs. Both have been abandoned, anyway, or at least shadowed by conventional technology, that presents itself as the result of rational reflection on the capabilities of building increasingly complex systems for practical purposes of controlling the world, and yet maintain and even increase man's distance from nature.

These systems or machines, in their turn, operate according to rules that refer not only to the natural world as an object to be controlled for achieving human desires, but depend on the machine as such and that are to be known and used according to the same criteria of the abstract technological thought which has given birth to them.

In this sense we can easily understand, without approving of all their views, the sceptical or negative reactions that bring together many philosophical traditions which are very different from each other. These include such authors as Hegel, Whitehead, Heidegger and Habermas, who shared the idea that technology detaches man from nature. Despite such a good premise, one of the worst consequences of these traditions has been to prevent a part of mankind from understanding not only the interest and beauty of conventional technology as such, that is to say of a genuine creation of reason, but also of understanding the deep difference between conventional technology and the technology of the artificial, and man's likewise different and illuminating connections with human nature.

Furthermore, as it has been underlined, the opposition to the technology often derives from a

> resentment of the device one needs, resentment at one's own need and guilt, and a Romantic dislike of the artificiality of the device that answers one's needs [and all this] marks most humanists' attitudes toward technology.
>
> (Landow, 1992)

Actually, we must understand that the artificial is setting up new realities (amongst which, for example, those denominated as virtual reality, artificial life or artificial intelligence are only special cases) whose study will only be sufficiently advanced when, to assume an amusing lexicon, all of us will share the exactness of an expression of the type 'that one is a genuinely artificial object'.

16. The latest challenges: from simulation to artificial life and virtual reality

Computer simulation techniques are a very old and well-established tool for reproducing the world although only in an abstract way. In other words, a simulation model does not aim at reproducing an object, a system or a process in real terms, that is to say, building up a concrete reality. Rather, it is able to conceptually reproduce the reality by transforming the empirical phenomena involved in a symbolic representation governed by formal rules which, in turn, should generate some other kind of symbolic representation according to the model adopted. Even computer simulation requires, of course, the selection of some observation level, of an exemplar and of an essential performance and, in this sense, it surely belongs to the artificialistic tradition though on a special level, owing to its non-materiality.

Nevertheless, the logical condition which requires that, by definition, an artificial object should be made of different materials and procedures is radically applied here: the 'different materials' are reduced to the most 'immaterial' ones, i.e. to concepts transduced into formal symbols and nothing else. The case of computer simulation is, therefore, a quite interesting one and deserves a study of its own in the direction we are proposing here.

At this current stage of our research, we wish to underline that advances in the techniques of computer simulation have made available several types of extensions of their working and, certainly, those which allow for the generation of graphic outputs – that are central in the so-called virtual reality – are of particular interest here.

In the field of artificial life, for instance, it is rather easy to discover what kind of essential performance the designers wish to artificialise, simulate, namely that of self-reproduction processes. In adopting recursive models, the concept of life is reduced to a process of self-referential computation which is very similar, on a formal level, to that of the development of a generic organism, assumed as an exemplar.

The purely informational observation level, of course, cannot guarantee anything but an analogy between the simulated process and the real one: nevertheless, an essential performance of this kind is quite consistent with our definition of the artificial beyond the allusive and binding terminology adopted to define this new area of research. As two designers have remarked:

> Our problem isn't that of re-creating ants but of reproducing some aspects of their behaviour. It is clear, for instance, that, unlike the computer, ants secrete pherormones. . . Once we get a satisfying simulation level we can experiment with unusual situations, changing the environment or adding some new rule, always local, for the reproduction getting, this way, a little speculation on the life-as-it-could-be.
>
> (Gambardella, Cattaneo, 1990)

The machines of the artificial have, as it were, a thin umbilical cord that connects them to nature and which, to some extent, could make them compatible with it: a characteristic absent, or only randomly present, in the products of conventional technology. In this sense, the question posed by V. G. Simons in 1983, *Are Computers Alive?* (Simons, 1983) could have a positive answer but only if limited to the observation level at which the concept of life converges with that of information processing. On the contrary, the claim, rather diffused in artificialism and in science itself, to reduce to one's attributions of 'essentiality' the whole meaning of a given system, does not possess, in principle, any hope of conclusiveness.

Even recently, Christopher Langton, to maintain the plausibility of artificial life being exactly like a form of life, proposed a principle – already introduced with some insistence in the domain of artificial intelligence – which seems to us quite unacceptable. According to this principle, namely the so called 'functional equivalence', several processes – such as intelligence or life – may be conceived as independent of the physical structure on which they are implemented.

In other terms, this principle states that physical matter is not important at all, since the only key point is the programme or the organisation of the system in itself and nothing else.

Unfortunately, we cannot agree with this claim. Here we shall limit ourselves to underline that such a principle holds only when we deal with formal or, to be more exact, informational systems or processes – like formal intelligence or formal models of life – just because these are, tendentially, independent on matter and energy.

Thus, a computer, as John Searle once said could be made of beer cans and string and, in the same way, a message could be transmitted in an emergency, without the use of words, using coloured flags or smoke clouds. All informational systems or processes are indefinitely replicable without depending, within certain limits at least, on material structures.

Yet a very different situation is the artificial reproduction – in concrete terms – of exemplars, structures or processes, of real matter, in the sense of empirical and material matter which incorporated the formal definition of a living system or human intelligence.

In this domain it seems to us that almost by definition physical structure plays an absolutely decisive role.

Often researchers seem to be inspired by the so-called 'emergence principle', according to which if one is able to set up the right structure – emulating the exemplar – then the properties of the exemplar will appear spontaneously.

Nevertheless, as a rule, from a concrete artificial object we cannot expect any emergence – beyond the essential performance we planned – which, as a miracle, would be similar to what we observe in nature. This is due to the fact that the observation levels of concrete reality – both of the natural and of the artificial reality – and their interplays have to be considered as infinite. In other words, the probability that the properties of the natural object and of the artificial object could overlap is a negligible one.

The success of the reproduction of an exemplar of concrete stuff may be defined as the achievement, by means of non-natural materials and procedures, of an essential performance that, at the selected observation level, is indistinguishable from the natural one. But only at that level, of course.

In this very close but realistic meaning even the successful artificialistic work demonstrates the validity of the idea of functional equivalence. An artificial kidney, for instance, reproduces rather efficiently an organic process by means of alternative physical structures and procedures compared to the natural ones.

It is also true, on the other hand, that the materials used cannot be chosen arbitrarily or at random: the strategic point is not the 'program' or their 'organisational architecture' (which are usually very different from those exhibited by the exemplar), but just their physical and behavioural compatibility with the performance, which is also physical.

Therefore, the materials are irrelevant only when the exemplar and the essential performance to be reproduced are not material, i. e. when it is purely informational. From this we see that the 'life' Langton has in his mind has nothing to do with real one and is valid only in the case of an informational understanding of this concept.

In a sense, we could confine ourselves to think of life according to our model – and this is just what happens when we write a program for simulating life – but this would involve only a representation of life and not a reproduction of it.

Being able to reproduce the autopoiesis process through a symbolic recursive system, for instance, means to establish a formal analogy – a simulation, in other words – between this informational process and the autopoiesis of the organic cells system and not to reproduce it. No specialist at NASA labs would pretend, I think, to define as artificial journeys their simulation models of the space shuttle.

But the machines of the artificial also show, in the essential performances that they sometimes succeed in reproducing, a context of real or potential performances which in no way overlaps the natural contexts within which they reveal themselves.

This point is very clear in the case of so-called 'virtual reality', since this branch of computer science directly tries to allow the user to experience usual or unusual situations provided he keeps in mind the observation levels pre-selected by the machine.

Even here the terminology adopted for defining the area is a somewhat ambiguous one: why should we define something which is virtual as reality; on the other hand, why should we call something which is real, virtual? The fact is that, as in the cases of artificial intelligence and artificial life, designers are motivated both from a need for distinction and from a need of impressing people's imagination.

Actually, virtual reality is a fictional technology characterised by what we could term a Tree-dimensional Dynamic Interaction (TDI) simulation. Showing TDI features, virtual reality may be seen as a different thing from other fiction or fantasy based processes or products, cinema, television and cartoons, since these exhibit only the second one or the first two of TDI properties, although they share the observation level which, in all cases, is human vision.

Furthermore, virtual reality is a much wider area than artificial life, since it may consist of several widely different machines oriented to several widely different aims, each of them representing some exemplar: houses or museums, landscapes or cellular structures and even completely imagined situations built up by means of simulation algorithms based on a mix of realistic and arbitrary rules.

Once again the artificial can work well, thanks to the great power of computers, on the one hand and, to the possibility to describe mathematically many, though not all, the contours of the world on the other.

As it has been remarked with excessive enthusiasm, after having quoted Galileo's view of the universe as a book,

> Maybe the universe is not a book so much as a computer, everything that exists within it is the product of some algorithm. If so, this would mean that Turing's universal machine would truly be universal: given the right table of behaviour, and sufficient time, it could reproduce an entire virtual universe.
>
> (Wolley, 1992)

To some degree, the concept of virtuality reminds us of the concept of potential introduced by Aristotle, while that of reality could be similarly related or defined as his concept of act: indeed, like a computer, the virtual reality machines, as potential things, are always waiting for some instantiation by an external 'engine'.

In this way, a virtual reality machine could be seen as a tool for transducing our projects and our desires into artificial objects which are *actual* at a visual observation level but *potential* in their purely informational stuff. We think we could say the same for holographic objects, even when they will join the technology of virtual reality.

What is clear, however, is that in every case we shall have some essential performance dominating another and, as is usual for the artificial, we shall have no serious possibility to design a realistically integrated device which is able to reproduce the interplay among different performances as it works in reality. This point is and will be very crucial in fields such as tele-surgery, within which the virtual reality device is designed for working as a reliable representation of the body of the patient on which the surgeon acts as if the patient were in front of him. Therefore, much more than in cases of established virtual reality tools – such as the military maps adopted by headquarters for managing a battle – the surgeon will need realistic feed-backs from the field requiring the reproduction of structures or processes belonging to more than one observation level.

Actually, beyond the available TDI features, in order to reproduce the world in a more accurate way, we should have to enter not only the informational reality but also the non-informational one, that is to say the concrete reality and its empirical dimensions. Thus, further advance in research into virtual reality cannot hope to fully achieve any significant success if they neglect to take account of the complex methodological difficulties, perhaps conclusive, which every attempt to cumulate multiple performances in an integrated artificial device is fated to meet.

The anthropomorphic preparation of an automaton at the beginning of the twentieth Century. Below, a doll that serves tea is a reconstruction of the designs involved in the Japanese Karakuri zui, *1796. In order that the exemplar can be recognized, a look is needed which matches shared human representations of it. This enables the artificial to be accepted by the culture. Source: M. G. Losano,* Storie di automi, *Einaudi, Torino, 1990.*

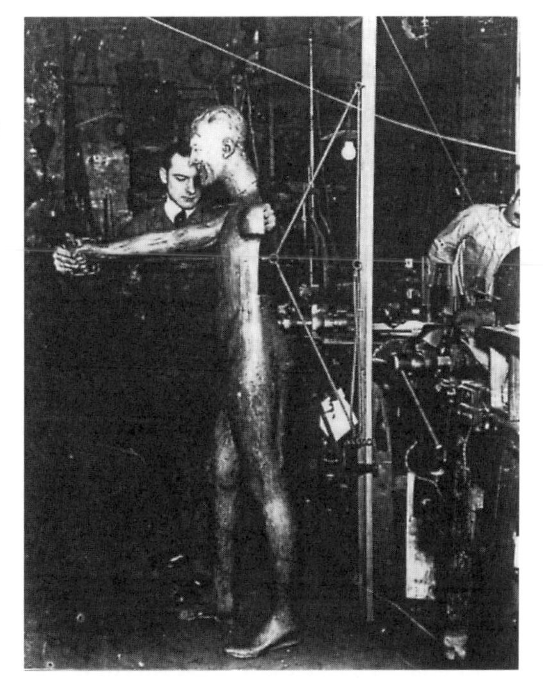

2. The Theory of the Artificial

1. Overturning a classical debate

After having introduced in the previous chapter the main terms of the TA (particularly those of observation level, exemplar and essential performance), we shall now expound the details of our theory, starting from its motivational premises. The long debate on artificial intelligence has brought up to date and renewed man's disposition towards the artificial and, consequently, has made it possible for us to advance a theory. Taking our cue from the ideas that have emerged from that debate, the TA intends to shift our attention from the first term of the binomial, intelligence, upon which the whole debate was centred, towards the second term, the 'artificial'. For years we have inquired 'what is intelligence?' but we never asked what the artificial is. Clearly we need a definition, both in general and analytical terms, explaining the concept of artificial not only in an adjectival and more or less negative sense, but also in a substantial sense.

In forming such a definition we recognise that the conceptual relationship between the artificial and the natural is remarkably close and straightforwardly constitutive, compared to the commonly held view.

First we note that while the 'natural' has, or we could assume that it has, an autonomous and independent 'status', the artificial would not make any sense without reference to something in nature, which is taken as a target of the attempted reproduction. The artificial, in other words, always exists in comparison to something else and it could be defined, tentatively at this initial stage, as an adjective to which a technological object can be assigned which is aimed at reproducing something using different materials and procedures.

In taking a second provisional step, we must recognise the impossibility for the artificial to reproduce all the characteristics of the natural object which is taken to denote an exemplar since, if it could do so, there would be no need for defining it as artificial. Instead, we would have to speak of a naturally replicated object. The generator of a replicated object, on the other hand, should be coincidental, in its turn, with natural generators. A replicated object, such as a clone, does not involve the reproduction of any particular aspect of the natural object but of all its characteristics and then this is only possible through natural processes.

The artificial is, therefore, an object that is forced to fluctuate between nature and conventional technology since it would not be able to identify itself either with the former or with the latter.

The artificial, far from bringing back what is simply 'non-natural' as a concept, depends closely upon the exemplar that it aims to reproduce whilst, as a concrete product, it depends, unavoidably and paradoxically, only upon conventional technology in order to become a reality.

We can now propose a synthesis of the above considerations through an indepth discussion of the three fundamental concepts of the TA: the observation level, the exemplar and the essential performance. (The whole set of the concepts introduced by the TA is, in addition, laid out in the 'Glossary' below).

2. The TA: observation levels

The observation level is the level at which the artificialist 'observes' nature and identifies, within it, a sub-system that he considers to be reproducible.

This is an epistemological premise that can lead to two different interpretations.

On the one hand, taking a realist stance, we may assimilate the observation level to a state of nature: in this perspective the observation level is an internal character of reality and the observer must necessarily conform to it.

On the other hand, taking either a subjectivist or constructivist position, the observation level is a necessary expediency of the human mind: the internal nature of our mind can ideate or select, for each unit of time, some homogeneous classes, or levels, of the real world which is, *in se*, a continuous whole. The important point is that, in each case, the observer selects different levels at different moments and thus isolates the reality, which regardless of his approach acts through him as if it possessed independent qualities: these observation levels are, however, the sole reality that the observer can interact with, although without any hope of being able to identify some definitive level. As Morin wrote,

> In the same way that every system escapes from some side to the mind of the observer for depending on the physis, every system, also the one which seems more evident from the phenomenic point of view, like a machine or an organism, depends also on the mind in the sense that the isolation of a system and the isolation of the concept of system are abstractions performed by the observer/ conceptualizer.
>
> (Morin, 1977)

Since the emergence of modern scientific research, this is a well-known question, though in terms perhaps more naïve but probably even more relevant for the history of science. During these times, the anxious search for instruments and procedures for surveying reality 'as it is' often led to many frustrations. For example, François Bichat, the founder of histology, referring to the reliability of the observations made possible by the microscope, said that, such instruments

> ne me paraissent pas d'ailleurs avoir jamais retiré un grand secours, parce que quand on regarde dans l'obscurité, chacun voit a sa manière.
>
> (quoted in Galloni, 1993)

In the perspective of a theory of the artificial, the most remarkable aspect of a methodological premise in terms of observation levels is their hereditary character. When man builds a machine or, more generally, when he behaves, he follows a plan which is oriented or polarised towards some target around which he organises his materials and his building procedures. In other words, he acts as if all the things were happening at the observation level he has selected.

But the result of man's action, the machine or the situation, will also be real from other, infinitely latent or potential observation levels, even though these were neglected by his plan. Reality is not, as it were, reducible: the construction of a machine which aims at some essential performance does not itself imply a lower richness of observation levels compared to those which characterise any other portion of reality.

The concept of the observation levels can also refer to the position that we take in the interval the 'micro-macro'. For example, traditional mechanics and optics are oriented to the study and production of machines that could be built and then used by man according to the position that he occupies to suit his nature in the above cited interval. Therefore, the machines have to be compatible with the dimensions of his hands, with the resolution of his eyes and with the range of frequencies of his ear, etc. But the availability of more sophisticated knowledge and technologies has recently allowed researchers to carry on studies and projects within micro-worlds which up to now have never been approached and which are characterised from phenomena which are not always understandable by analogy with other levels. It is enough to think, for example, of the fields of micromechanics and binary optics. Further, the problems related to these new observation levels will involve, quite naturally, the technology of the artificial itself.

3. The inheritance principle

This frequent and unavoidable technological delusion comes from the tacit claim that organising any matter according to a pre-organised plan forces the machine to be only what is established by the design and, therefore, what the selected level allows one to see, as if, in other words, all its constitutive or observable levels would obediently orient themselves to the target desired by the planner.

However, what happens in reality is described as a sort of revenge: the reality will be present and act with all its features and not just through those which have been selected by the designer according to a given observation level. This is what we call the 'inheritance principle'. It governs not only the work of artificialists but also any action by man.

This is a well-known effect in pharmacology: the side effects, or so called sudden events, are often just the result of an interaction between the drug (components of the drug) and the guest system (i.e. the components of the system). Any drug, though polarised to some 'effect', always implies a 'machine' that inherits all the levels, both known and unknown, which characterise the whole structure of its components.

More generally, the best example for clarifying this point could be what we will call the illusion of the perfect crime. Even if the criminal is very careful in preparing his crime, he cannot check all the observation levels involved or 'inherited' by his action (macroscopic actions, biologic, physical, chemical, social traces, etc.) and it is just at one of these levels that the scientific police, actually or potentially, will find some unchecked sign, which will enable them to discover the culprit.

The observation levels could depend on dimensional natural factors and on cultural paradigms. The attraction or motivational power of some aspects of the objective or subjective reality could sometimes be strong enough to set the level at an apparently optimal level, 'real', 'essential', and 'true', yet not 'unique'. A painting by Brueghel will explain this point better than a long discussion. The traditional representation of

Jan Brueghel the Elder, The Entry of the Animals into Noah's Ark, 1613. Source: Paul Getty Museum, Malibu, California.

Noah's ark may help us to understand how man is naturally oriented to perceive reality in anthropomorphic terms: all the animals which were selected to survive have physical dimensions which are compatible with our senses, while microbiological living systems are fated to extinction. The love for a certain animal species, furthermore, often imposes an observation level which is functional to the affective character that we attribute to it. This polarisation leads us to neglect those levels at which we could observe the brutality and cruelty of the observed species towards their preys.

3.1. The TA: exemplars

As we have already outlined, an exemplar is an object, or a sub-system of a natural system, which the artificialist assumes as the target of the reproduction. Usually it is a sub-system of a system which apparently could be easily isolated from its context, but in some cases it could also be a discovery or a hypothesis about the structure of the world.

Furthermore, when looking at an exemplar we cannot but assume a given profile (e.g. the histological structure of a muscle) since even the isolation of the exemplar as a sub-system is insufficient to reduce local complexity. It is also worth noting that, on occasion, the selection of an exemplar depends on a previous selection of an essential performance which attracted the attention of the researcher. Researchers often look for a structure to attribute to a performance whose reality is given with no clear idea of its source (this case is greatly diffused in artificial intelligence).

Within the study of mental states in psychology, the exemplars are necessarily subjective. They are more difficult to define, as representations are, and less acceptable as being a real state of nature. In these cases (and this is always the case for artificialism), the success of the reproduction will firstly depend on the degree of likelihood of the existence (assumed) of an exemplar as a meaningful object or process. For instance, the shared belief that there exists a faculty of the mind named 'intelligence' leads us to try to reproduce it as if it were an object or a process, isolated from the context.

Within artificial intelligence, the so-called context-free reproduction of intelligent behaviours, it is impossible to maintain that human intelligence can be clearly isolated from the context of the mind. Thus the advances in the building of intelligent devices generate many kinds of intelligence. Although they are in principle all possible for the human mind, they will increasingly transfigure the purely imagined exemplars they come from. In other words, they will be really intelligent but this will be a sort of distilled, or purified, intelligence rather than human-like.

Artificial intelligence devices seem to be similar to certain metallurgic experiments carried on board artificial satellites in order to avoid the interference of atmospheric phenomena. However, there is evidence that human intelligence is not altered by the interference of the world (owing to the activity of the brain) but is possible thanks to the relationship with the environment. In this sense, when artificial intelligence devices work well, they set up a Platonic kind of ideal world which is only useful for accomplishing very formal reasoning tasks, that is to say, when man has to work in an extremely pure and fatiguingly abstract context.

Finally, the concept of an exemplar is a crucial point for understanding the artificial since it lies at the centre of the artificialistic project. On the one hand, we can conceive of the things in the world as objects or processes which we can empirically and successfully separate both in order to study and to reproduce them. On the other, we cannot ignore that the level at which we observe the empirical world acts as a filter preventing us from observing other features of the exemplar we have selected.

For this reason, the behaviour of an artificial device will always resemble closely the human exemplar, depending on the extent to which the observer or the user closely sets himself at the same observation level as the designer.

Of course, if the observer or the user were to deal with a new or a strongly subjective observation level, then he would face more problems in recognising the closeness of the fit of the reproduction. This is not only the case of artistic reproduction, which is innovative by definition, but it happens also in science. Indeed, the reproduction of the Copernican solar system through a mechanical device would have been not so easily understood, nor appreciated, at a time when Aristotelian representation was the commonly shared model. On the contrary, in mechanistic culture, towards the end of the sixteenth century, Kepler could design a three-dimensional reproduction of the universe, *the Machina mundi artificialis*, which was given as a gift to Prince Friedrich von Württemberg. At the same time, the mathematician Henri de Monantheuil maintained that

> the man, being an image of God, was invited to imitate him as a mechanician and to produce objects that could compete with those made by nature.
>
> (Bredekamp, 1993)

In conclusion, the exemplar is the 'what is it?' feature of the object or process we are trying to reproduce and, since the exemplar is incorporated in some specific word and in some more or less shared representation, its accurate description and isolation within the natural context seems an easy affair.

3.2. The TA: essential performances

The essential performance is the performance of the object, the process, or the sub-system which is characteristic of an exemplar and is the specific target of the reproduction process. In other words, the essential performance is the behaviour or the performance of an exemplar with which it is deemed to have a univocal or exclusive relationship: that is, the one which best describes the specificity of the exemplar. The exemplar can often be 'isolated' simply because of the performance it exhibits when it is described at a particular and shared observation level.

The core of a performance will almost always depend upon our decision, rather than its emergence from reality. Furthermore, our more or less shared judgement will be of great importance: nobody will deny that in man the kidney has a filtering function. But the selected observation level could, in principle, conceal some alternative performances which could arise later, thanks to new scientific explorations, say through the setting of new observation levels.

The concept of an essential performance ultimately derives from the exemplar which confers onto it its dynamic features.

The essential performance is, thus, the 'what does it do?' of an exemplar. The essential performance often replaces totally the exemplar itself, in the sense that we are more interested in reproducing the performance rather than the object or the structure which produces it in nature. This is often the case, particularly when the artificial we are trying to build is not important as an analytical reproduction but merely as a useful source of outputs, for instance when we invent sources of warm light or even when, in chemistry, we are able to synthesise various kinds of organic or non-organic substances useful to man.

To a large degree, this is the real destiny of all the artificials owing to the transfigurations that every artificial system will show during its advancement. They often start as more or less reliable reproductions of some exemplar but develop as machines, capable to generate unexpected and useful performances, often deriving from the amplification or 'purification' of performances which were indicated as the essential ones in the exemplar itself.

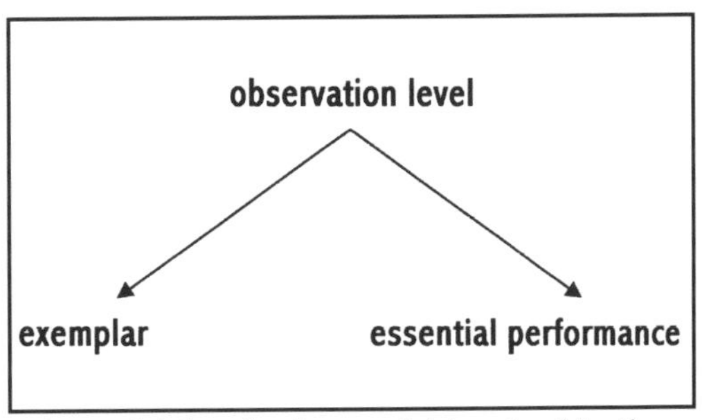

The multiple selection model involved in the design of an artificial object

The selection of an exemplar and the selection, or the attribution to it, of an essential performance depends on the previously selected observation level.

Although the TA will also concern the above cases, it is more interested in the study of artificialism in its, so to speak, genuine and pure aspects: those aspects in which artificialists try to reproduce a natural object, process or system as it is or as it results from the established and commonly held scientific view. In these cases, the deviation, whether qualitative or quantitative, of the essential performance from its model, as it is known in the natural world, would be taken as a failure, even if it exhibited useful applications.

A Minimal Glossary of the Artificial

Meta-artificial: mental voluntary and not voluntary representations of things or events in the external or internal world.

Artificial: an object, machine or process designed and carried out, based on a natural one (i.e. on the basis of its representation), and is taken to be an **exemplar** at a given **observation level.**

Analytical artificials: **artificial** objects, machines or processes which pretend to be a reliable reproduction of an **exemplar** and of its **essential performance** on the basis of its analytical knowledge, as it is described in some established scientific theory or model.

Aesthetical artificials: **artificial** objects, machines or processes which do not pretend to be a reliable reproduction of an exemplar and of its **essential performance**, but only to reproduce them in aesthetical terms, as an intentional fiction, more or less easily recognizable.

Structure oriented artificial: the artificial which aims to reproduce the structure of an **exemplar**. The **essential performance** is expected to 'emerge' from the structure, as if it were a function of it.

Process oriented artificial: the artificial which aims to reproduce the **essential performance** directly, without reproducing the structure of the **exemplar**.

Conventional technology: the technology which builds up original objects, machines or processes, which are not oriented to **exemplars**.

Essential performance: the performance which, at a given **observation level**, is considered to be typical and characterizes the **exemplar**.

Exemplar: the natural object or sub-system, at some **observation level**, to be reproduced in order to get the **essential performance**.

Inheritance principle: every **artificial** object will possess all the known and unknown properties, and the performances embodied in the materials and the procedures adopted to built it.

Homologous components: components of the **artificial** system and of the **exemplar** which exhibit, at least ideally, the same structure and/or the same functions

Isolability: the disposition of a sub-system (assumed as an **exemplar**) to be heuristically isolated from the global systemic context without any meaningful loss in the conduct of its **essential performance**.

Observation level: the level, selected by the researcher or the designer, at which the **exemplar** and its **essential performance** are described. (It is strictly related to the generation of mental and cultural representations).

Performance spectrum: the group of performances of the **exemplar** or of an artificial system

Reproduction: in general, the activity of designing and constructing an object, a machine or a process which is able to generate the **essential performance** of an object or a process, taken to be an **exemplar**. It is synonymous with 'making the artificial'.

Sub-system: a part of a given natural system which is characterised by peculiar performances. It is closely connected to the global systemic context, but it demonstrates heuristically some **isolability** from it.

Transfiguration: the transformation in the range and in the quality of **performances** that the **artificial** will exhibit as compared to the **exemplar**. The transfiguration is unavoidable because of the multiple selections implied by the design process and of the inheritance of the different materials that the **artificial** has to, by definition, adopt.

3.3. Development of the artificial: naturoids and technoids

The constraint of the observation level acts both when one indicates that an object or a sub-system will be an exemplar and when one attributes to the object or to the sub-system one or more essential performances.

Using the three basic concepts, which were introduced above, the artificial could be defined as being an object or a machine that reproduces the *essential performance* of a natural object or sub-system which is taken to be an *exemplar*, at a given *observation level*.

It is very important to understand that the contribution of conventional technology makes the artificial not only able to reproduce the natural performances of the exemplar but also to generate side performances which are almost always unforeseeable *a priori*. This explains why, as a paradoxical rule, the more an artificial device advances, the more it tends to move away from the exemplar and from its essential performance.

The artificial, in conclusion, is conceived and present in the first phases of its existence as a *naturoid*, an object achieved by man and oriented to some natural exemplar as it is seen at a given observation level. However, it soon becomes, or reveals itself to be, a *technoid*, that is to say, it becomes an object that exhibits characteristics which exceed those of the exemplar and either strengthens, reduces or somehow transfigures some of these, as if it had to redraw the exemplar not as it is but as it should be. Furthermore, as we have already pointed out, the artificial is constrained to fluctuate between nature and conventional technology: the identification with either the former or with the latter would, in fact, remove its peculiarity.

Interestingly and quite independently of our study, a recent report from the Biomedical Engineering Center of the Minnesota Institute of Technology (1995) introduces the concept of *organoids* to refer to the devices which in the future will

> expedite millions of years of evolution by assembling bioartificial membranes, tubes and neurofilaments.
>
> (Hoffman, 1995)

although,

> Artificial substitutes for failed or damaged tissues and organs have been around for more than 40 years, but the limitations and side effects make clear the need for better solutions.
>
> (Hoffman, op. cit.)

Ideally, advances in the field of many artificial devices, must necessarily take into account the growing number of observation levels or scales, since

> If we want to engineer a material that has the characteristics of soft composite biomaterials, we have to understand the interactions at all scales, from the molecules, up to the cells, and up to the macroscopic properties of tissues
>
> (Tirrell, 1995, in Hoffman, op. cit.)

But this would ignore, at least in principle, the fact that every material adopted at a given observation level will behave according to its own rules and that these rules will show a different range compared to natural ones. The overlap among all the ranges of materials will intrinsically generate an unpredictable quantity and quality of phenomena, even if the resulting device exhibits a behaviour which is more compatible, on a local and regular basis, with the requirements of the natural exemplar. This problem would be avoided if, and only if, all the structures and all the functions which characterise the natural system, that is to say all the potential exemplars and performances of it, were to be substituted according to a one-to-one criterion and, of course, with of the same materials adopted by nature. This would mean, in turn, the setting up of a replicative design rather than an arificialistic one and this would be, as we shall see later in this book, a quite different and impossible affair on an analytical basis.

Our hypothesis is that the development of subsequent generations of the same artificial object fundamentally possesses an intrinsic orientation towards the new, as is typical in conventional technology. The latter is, in fact, not only essential for generating the initial release of a machine which is able to reproduce exemplars and natural performances but it is also the only source of knowledge (on materials and procedures) for advancing the artificial and for expanding its potential. The further introduction of conventional technologies, heterogeneous by definition, compared to the components of the exemplar (or at least compared to the components which are unavoidably neglected from the observation level assumed by the artificialist) will always remove the artificial from the exemplar.

This intrinsic destiny of the artificial is not necessarily related to a loss of effectiveness in the reproduction of the essential performance towards which it has been oriented. Rather, we will simultaneously get contingent improvements in the performance and losses or metamorphoses within other related performances present within the exemplar and also new performances. As we shall see later in this book, the perspective which is being analysed here assumes that there is a particular relevance in those of man's activities which, though they do not reach a finality in the physical production of a machine, reveal internal characteristics such that one can justify their interpretation by means of the TA itself.

It is not uncommon that sudden events and side performances exhibited by the artificial persuade the artificialist to follow new plans which are induced just from that unexpected phenomena or behaviour. This is often a better decision than insisting on the consistency and amelioration of the original performances, which is an effort that always involves, beyond a certain threshold, exponentially growing costs and marginal effectiveness. There is a frequent tendency for this, for example, in the field of synthesis pharmacology but also in artificial intelligence, electronics, bio-engineering (remember the so-called 'bionics' of the late fifties?) and in many other fields of advanced research, amongst which are the phenomena of computer art (Bertasio, 1992) and computer music (Baggi, 1992).

In all these cases the conclusion is that the artificial, beyond a certain threshold of complexity, tends to transform or enrich the exemplar and its performances. This is both for the internal reason that it is a machine and because it deepens the characteristics of the exemplar 'which is isolated' from its context at one observation level and does not embody the levels that constitute the real object or sub-system.

Of special importance, of course, is the heterogeneity intrinsic to conventional technology, unavoidably adopted by the artificialist, which we have been cumulating since, at least, the seventeenth century. In fact, it is a kind of activity based on an abstract rational way of studying and controlling the world by grasping and exploiting its uniformities through means of mathematical models. Therefore, we should not forget, as Poincarè rightly states, that

> The genesis of the mathematical creation is. . . the activity in which the human mind seems to take very few from the external world, and in which it acts or seems to act only by itself and on itself
>
> (Poincarè, 1952)

Further, man's inclination to invent something new by firstly imitating something that exists is a very ancient one and it is always related to the rise of 'abstract' technological knowledge or rules. The anthropologist Franz Boas maintained that within the symbolism of primitive art one can find two distinct moments: that of representation (drawings reproduce aspects of the natural world, such as fish, snakes, men, etc.) and the other which he rightly calls purely conventional. The latter, however, could arise, according to Karl von der Steinen, from the former. In other words, in the initial stage the drawing (or the design) starts from nature by imitating some aspect of it. In this way stable styles will develop. In a second stage, the forms which have been generated in this way take on a reference value and their further development may become autonomous as innovative research. Thus, the forms move further away from the direct influence of nature and set up truly cultural models at a second level, which is more predisposed to new abstract and creative evolutions. In fact,

> the weaver 'plays' with his own technique, that is to say when, no longer satisfied to weave forward and back, he begins to skip the wires introducing then more complex rhythms of movement.
>
> (Boas, 1927)

It is easier to understand the above quotation in a wider sense if one conceives of the weaver as a universal category, or model, which depicts the natural way by which man develops technology.

3.4. Instances of advanced artificialistic attempts

It might be interesting, at this juncture, to consider some statements from a real artificialistic experience. From these we will easily recognize, the selective steps and concepts of observation level, exemplar and essential performance, as well as the roots of the advancements that designers imagine for the future. The case is that of the attempt to reproduce the retina of the human eye.

Observation level

> For years biologists have tacitly pretended that once we understand how each molecule of the membrane of a neuron operates, it would be possible to understand the operation of the brain. Nevertheless, both the digital processing paradigm and the analogical one demonstrate the groundlessness of this hypothesis.

Exemplar

> The first three layers of the retina, those of the photoreceptor, of the horizontal cells and of the bipolar cells, are the most well known. Our silicon retina is just an imitation of the organisation of these external layers.

Essential performance

> In building a silicon retina, our purpose was not to reproduce the human retina to the last detail, but to get a simplified version of it which contains the minimum necessary structure required to accomplish the biological function.

Further developments

> The real vision. . . will probably require that artificial retinas contain 100 times the number of pixels and auxiliary circuits, to imitate the functions of perception of the movement, and to intensify the contours performed by the amacrine cells and by the ganglionic cells. Finally, these systems will also include additional electronic circuits for recognising configurations generated by the retina.
>
> (M.A.Mahowald, C.Mead, 'The silicon retina', Le Scienze-Scientific American, 275, 1991, retranslated from the Italian edition).

Another typical case, which is analogous to the previous one, is the attempt to reproduce the propulsion of fish by means of a robotic model. Up to now,

> It is almost impossible to reproduce the performances of fish simply by imitating their form and function, because a vehicle able to set up uniform and continuous flexes, having a body similar to that of a fish, is quite beyond the state of art of robotics
> (Triantafyllou E. Triantafyllou, 1995)

Nevertheless, it is possible to imagine that

> In the future, such creations which are inspired by nature, will perhaps improve their biological models for some specific task, like, for instance, the exploration of the sea-bottom.
> (Triantafyllou E. Triantafyllou, ibid.)

It is very probable that with future advances we will discover that the silicon retina performs in very different way from the natural one and that these differences will allow for interesting or even strategic performances which are not possible by the human eye. In other words, this instance of the artificial will also shift it from a naturoid status to a technoid one as has happened in almost all cases where human beings have attempted to reproduce nature.

We should not ignore, then, the growing area of artificial organs, where artificial hips, arms, hands, wrists, legs and feet are currently very advanced. Within this area, along with very advanced projects like that of the artificial kidney or artificial heart, much work has been done to reproduce the essential performance of the pancreas, the liver, the eye, the internal ear and others.

Unfortunately, in all cases in which the project involves placing the artificial device inside the host organism – that is to say, its working environment – the problem arises of the immunitary rejection.

Recently, a new strategy has been developed that avoids this problem, the design of bio-artificial devices or 'organoids'. These are devices made of a bio-compatible or inert membrane which has to defend a set of natural cells given by a donor – for instance, the so called Langerhans islands, finalised to the production of insulin.

The protection consists of the fact that the technological membrane has to allow the passing of fluids, like the metabolits, necessary for cell life, but must also prevent access to the mediators (antibodies, T lymphocytes) which would intervene in order to destroy cell transplantation.

It is a matter, in the end, of a new and brilliant technological expedient, rather than of an artificial expedient, to 'cheat nature' – to use the words of Prof. Willem Kolff during the interview we shall report in a moment – rather than to reproduce it.

In fact, insulin, produced in natural ways by the cells given by the donor, will be able to do its work of holding constant the amount of glycemia as if it were produced by the host organism, which will not perceive what is really happening.

The whole game will be played, then, around the precision of the 'cheat': the membrane will be, at the same time, 'inert' in relation to the organism and 'active' in protecting and implementing the regular biological activities of the transplanted cells.

A dramatic contribution will be made, now and then, by an innovative project made possible by the materials and procedures of conventional technology.

The aspect of the boundaries between the artificial object and the environment or the context which includes it is very general. It involves not only the theme of biocompatibility in bioengineering but also all those problems which we usually refer to as *interfacing* issues. It is a problem which characterises all machines – even the conventional technology machines, of course – but it shows special features in the field of the artificial.

To give another instance, rather different from the bioengineering ones but exhibiting the same logic, think of a modern zoo.

Ken Sanes, among the others, has studied the strategies of designers of artificial environments *(artificial naturescapes)* destined to 'cheat' or to illude visitors to a technologically advanced zoo. Obviously, the first task to be accomplished is that of observing, directly or indirectly, the environment in which the exemplars live. For the project of the Lied Jungle at Omaha, Nebraska, several specialists from the building companies visited Costa Rica to study the characteristics of the trees needed to reproduce the forest.

The main activity was to draw the external form of the bark by means of latex layers. After drying the latex, the designers had the pattern of the tree. Once they were transferred to the Lied Jungle the patterns were pressed onto concrete columns, conveniently tree-shaped, 50-80 feet high, to obtain a 'replica' of the bark. The same technique was used for the reproduction of rocks, which were then worked by hand, as were the trees, to apply colours as close as possible to the natural ones.

After this phase the artificial trees are erected among natural ones with the result that visitors, looking at the landscape, lose their ability to distinguish the natural from the artificial.

At Jungle World – another artificial naturescape – the visitor, from a given position, sees two layers of leaves: those in the foreground are made of polyester while those in the background are ficus; it is impossible to distinguish them.

At another observation level, the acoustic speakers hidden in the trees continuously emit choruses of birds and insects, recorded in a Thai forest, which blends with the sounds made by the animals in their cages at Jungle World.

The separation of the natural (the public which must be illuded) from the artificial (the illusory devices) is, therefore, done accurately, just as bioengineers do when they try to separate an artificial organ from the host organism. But at this point,

> we have barely begun to scratch the surface of illusion. As we do so, we discover that immersion landscapes also rely on stealth simulations, which is to say, they use partial invisibility, cover-ups, distraction and disguise to hide features that might interfere with the illusion. As in any good magic act, the art is in what the audience can't see and what it fails to notice.
>
> (Sanes, 1998)

Rightly, Sanes underlines that

> With some variation, these qualities can be found in all the invented 'worlds' that make up popular culture, from theme parks and movies to virtual realities.
>
> (Sanes, op. cit.)

Furthermore, to avoid any contact among organic elements (the animals of the zoo) which could be, so to speak, 'rejected' by the host organism (the public and the surrounding structures), while allowing people to enjoy a realistic environment (the true essential performance), a series of expedients are used. These include: artificial rocks and islands on which animals may be observed and, at the same time, isolated; small wires conducting electrical currents to surfaces and even the application of vaseline to some rockfaces and beams to prevent monkeys from climbing. Sanes concludes

> it becomes obvious that there is a drama going on here that is very different from the pretence that visitors are looking at animals in a natural habitat . . . One might say that artificial rain forests are forms of theatre that have a captive cast of animal-actors who keep trying to leave the stage.
>
> (Sanes, op. cit.)

A great contribution is, of course, made by conventional technology: air conditioning devices, drainage and irrigation lines, ground supports, power suppliers and everything necessary to facilitate the sensation that one is in a tropical forest are well hidden in the rocks and the trees or behind other perceptive obstacles.

Nevertheless, things – such as the side effects which always occur with the artificial or the infections which accompany artificial organs – happen unpredictably which challenge the maintenance staff. For example, artificial rain forests are ideal habitats for mice and roaches, which find a comfortable climate and plenty of food and hiding places.

As a result, the maintenance staff – just as a highly selective drug – are always at work not only to keep alive certain animals but also to eliminate other living forms. For example, toucans were removed from the Lied Jungle because they exhibited unacceptable behaviour, destroying nests and taking away fledglings and eating many types of frog and lizard.

3.5. Types of exemplars and essential performances

From a more analytical point of view, the history of technology demonstrates that the artificial is sometimes the result of the attempt to reproduce exemplars as structures from which we want to derive given performances. In other cases, it (the artificial) is the result of the attempt to reproduce exemplars as processes, that is to say, to reproduce the performances directly, independently of the sub-system that generates them in nature.

In other words, whilst in some cases the capability of reproducing the essential performance is considered to be closely related to the capability of reproducing the structure of the exemplar, in others the capability to reproduce the essential performance is conceived as independent of this necessity. The Babbage machine was intended to reproduce a process and not the structure of the brain which does computations, which is what happens to a large extent in artificial intelligence projects. In fact, such projects almost always seem to base themselves on the previously discussed principle of functional equivalence.

In the field of AI, after some initial enthusiasm about reproducing the human mind as a structure, the research quickly oriented itself to the reproduction of intelligent processes, in whatever manner they could be generated. As Langton wrote

> The consequence is that artificial intelligence has embraced since the beginning a methodology for the generation of intelligent behaviours that doesn't have any demonstrable relation with the way in which intelligence is generated in the natural systems.
>
> (Langton, 1992)

During the process of software design in AI, the designer gets the computer to substitute or to imitate. Only by putting himself in the shoes, as it were, of the machine, of its potentiality and limits does the designer succeed in imagining and possibly in implementing decisive processes, which vary in their nature. In some ways, the mind of the designer prepares to reproduce the structure and the dispositions of the computer as an exemplar. In so doing he attributes to the machine some unusual performance of his own natural mind (Negrotti, 1991) which is purely informational, but which is suitable to the nature of the tool, which will then have to implement and execute it.

This underlines once again that the reproduction of an external reality in man's own mind is certainly one of the fundamental dispositions of human nature.

Several other examples demonstrate the frequent resort to the separation – always possible and sometimes effective – between structure and process.

The ancient and vain attempt to reproduce flight assumed the exemplar of the wing sub-system of the bird. The reproduction only succeeded when the exemplar-like process (the performance of the flight *in se*) was separated from the exemplar as structure. Ever since the success of its early models, airplane flight has, in fact, been based on completely different principles from those of animal flight.

The act of separating, which lies at the base of the whole of scientific research and of artificialism itself, coincides with what has been called the 'fractionability' of reality, thanks to which, just as in the case of flight, one refers first of all to the

> separation or segregation of the flight from the bird. This kind of fractionation is what I have elsewhere (e.g. Rosen, Fundamentals of Measurement, North Holland Pub. Co., New York, 1978) called alternate realisation, in this case of a function (flight) by distinct and otherwise unrelated material structures (bird and airplane).
>
> (Rosen, in Karlqvist et. al., 1993)

3.6. The exemplars in human communication

An exemplar, as an object to be reproduced, could belong not only to the external world – though it is always mediated by the internal one – but also to the internal one itself. By this we mean that the concept of exemplar not only concerns the artificialist but also man whenever he communicates something. This type of exemplar, which we will call subjective, includes mental states such as: thoughts, representations, intuitions, analytical or synthetic visions, images, scenarios of lived experience, etc. The reproduction, that is to say, the communication of such exemplars and of their essential performances, which are subjective in their turn, appears closely analogous to the concrete production of artificial objects. In the case of representations, in particular, we set up a second order process of reproduction, since the representation is a subjective reproduction of reality, and its further reproduction during communication will generate an artificial that takes a meta-artificial object – namely a subjective representation – to be an exemplar. In parallel, the selection of the essential performances will occur in two ways: the first is when the mind generates the representation of reality and the second is the moment at which it tries to communicate it.

Reproduction always and unavoidably concerns the selection of something essential from some observation level. It does not concern the complete mental state, whose wholeness could only be replicated by reproducing the exact and complete mental context of a subject in the mind of another. This formulation bears some similarity with N. Luhmann, who speaks of communication as the 'transfer of a reduced complexity' (Luhmann, 1975). However, in our case, the emphasis is placed upon the arbitrary effort of the actors in selecting the observation levels and the essential performances required for communicating.

This effort sometimes involves making rational selections using information techniques (take the case of standardised ideograms used for informing people at an airport) but more frequently such an effort is achieved linguistically, where semantics and style offer a relatively poor formalisation.

Lack of formalisation plays the precious function of allowing people to communicate with a highly expressive and interpretative flexibility. However, it also carries an enduring vagueness, particularly when we have to deal with mental or sensorial processes that are neither objectifiable nor measurable. This happens in the case of taste, the sense of smell and physical pain, and also for many other psychic episodes. In all these cases, and in many others, the adoption of linguistic technology and the reproductive power of semantics does not guarantee success.

When they communicate, people reduce exemplars and performances to some type of familiar symbology or to shared reference concepts drawn from disciplines or activities that, at least on a conventional basis, offer a certain inter-subjectivity. Thus a perfume becomes 'soft', the taste of a wine 'round' or a pain 'acute', but also a discourse becomes 'flat', a personality 'spiky' or an expression 'icy'. Such expedients or metaphors introduce standardised exemplars and performances which are in various measure distant from the specificity of the exemplar and of the essential performance that is to be reproduced. In addition, despite their pragmatic effectiveness, as in Peirce's sense, they assign a rather standardised nature to daily communication.

In some sense, we may then assign to the daily communication a dynamic which is similar to a bounce. The specific meaning of the message, stored in A's mind, is translated as something artificial, constituted by the linguistic elements that A thinks of sharing with B and is then deposited and reproduced in B's mind. But it also returns to A, who judges the effectiveness of the message as if he were a listener. Communication generates an artificial which, first of all, has to work well according to the criteria of the transmitter: in this sense, the process of communicating is sometimes persuading but is always self-persuading.

4. The exemplars in the arts

The composition of a work of art relies simultaneously upon systems of rules and the flexibility of their use. However the ambiguity of the final product is not only harmful as it is in the ordinary communication of mental statuses, but is meant to be enjoyed like an aesthetical event. The transfiguration of the exemplar and of its essential performance – which is the cause of the ambiguity – is the central and intentional objective of the artist. The ability of the artist can be defined as the ability to generate an artificial using the tools of language, painting, poetry, music and technology, whose harmony and completeness are definitive: although they are open to different interpretations, their content cannot be modified. While our daily speech often has a shapeless structure, circularity, deviations and breaks, a painting or a musical composition cannot be altered or 'summed up': its complexity cannot be reduced without a loss of aesthetic content. It is not possible to change at random some note in a musical score or some words in a lyric without imposing a potentially heavy loss in the beauty of the whole. Just as with a technical drawing or a computer program, although these are genetically different matters of production, the manipulation of an artistic text will always be an arbitrary act that will destroy its aesthetical value. As a result the exemplar would lose the capability to transfer itself and the transfer of the essential performance which the author has decided to make coincident to a precise whole of the technological and technical elements. Paradoxically, the ambiguity of art is the deliberate result of rigorous decisions and actions, which cannot be separated from it, just as form is inseparable from content.

Periodically in the history of thought since Aristotle, we see the appearance of aesthetic descriptions which are oriented to an imitative conception of the processes involved in the composition of art. In this vein, an interesting Italian scholar and scenographer of the nineteenth century wrote,

> the principal purpose of the imitative Arts is to represent through their special means the productions of nature.
>
> (Blasis, 1844)

The adoption of 'special means', that is to say of conventional technology such as the tools of the painter or of the musical composer, or the idiom of the poet or of the playwright, is one of the fundamental causes, as we have maintained several times in this work, of the transfiguration, dictated by the artificial product. This is in contrast to the exemplar. Thus, at the end,

> The imitators normally go beyond their models to such a degree that the eccentric fictions insensibly multiply, all is denatured.
>
> (Blasis, ibid.)

In the same vein, Oscar Wilde writes,

> The purpose of art is not simple truth but complex beauty. Art, in the end, is a form of exaggeration of things, and the selection of these things themselves, that is the soul of them, is nothing but an intensified form of emphasis.
>
> (Wilde, 1901)

Other, more classical references to the old problems, only briefly sketched here, link the nature of artistic production and its relationship with the essential performances of an exemplar and its 'imitation'. These can be found in this book in the chapter by Bertasio.

5. Epistemology of the artificial: the observer and his bets

The essential performance of a natural object or sub-system, at a given observation level, seems to be peculiar or characteristic of that object or sub-system. Science, like the activity of the artificialist himself, develops by means of 'bets' or decisions on the essentiality of the performances of a sub-system and then, implicitly, upon the decisive character of the assumed observation level. The essential performance of a leaf in a tree, at a certain level of observation, is photo-chlorophyllian synthesis; at another level the essential performance is the mechanical function of harvesting water, and at another level yet, some nutritional function. The debate on artificial intelligence has highlighted this methodological aspect.

Each performance of a computer, programmed for intelligent behaviour, either implicitly or explicitly, refers to the mental performances exhibited by the human mind but at very different observation levels according to the purpose: computational, inferential, associative, etc.

Furthermore, it is interesting to underline the analogy between the couple cause / effect in scientific activity and the couple exemplar / essential performance in the technology of the artificial. In both cases the researcher adopts assumptions and techniques for isolating phenomena which in nature are connected to the guest systems (Collins, 1990) and which relate to an endless spectrum of potential levels of observation.

The disposition to single out homogeneous classes of phenomena for scientific or applicative purposes is the basis of the human way of facing the world, albeit its achievement is not without cost because it entails the loss of wholeness. In any case, such a process of separation constitutes a fecund means both for knowing nature and for getting effectiveness from machines. The science and technology of the artificial, being bounded by the selection of observation levels, can only adopt strategies of conceptual isolation and assumptions of the *coeteris paribus* type. These strategies are based on the implicit assumption that there is a world to observe but that, at the same time, we cannot capture the world in its wholeness on the basis of empirical observations.

Furthermore, scientific reason tends to select what it judges as relevant from the world, as wisely underlined by Max Weber when he says

> All conceptual knowledge of the infinite reality by the finite human mind rests on the tacit assumption that only a finite part of the reality should form the object of scientific consideration, and, therefore, result 'essential' in the sense of being 'worth to be known'.
>
> (Weber, 1904)

With reference to this, the TA emphasises a conception that could be defined as objective relativism.

The problem of observation concerns both science and technology as well as daily life. Perhaps the central question is: 'When we observe something, do we see the reality as it is or do we observe only something coherent and dependent upon the physical or cultural system to which we belong?' As we have already remarked, by accepting the first alternative, we choose a position that could be defined as empirist or objectivist; if we accept the second, we choose a position that can be defined as relativistic, constructivistic or neo-systemic.

Objective relativism tries simultaneously to avoid the sceptical results of relativism and of the metaphysical kind brought about by positivism. According to the relativistic-objective perspective, which is only pointed to here, the observer is constitutively and then fatally situated in a system, and he observes according to implicit constraints. But a large part of what he observes could be observed in the same way by whoever follows the same operations and is placed in the same system. The observer can declare objective or inter-subjective judgements.

As far as scientific research is concerned, there is no need for self-referential premises (Maturana & Varela, 1986) or to assume the anthropic principle which is being developed in the wake of quantum physics. Perhaps the function of such epistemological assumptions is rather that of claryfying the roots of knowledge and not of depicting the real cognitive value that men actually produce. This is useful for explaining and predicting, which we can achieve if we start from the recognition that we exist as parts of different systems at different moments.

In other words, the unavoidable position of the observer within a system implies that it is impossible to observe the real world *in toto*, but it allows us to perform our observations with all their real effects. Among the several questions that we cannot discuss here, it remains open as to what the boundaries of the systems we belong to are at a given moment, what we can ultimately claim when we point out one as being distinct from one another. It is clear that the necessarily arbitrary attribution of a systemic character to some reality is, in itself, a further consequence and proof of our necessary choice of observation levels. Whether such levels are internal to reality, and can be isolated in terms of discovery, or extrinsic and dependent on our physical and mental or cultural structure, is a rather fascinating problem but completely irrelevant to our aim of acquiring effective scientific knowledge, particularly in fields such as that of the artificial, which have been recently explored and are still dense with macroscopic phenomenologies. We mention the methodological and epistemological aspects of artificialism to reveal the character of the processes which occur before the concrete generation of the artificial.

6. Epistemology of the artificial: selection and reproduction

In order to reproduce something which exists, man must first be conscious of its existence and of its characteristics.

Similarly, it is valid to pose more specific questions of the type: what does it mean for us to prepare ourselves for building an artificial brain? After taking the first fatal steps, the artificialist who embarks on such an enterprise will reveal his implicit or explicit selected observation level: organic, biochemical, electric, informational, mental and so on. Such revelation holds for other, apparently simpler, kinds of exemplars: for example, 'what aims does the reproduction of a flower exhibit?' We could not aim at the total reproduction of a flower using the same natural materials (even if it were possible, it would be a natural flower), but, at the same time, we can immediately see that we cannot adopt totally exclusive heterogeneous architectures and adopt some which are extraneous to the exemplar (it would be quite another thing). The observation level selected for pointing out the flower-like exemplar (micro, macro or something intermediate), will induce us to attribute to it some essential performance (e.g. the form, the colour, the perfume, etc.) and to neglect other possibilities (the consistency, the cell dynamics, etc.).

The entire process of ideation and of design consists, therefore, in a series of increasingly narrow inclusive selections that take us far from the exemplar as a whole; they describe in some way and measure how we enter into reference systems which are more and more specific and cogent.

The relativistic-objective observation is the only one at our disposal and it depends on those systems of reference within which we are situated and also upon others that we deliberately assume through rational decisions. The latter case is exactly that of scientific research and also of artificialistic activity. On a scientific basis, any research aimed at reconstructing reality as a whole (that is to say, from all the possible observation levels) is without hope: it would be a purely metaphysical enterprise. In the same way, attributing an absolute and exhaustive status to the facts which we observe at a selected level would be a reductive process that would prevent us (and this has happened many times in the history of the scientific ideas) from studying them at other levels. This is a 'temptation' which has occurred many times in the course of history: think of electricity, to which were attributed central roles in several phenomenologies, including the sexual act (Leschiutta, Rolando Leschiutta, 1993).

The objects that we perceive from the observation levels that we assume in each unit of time and of space are not 'pieces' or partial spheres of reality: rather, they are the verifiable reality that we can grasp from those selected levels.

When we look at reality, we always have in our mind some kind of filter which is in tune with our interest at that moment. When we check a map we do it in order to seek out some selected information. Hence we use, for example, a motoring map instead of a weather or physical or demographical one. While it is impossible to conceive of, and therefore use, a map covering all the known observation levels, it is quite reasonable to assume that each thematic map describes a true reality.

Scientists, just like ordinary people, form a community (this enables them to be successful in communicating) which shares the same observation level, whose common selection at a given moment and place depends upon different cultural factors: freedom, convenience, knowledge needs and urgency.

Scientists can easily agree that their work upon similar types of empirical levels is due to the sensors human beings are equipped with, the sensitivity of which is largely tuned in the same way and extension. The system itself is a linguistic convention which in the end must allow some sensorial interaction with the measured object.

On the contrary, when men deal with psychological or cultural levels they cannot simply rely on some shared physical structures; rather, they must rely upon some kind of subjective or cultural construction of meaning. Therefore, the overlapping between areas of possible agreement becomes unpredictably narrower and narrower and may even disappear, as if it were a hallucination.

The artificiality of science itself (Churchman, 1970) does not consist in it being merely a product of man, but in being the result of a reproduction of representations, visions, landscapes and images that are created in the mind of the scientist who looks at reality to gain some understanding of it. Scientists are successful when they are able, by means of clauses that select observation levels, to achieve a shared agreement about the characteristics and behaviour of an object, by starting from the selected image which they developed in their own mind. The inter-subjective agreement on the behaviour (or the essential performance) of the object they study, according to those clauses, is a proof that the real world exists independently of us and that it is accessible from many alternative levels. Reality is not a radical construction of reason, as is the case for a theological or philosophical system. What is true is that we could have different scientific systems according to different observation levels, tools of representation, and mental styles (just like we have different but real artistic representations of the same exemplar). It is not true that the science we have created through the centuries does not have any objective reference in reality. Rather, objectivity could also reside in small regions of knowledge and relativism does not prevent us from approaching it.

7. Epistemology of the artificial: the impossible synthesis

What we cannot claim, as we have suggested above, is the accumulation of knowledge for rebuilding the object of study from all possible levels. The conjugation, in fact, of two or more levels of observation implies – when it succeeds – nothing more than the building of a new level of observation.

It is a matter of fact that man, according to his nature, can select only one observation level for any unit of time. We may observe the social structure of a community and, then, its economic structure. But a true socio-economic observation cannot be built up by simple addition nor the cumulative synthesis of the first two. Rather, and this is what really happens, we can define a third observation level of a socio-economic order that will exhibit different characteristics and even autonomous terminologies and definitions compared to the first one. This will also be true, of course, for future socio-economic-political levels, and so on.

The many typologies of man proposed by philosophers, sociologists, economists and psychologists well describes this point. When we speak of man as being a *political animal, homo faber, homo sociologicus, homo oeconomicus, animal simbolicum or ludens,* we clearly reflect the observation level we have implicitly chosen and the performance we claim to indicate as essential. The claim for a definition of man *in se* would fall into silence, since at the moment we begin to speak, even at a metaphysical level, we select some observation level *a priori*.

It is important to underline that the phenomenologies we can capture from a certain observation level will always tend to show uniformities and models which are relative to the system or level of reference but are objectively controllable.

The knowledge which was generated at other levels will only partially contribute to the definition and explanation of those uniformities and models. This is also the case when both have to deal with the same empirical phenomenon. For example, the essence of suicide does not consist in its psychological nature any more than in its sociological nature or vice versa. Any book on this theme which claimed to synthesise the two observation levels would present itself in two parts, one on the psychological and one on the sociological aspects, provided that the author does not introduce a third level of observation, for example the psycho-social.

In the latter case, in order to avoid simply listing psychological and sociological aspects, the author adopts new concepts which are not reducible to one of the previous levels. The result of such operations does not guarantee that, by beginning from the new observation level, it is possible to build explanations and predictions which are necessarily coherent with those attainable from the two lower levels, as we would legitimately expect from an accumulative synthesis of knowledge. If we define the psycho-social analysis as the study of the relations between the psychological and the sociological dimensions, it is clear, in fact, that knowledge of the two related areas is only relevant because, in the relationship between the heterogeneous entities, they tend to present themselves as a phenomenological *novum* and not as a simple linear resultant.

'*Senatores* are *boni viri* but the *senate* is *mala bestia*' is an ancient and common remark - that is to say, 'Senators are good men, but the Senate is a bad beast' – which field theory, systems theory and structuralism have only formally pointed to. In fact they underline that within a scientific approach, the different observation levels pose a precise methodological constraint without alternatives.

The greater the number of heterogeneous elements in two observation levels, the more the resulting third level will lose the richness available at the lower ones: in fact, it will achieve a new richness of a different nature. Consider, for example, Heisenberg's well-known parable about the mountain climber who, in climbing, gains an ample view but loses the detail and, in descending, experiences the reverse.

Drawing further upon Heisenberg, we could speak of a sort of generalised indetermination principle: the choice of an observation level allows us to capture a true reality but only the one which is compatible with that level. In more general terms, one could say that in selecting an observation level,

> we force the matter to choose a configuration among those that are available.
>
> (Regge, 1994)

Likewise, the synthesis of the concept of man, or the concept of mind, is impossible by following a sort of bottom-up strategy which claims that in climbing towards levels of synthesis starting from lower levels we increasingly approach the wholeness. On the other hand, a top-down strategy suffers from the reverse weakness of the unjustified pretence to know in advance the essential meaning of a system which we have actually depicted at only one phenomenic level, arbitrarily assuming it as if one were the matrix of each other. The twofold conclusion is that

a) every observation level is valid in its own right under precise conditions concerning its power of explanation, of predictability and;
b) there is no way of simultaneously considering more than one level, i.e. no level can include another rationally or to be included in another level without a loss of knowledge.

Furthermore, the phenomenology of art itself shows clearly a specialisation of the levels of observation not only among different arts but even within each specific art. The claim that reality consists in unity is perhaps plausible in purely metaphysical terms but it is quite inappropriate when applied to actual achievements.

A product of art is always a piece of music or of theatre, a painting or a poem; we do not know of any serious proposal for generating something that could present itself as a total artistic fact, ignoring the fact that some aspects may prevail on the others.

The current attempt to set up artistic works exploiting the so-called multimedia technology is just at its starting point, but it easy to predict that, within it, some of the 'media' will prevail, or, as a sole altenative, such an art will generate some new kind of *kitsch* rather than a new profound and durable aesthetical knowledge.

Nevertheless, we know, as we will underline in a later section, that the effects of whatever fact, be it technological, artistic or communicational, will always cover a wider number of levels than the one within which our actions are involved.

Actually, according to the inheritance principle, the consequences of a fact which is intentionally oriented to pursuing some goal will have many of their causes inside the generated fact and will be able to act and possibly to reveal themselves at different levels of reality or of some observer. This is why, for instance, music may have no meaning in a properly semantic definition (Sloboda, 1985) but it surely has extra-musical effects, for example on some classes of physiological phenomena, exactly as a drug may produce biological dynamics which are different from the action level at which it was designed and tested.

The relevance of all this for the study of the production of artificial systems is clear: to reproduce an exemplar which synthesizes the various levels of observability is absurd, even if one ignores the question of comparing different materials and procedures to those of the exemplar, just because its whole rebuilding is not open to scientific speculatation itself. As far as artificialistic projects are concerned, we can argue that the main difficulty in reconstructing the exemplar as a whole arises from the fact that the relationship between two performances, even if observed at only one level, depends on the nature of those performances as much as on the nature of their relationship and on the quantity and quality of other performances involved by it.

As a typical problem of this kind, let us quote a biologist involved in understanding some aspects of the sensorial functions of the Nautilus:

> Another fascinating problem is the relationship between visual and tactile learning. . . Since the two systems overlap in the vertical lobe, maybe there is some kind of co-ordination between them. However, it has been demonstrated that the objects detected by sight are not recognised by touch.
>
> (Young, 1974)

The attempt to reproduce the co-ordination between tactile and visual learning will imply the discovery of the stuff it is based on, and, thus, a third observation level should be selected. On the other hand, if we know the stuff of the co-ordination performance, we have to make the tactile and visual performances able to work according to the rules of this stuff. This could introduce some additional problem which we did not face when we only had to reproduce the two performances as stand-alone functions.

If these additional problems can be solved then the resulting artificial system will work well at the observation level described by the co-ordination performance if, and only if its working is locally determined; that is to say if and only if the sub-system is a rather locally self-sufficient one which does not involve a linkage with any other sub-system to the co-ordination performance, and this is, of course, a very rare case. In other terms, the stuff on which the co-ordination works could impose a complete re-design of the two performances, visual and tactile learnings, in accordance with the needs of other systemic levels that govern the co-ordination itself. Apart from the heterogeneities introduced by the materials and procedures adopted by the artificialist, the bottom-up strategy sketched above will clearly trigger a discouraging sort of *petitio principii* that, in an ontologic sense, establishes a limit to scientific knowledge too.

Each time we select an exemplar from a whole object or system, we eradicate it from the global context. Each time we eradicate a performance, which we consider is essential in an exemplar, we also eradicate the linkages which connect it to other performances. Each time we eradicate a relationship, i.e. by indicating it as our essential performance, we eliminate the features of the other performances linked to it, which are not highlighted by the nature of the relationship we have selected.

8. Logical limits in cumulating essential performances

The common sense but also concrete practices of scientists and technologists implicitly assume that the strategy of successive approximations could be used also to rebuild exemplars drawn from the natural world. The core of this reasoning is that:

1 if we know, perhaps scientifically, the performance P1 of an exemplar system S, then, provided we have the right technology for exploiting, we can reproduce S in terms of a machine able to reproduce P1;
2 if we could know, in a second stage of scientific advancement, the performance P2 of the same system S, then, provided we have the right technology, we could reproduce S in terms of a machine able to reproduce P2;
3 thus, in a third stage, we shall have the possibility to rebuild the system S in more accurate terms, since we shall be able to give it two classes of performances (P1 and P2) and no longer one only.

The tacit assumption is that P1 and P2 could be simply summed up in order to get a more accurate reproduction of the system involved.

Normally, if S is a real system – in the case of a formal or informational one the situation could be different – this strategy will fail, even if P1 and P2 belong to the same observation level.

The are many reasons for this failure.

First of all, P1 and P2, as a rule, are linked together by some kind of direct or indirect relationship R within the system S. This relationship should be known in order to reproduce it. If this relationship is a simple one, that is to say if it does not involve anything more than putting together two or more parts in order to get a more accurate reproduction of the exemplar, then no particular problem will arise. Actually, in these cases, the essential performance may remain those already reproduced.

But usually the exemplar is more complex than one would think. For example, although the essential performance in the design of artificial bones remains a mechanical one, a great relevance is given today to a number of related problems, amongst which the relationship between the artificial device and the muscles or other bones is one of the most important. Thus, owing to the delicacy of such problems, among others, the fact that

> joints are trouble-free for 15 years [may be evaluated as] a remarkable record considering the harsh biomechanical and biochemical environments of the body.
>
> (Keaveny, 1996)

In other words, and quite often, the relationship R reveals itself to be a very complex function, involving other observation levels and performances which are not considered in the model. In many cases, R is effective if and only if some other sub-system of S performs in such a way that P1 and P2 could communicate or, at least, be related each other. Biological systems frequently exhibit circumstances in which two or more organs or processes are regulated by a third sub-system, for instance through some hormone production.

Furthermore, there is a more subtle logical reason for that failure. If P1 and P2 are different enough in stuff, R could not work based on the stuff or the rules of, say, P1 rather than of P2 or vice versa. R would need to consist of a function which is able to 'understand' both P1 and P2 and this implies that R has to be a more general process than P1 and P2. In other words, R can only be performed by a structure whose core should be able to transduce the states of P1 and P2 in something that could be useful for triggering the process R. Thus, that structure will belong to a specific observation level from which P1 and P2 disappear, in the sense that they no will longer be the focus of the model, which needs always to work on only one dominant observation level.

This is why, at the end, R should be considered a new essential perfomance in itself, at a specific observation level: actually, we could reproduce R as an essential performance of S, even ignoring P1 and P2 or forcing them, so to speak, to behave according to the functional requirements of R and no longer according to their own nature.

Formally, if we assume that the probability of an effective reproduction of P1 is p(P1) and that of P2 is p(P2), both being less than 1, of course, then the probability of getting an accurate reproduction of both, in the case of a pure sum of P1 and P2, will be $(p(P1) * p(P2)) + K$, where K represents a constant which depends on the nature of R: if R is not reproduced but, for example, depends on the direct interaction of P1 and P2 (independently of the materials adopted) and not on some third structure, then it will be greater than zero; if R (and this is presumably the most frequent case in nature) depends on a third structure and it is not reproduced, K will be less than zero, impoverishing the total probability. The reason for this greater failure is that, as far as the separate performances are concerned, P1 will have its own probability p(P1) and P2 its own p(P2), but when they happen or are considered together, the absence of R will fire some unpredictable event which will, however, be very far from the original R.

On the other hand, if one looks at S at an observation level from which R is focused as an essential performance, then the probability of R will be p(R) and we cannot say anything about its value compared to $(p(P1) * p(P2)) + K$.

The two cases mentioned above well describe the pitfalls of both the bottom-up and top-down strategies: in fact, in both design paths we meet a point beyond which we would need knowledge on a level which has been absent from our choices and, more substantially, on the way to connect with that level.

For instance, if we take a flower as an exemplar and we reproduce, using different materials, its colours (P1) and some of its fine structures (P2) we could not expect to get, as a magical result, its typical perfume, assuming that such a perfume in the exemplar depends on the relationship R between P1 and P2. On the contrary, if we decide to choose the perfume as the essential performance, then we can easily reproduce it without setting up any kind of relationship between P1 and P2: in fact, P1 and P2 could be totally ignored. But, of course, this will be quite a different kind of work.

The above discussion is not only an academic one: it deals with well-known real problems, for instance, in biomedicine, where in order to avoid trouble coming from the interplay among what we call here different observation levels,

> Until recently, most research in the field [of cell transplantation, n.d.r] has focused on minimising biological fluid and tissue interactions with biomaterials in an effort to prevent fibrous encapsulation from foreign-body reaction or clotting in blood that has contact with artificial devices. In short, most biomaterials research has focused on making the material invisible to the body.
>
> (Mikos et. al., 1996)

It should be added that, in this field, the most advanced research trend is now of active biomaterials and, therefore, of devices which begin to be named as bioartificial: those materials which, in other words, are able to interact in a controlled way with some specific aspects of the body, rather than remaining intentionally separated from it. This means that, if the points we have discussed have some prospect, they will enter the scene very soon.

9. Aesthetical artificials and analytical artificials

This point allows us to establish another important difference between reproduction attempts aimed at reproducing the world as it is, i.e. as it is for some established analytical ways of looking at reality or constructing it, including science, and those aimed purely at external resemblance. We could name the former as analytical artificials while the latter could be referred to as aeshetical artificials.

The analytical artificials are, in other words, objects, machines or processes which pretend to be a reliable reproduction of an exemplar and of its essential performance and are based on some established analytical theory or model coming from science or, at least, from some established and shared knowledge system.

On the contrary, aesthetical artificials are objects, machines or processes which do not pretend to be a reliable reproduction of an exemplar and of its essential performance but seek only to reproduce them as an intentional fiction, which is more or less easily recognisable.

While an artificialist who is oriented towards an analytic reproduction is tacitly or explicitly always expecting, from the final result of his work, an object which will behave like the exemplar, an artificialist oriented towards reproducing resemblance will not have such an expectation.

While the logical and methodological problems seen above about the cumulability of performances in an integrated artificial system are surely valid for the analytical artificials and constitute a serious difficulty for their advancement, they can be seen as quite negligible for almost all the purely aesthetically-oriented artificials.

Actually, nothing prevents us from reproducing a flower, or any other system, by just summing up a number of performances: a gadget which looks like a flower both in terms of colour and structure and which is, furthermore, able to provide its typical perfume, is a possible reproduction target. It could be even greatly amusing and appealing for many people. On the other hand, if our aim is not to achieve an external resemblance level but to reproduce the flower in its real structure and processes as scientifically represented – if, in other words, the artificial flower is to be a valuable simulation of the natural one – we cannot avoid reproducing the relationships among the performances and their logical traps.

We can only remark, on a speculative level, that it is difficult to establish a broad line between the two kinds of reproduction discussed above. This fact makes the concept of the artificial fascinating.

Indeed, man always seems to be looking for 'realistic' reproductions but he knows, or gradually discovers, that this aim is beyond his possibilities. Every manufacturer of artificial flowers would be happy to be able to imitate nature to such an extent that it would be impossible to tell his products from natural ones, even to the eyes of a botanist. What really happens is that he stops his attempt when his reproduction meets public agreement, that is the way people, depending on their natural or cultural perception constraints, think that the natural system has to look.

On the scientific side, scientists would also be glad to be able to understand the nature of the world with total accuracy, although they will stop their efforts when their models appear to control enough of the phenomena concerned, at some observation level. In the end, both types of human action, manufacturing and science, seem to be oriented to solutions that work according to some general understanding of the pragmatic role of science and not according to some approximation to the truth. If they were to do so, then they would be unable to do anything.

The same impossibility to synthesise two or more observation levels applies to the synthesis of two or more essential performances. Of course, if the essential performances I would like to synthesise involve or belong to different observation levels, the above impossibility is even clearer. But also in the circumstances where they belong to the same observation level, the impossibility of a synthesis depends, in the end, on the fact that our selection of some real performance as being essential, according to some criterion, always consists of a low probability process. In other words, when we attribute an essential performance to an exemplar we unavoidably ignore the remaining performances characterising it, not only at the considered observation level but at all the other ones, also unavoidably ignored in our work.

The ability of science and technology to know or reproduce some performances of natural systems or, more accurately, sub-systems, is due to the fact that within the narrow limits of the selected observation level the essential performance observed in the exemplar appears and is controllable in our scientific model or in our machine. Nevertheless, in the same way, the artificialist can reproduce a performance using quite different materials and procedures compared to those of the exemplar.

The scientist would also be able to describe, explain and predict the behaviour of a system through quite a different logic from that which nature follows.

This is the real situation in which science works, for instance in attributing some mathematical model to the movements of living systems, or even physical ones, which of course behave without applying any mathematical rules; their dynamics is based, on the whole, on the intrinsic interplay of their components. Once more, the problem of the essential truth is beyond the possibilities of human effort and the only strategies available to man are those of knowing or reproducing the world through operational expedients that pragmatically capture what is compatible with the assumed model and the multiple selections it implies.

In the field of the methodology of science the above arguments could have interesting consequences. For instance, in the area of quantitative simulation, where the notion of relationships among two variables, say P1 and P2, is well-known, the mathematical model treats the relationships at their own formal level which in the past demonstrated itself to be powerful enough to predict the behaviour of both P1 and P2. In other words, the pragmatics of quantitative simulation does not rebuild the relationship but limits itself to symbolically govern the dynamics of P1 and P2 which, in turn, represent some real phenomena that has previously been observed at some level, according to the properties that belong at its own formal level as variables included in a computational system.

The failure of the simulation attempt has to be ascribed, in this way, not just to the formal methods in themselves, but to the uncontrolled, and uncontrollable, interplay between the two classes of observation levels: the real and the formal ones. While the former will enter the scene under the principle of inheritance, which means that all the observation levels implied by P1 and P2 will act and relate to each other, no implicit inheritance is working in the formal models, apart from the ones that arise automatically from the formal interactions between mathematical structures, which will take the overall simulation further away from reality.

The formal model will focus on some formal measures of P1 and P2 at the empirical observation level selected by the specialist. This implies that the simulation process –

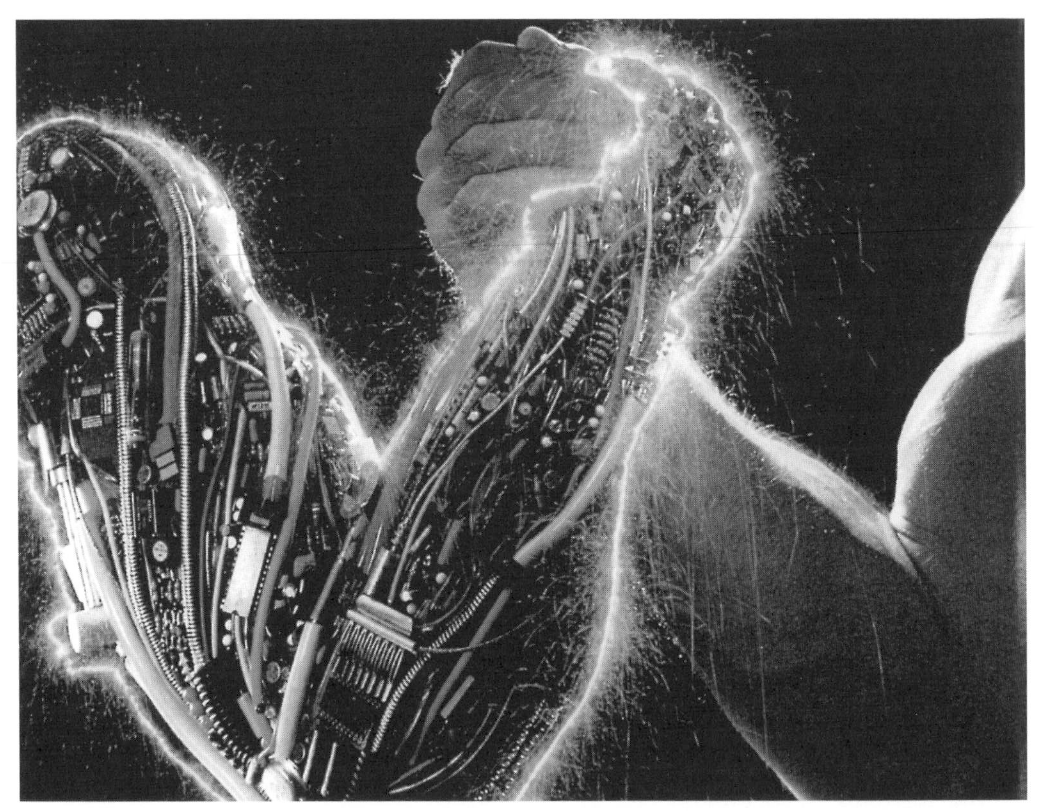

The internal structure of an artificial device advances with the growth of sub-systems of conventional technology and additional materials. This serves to increasingly make the performances of the artificial differ from those of the exemplar it evolves from. In general, the differences range from sensitivity, power, exposure to sudden events or side effects, resistance, and so on. Source: "Scienza & Vita", Rusconi, Milano, 6, 1996.

like any other artificial device – could sometimes work, paradoxically, both well and badly: well at the considered observation level and badly if other levels were to be concerned. There will be a clear failure when some neglected level makes its presence tangible and exerts its power in influencing, directly or indirectly, some considered variable or interaction between variables.

Accordingly, the improvement of any simulation technique cannot hope so much from the improvement of the formal calculations. Rather, such an improvement, though it is very limited in principle, could be pursued by means of an analysis of the compatibility among the observation levels assumed in the first stages of the construction of the model, bearing in mind that the simultaneous treatment of more than one observation level is impossible except by assuming some new level, the formal one, for instance, that will sometimes be pragmatically useful but also will bring us back to the above unavoidable problems.

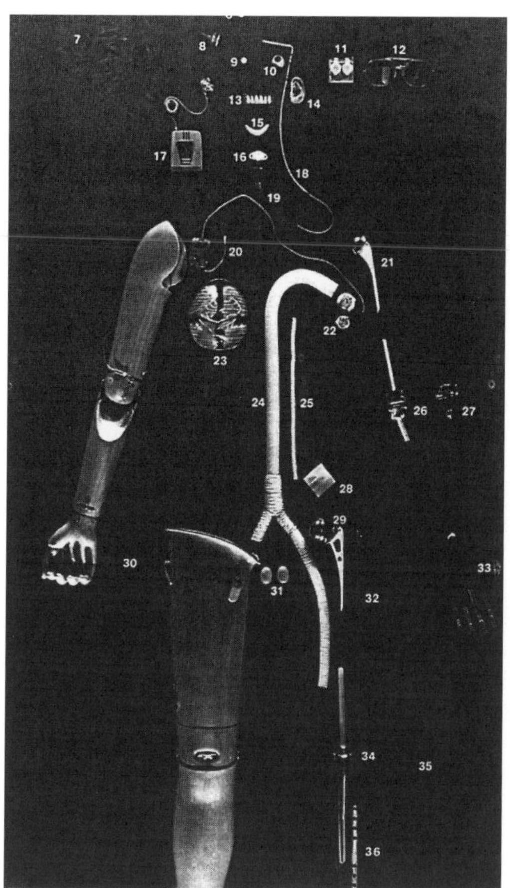

In 1980, a list of the human body's sub-systems that can be replaced by artificial devices was produced. The list has since grown, particularly in the fields of artificial bones and other tissues, but also in other crucial areas, such as vision and hearing. The relationship among artificial organs, particulalrly when they are be functionally close to each other, remains a very difficult problem both from a bio-techological viewpoint and from a methodological one. "Nel mondo dell'incredibile", Selezione del reader digest, Milano, 1981.

10. Sharing observation levels: gains and losses

It is easy, at this point, to understand why no particular difference exists between the situation in which the artificialist looks at reality as it is and the one in which the artificialist constructs reality, i.e. sees what he wants to see.

In fact, nothing prevents us from reproducing systems which have no evident existence but of whose features we are firmly persuaded: if we are persuaded that Martians exist and we have reason enough for attributing some set of physical or even psychological characteristics to them, then we could try to reproduce artificial Martians, in some of their supposed performances. The history of civilisations shows clearly that, from the arts to alchemy (Pereira, 1995), the collective beliefs and related representations serve as observation levels from which exemplars (demons, gods, forces and other entities) and essential performances are drawn and reproduced in many ways.

When objective nature is unable to convince man to select some observation level, for instance when the 'observed' exemplar does not empirically exist, it is replaced by culture, which forces man to agree upon some criterion by means of which it is legitimate to conceive, to define and 'to see' some non-material entity. Even in these cases, the artificialist, be this a technologist, an artist (any kind of reproducer), is cut off from the possibility to reproduce the exemplar in its wholeness, that is to replicate it. The final artificial product will, therefore, always resound with the multiple selections or attributions (true 'interpretations' and transfigurations) decided by him.

The constraint of the observation level is, in conclusion, the first, unavoidable and insuperable obstacle in the way of the replication which is conceived as a procedure

Artificial fruits are mixed in with natural ones. If one assumes the same and sole observations level as the artificialist has chosen, the artificial device, in reproducing a given essential performance (in this case, a purely external resemblance), easily passes a Turing-like test. Source: "Scienza & Vita", Rusconi, Milano, 1995, 3.

made possible using analytical techniques. Such a constraint forces man to generate the artificial.

The knowledge, but also the control and the reproduction, of objects or real systems from all the possible observation levels is pure utopia. For instance, as far as the artificial intelligence project is concerned, it is enough to refer to the sceptic's easy challenge which consists of the attempt to embarrass the machine, a behaviour which coincides with the attempt to bring the interaction with it to a level ignored by the designer.

On the other hand, and despite every good analytical and selective intention, it is fundamental to bear in mind that any action, gesture or product of natural origin possesses or, rather, inherits its own structural wholeness. This involves a wide spectrum of consequences or a co-production of effects at endless levels of potential observation, beyond those which we have deliberately selected. The artificialist, like the scientist, the

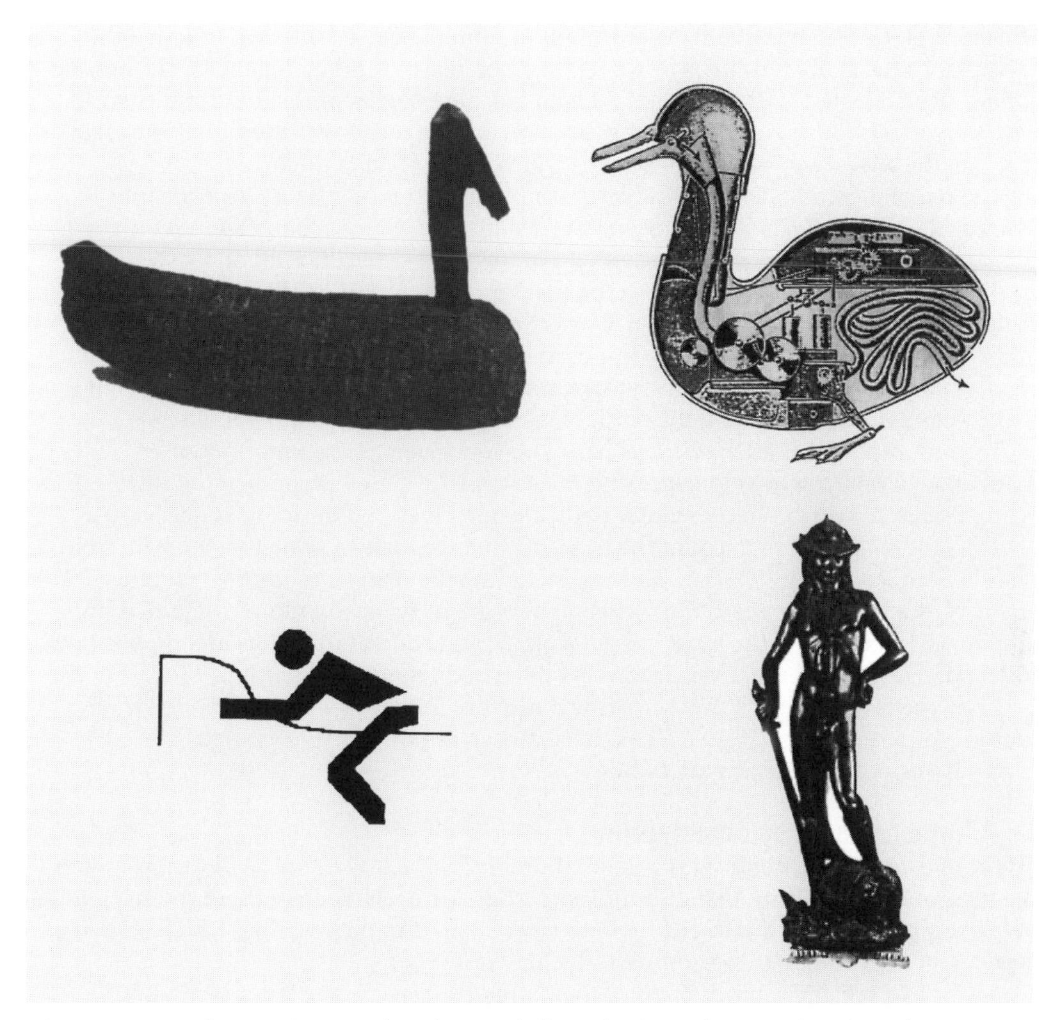

The same exemplar can be reproduced quite differently depending on the selected observation level and essential perfomance. In the far left, we see a primitive version of a duck-decoy, and to it's right, Vaucanson's famous duck. Even at the same observation level, the same exemplar can be reproduced differently in accordance with the different essential performances. In the lower right, we have the David *by Donatello, and to it's left is a contemporary ideogram. Sources: La nuova enciclopedia dell'arte, Milano, Garzanti, 1991; "Provincia nuova", Cremona, 1996, 1.*

conventional technologist and also man in general, tends to concentrate his attention on the reproduction of the essential performances of the exemplar and feels satisfied when he succeeds to an acceptable degree. Nevertheless the device or, more generally, the behaviour, that he sets up, by adopting available materials, structures and processes coming from the conventional technology, will possess a richness of observation levels which is not lower but is qualitatively different from the one which characterised the exemplar or the goal of his behaviour. It is just because of this heterogeneity, richness or complexity that science finds it impossible to grasp causal linear relations in the world with the same facility with which we pluck flowers in a meadow, although it is not so rare that the bets or hypotheses of scientists have some local good luck.

The remembered and unavoidable assumption of the *coeteris paribus* principle, discussed above, reveals its illusory or, at least, its provisional character, not only in the domain of scientific enterprise since it will in turn present itself with all its strength in the field of the artificial too. This is a logic that may be found in all the circumstances in which man has to behave. Consider, for example, the action of drugs and the concept of innocuity: a feature that is literally impossible to verify except within the limits of a group of already known variables, structures or organic phenomena which, even if it is wide, surely does not exhaust the endless variety of possible observation levels.

The assumption of *coeteris paribus* has to be conceived as the proof of our inadequacy or narrowness in capturing the essence or the wholeness of the things. This is an exercise to which we constantly dedicate ourselves and in doing so we almost always ignore the fact that just at the moment that we make a selection, we gain from one side but lose from the other. Nature, including the one we rebuild within the artificial, does not have regions or levels which are intrinsically more essential than others. Also, and this is the most crucial aspect, none one of them has any disposition to remain inert just because our interest is polarised on one or the other.

In this sense the marvel that scientific discovery induces (as Popper (1968) states within a different context), as well as the achievement of effective artificial systems, certainly resides in their low probability.

11. A further remark on cumulability

The above discussion deals with a general problem which we think will increase with the future of artificialism: that of building partial artificials, each of them referring to its own exemplar and having to put them to work in an unique machine, which should correspond, of course, to an exemplar of a higher level.

As far as a reliable reproduction of the higher level exemplar is concerned, excluding, in this way, the reproductions which are only aimed at mimicking it, there will arise a problem in the relationships between the partial exemplars and, therefore, between the partial artificials. On an intuitive basis, the artificialists often seem to think that the sum of the partial artificials would be a good strategy. For instance, during a talk in Salt Lake City with Professor Kolff – one of the most important contemporary artificialists, the designer of the first artificial kidney during the second world war and who then worked on artificial hearts and other leading projects – this question was posed.

Professor Kolff's view is that if two partial artificials were to work well as stand alone devices there would be no reason to predict some failure if they were put to work together. According to the above discussion, our opinion is that the final result of such an attempt will depend on the 'distance' between the two exemplars inside the higher level one, that is to say, the sub-system which governs or hosts the two exemplars.

By distance we mean the quantitative and qualitative relationship which exists between the two exemplars: if the distance is near to zero, that is to say the exemplars are very close to each other in terms of mutual relations of some kind, then the knowledge and the reproduction of these relations will be unavoidable if one desires to build up an artificial which respects the overall behaviour of the higher level exemplar. On the other hand, if the distance is very great and could be taken as non-existent, then the working of the two partial artificials will pose no problems.

The entire matter, in other words, depends on what we know or do not know about the relationships that exist between two or more sub-systems of a whole system. Nevertheless, since a relationship between two exemplars has to be understood as an essential performance of an exemplar constituted by the two previously selected exemplars, the problem once again becomes that of being able to reproduce that performance as a product of the higher level exemplar rather than expecting it to arise just from the mere 'sum' of the two partial artificials.

This is really a logical trap, because each time we consider an exemplar, we place ourselves on an observation level which is consistent in its own; that is to say, it tends to hide from our eyes all that does not belong to that level. As a consequence, the artificialist will almost always concentrate his awareness and his design efforts on only one exemplar and one essential performance per unit of time, rather than take into account the complexity of an exemplar which implies more than one observation level and more than one essential performance.

A rather typical case, which allows us to understand the general relevance of the above argument, could be that of the association of two drugs. While each drug can have predictable effects, the association of the two drugs can generate unpredictable events. If one of the side effects generated by the association is a good one – if, in other words, it is interesting in itself – then it could be assumed as a new target of research. However, further improvement of it will soon require studies which no longer will consider the two earlier drugs as they were previously considered, as a means to achieve some specific therapeutic result.

In fact, the new target of research will require a look at the dynamic of the association, i. e. the relationship in itself, and this, in turn, will require an investigation into the structures of the drugs, concentrating the analysis of their actions at the new observation level.

3. Deriving generalisations from the TA

1. Selecting and attributing essential performances

The implicit limitation in the process of selection is a constraint that we cannot avoid when we study reality. This limitation is also a fact that we must bear in mind when we claim to have reproduced reality. As has been maintained:

> Within a particular 'level' of phenomena (i.e. physical, biological, psychosocial), prediction which pertains to the goals of a designed system is almost invariably superior to prediction in unaltered phenomena.
>
> (Henshel, 1976)

Naturally all this is only true at the considered level and it does not concern events belonging to other levels, which are, in any case, inherited and involve that which explains or forecasts.

The result of a technological reproduction could reflect the selective perspective that we would have chosen. Its correspondence to reality, in the best of cases, will be acceptable, but only at the same level from which we departed. The attempt to reproduce artificially more and more inclusive systems possesses the same insufficient plausibility as the attempt to unify science in a unique body which pretends to reflect the whole reality.

This position is crucial for depicting and discussing cases which are very different from each other. For example, if we assume a physiological level of observation, then it is clear that attributing the essential performance of blood being pumped in the circulatory sub-system to the animal heart would obtain widespread agreement. On the other hand, attributing to the human brain-mind sub-system the essential performance of symbolic processing and then attributing intelligence to it and performances of a problem-solving type, would get only a partial agreement. In fact this is what has happened during the debate on artificial intelligence, leaving room for attributing essential performances to the mind which are very different from each other.

With regard to this, it could be of some interest to take into account the positions which have been recently assumed in AI by two authoritative scholars in the field. The first one is that of 'selection' of what should be judged as essential in the human mind, proposed by Roger Schank:

> One of the more real themes of artificial intelligence is that of the sizes. . . the truth is that the sizes are the core of the human intelligence.
>
> (Schank, 1991)

The second is the recognition by Marvin Minsky, in discussing the difficult theme of the definition and reproduction of common sense, that:

> every particular type of structure of data has its own virtue and its own shortcoming, and no one as such seems to be suitable for all the functions implied by what we call common sense.
>
> (Minsky, 1991)

This was very illuminating to the subject of the different selections regarding the deep nature of the mind (Dreyfus and Dreyfus, 1990).

This problem, however, does not alter the correct use of the concept of the artificial, provided we bear in mind the above considerations made on the selected character of any sub-system and of some of its performances which are isolated from the whole original context. While natural procedures allow for the generation of systems that 'automatically' include all the possible levels of reality and of observability, the artificialist must choose, decide, gamble upon something as being essential. After this, in order to construct, he has to address the conventional technology, which is quite heterogeneous compared to natural systems. In doing so, he sets up systems that will possess a wholeness in themselves, characterised by infinite observation levels, of which only one will overlap the level which was originally assumed in order to select the exemplar.

Both the artificialist and the scientist adopt the principle that, for a given system of events or a context of variables 'that variable is the most relevant', let us say the essential one. For example, the attempt to build a pond as such would be meaningless: we commonly do this kind of thing with some particular aim in mind, for instance to have animals or plants that interest us and live in such an environment. We would be satisfied by the enterprise when, under the polarising effect of our selection, the species in question seem to survive in the artificial pond just as well as they would in a natural one. In fact, we would have to set up a pond for that species, and for other possible unforeseen collateral species, but not necessarily an environment suitable for all the species living in a real pond.

2. On replication: the inheritance principle at work

These remarks allow for a better definition of the concept of 'replication' or 'copying'. In fact, at this point we can define A as a replication (in empirical terms and not logical) of B if A is the result of a reproduction of the exemplar B at all its observation levels by using the same materials and, more importantly, by drawing upon all his performances, without making any selection of essential performances. The sole acceptable difference between A and B will be in the names we give to them, and in their different placement in space or in time or in both.

This is true not only for the replication of structures but also of processes, that is to say, of structures that are changing with time. A process will then be replicable if and only if it is possible to indicate its starting conditions and the complete rules of transformation, just as in the case of the behaviour of trivial machines (cfr. Von Foerster): once more, true replication will only be possible if the description of the process is feasible at a wholly formal observation level, as in the case of computer operations or operations by any other entity that work perfectly according to a finite and complete set of rules. The models based on the work done by Von Neumann seem to belong, in fact, to this field and have to deal with replications of formal systems, as all the models of *artificial life* do.

A case apart seems to be that of the synthesis of molecules, since these could be defined as being 'identical' to those which exist in nature. It seems reasonable to assert that, in this kind of circumstance, the concept of synthesis, rather than that of the artificial, is applicable since the latter must adopt materials and procedures which are different from those that constitute the exemplar, whereas the former, by definition, does nothing more than suitably combine natural constituents. In other words, replication by synthesis is merely the generation of natural structures generated by the man who controls the required natural constituents.

A good further example that does not involve synthesis but does involve the deliberate combination of constitutive natural elements is artificial insemination. It represents a typical case of the reproduction of a process: the matching of two natural elements from which a new living system will develop is due not to the two systems they belong to but to a third actor that is charged with this enterprise.

It is interesting to note that the replication of structures or processes which are empirical and not formal is impossible in terms of rational and analytical planning, but is quite easily and, so to speak, automatically generated by natural systems in non-rational circumstances, including human beings at the moment at which they generate another human being. Incidentally, we could note that nature itself is sometimes able to generate an extremely faithful representation of its own reality by selecting its own observation levels, exemplars and essential performances: a footprint on the sand or the shadow of an animal cast on a wall are examples of this disposition.

In the field of devices or machines produced by technology, things are arranged differently from the field of natural exemplars. Take the case of serial production, all the operations involved in replicating artworks of various kinds, where the details of planning, materials and procedures of construction are completely known.

We could state that in these cases the level or the observation levels adopted in the production of the original prototype are known and that those which are unknown are implicit or, to rephrase, inherited from those which are known.

For example, a chair which has been built according to a certain project with a certain set of materials could be easily reproduced (replicated) by adopting the same project and the same materials. The latter, wood, cloth, etc., could be described at an endless number of observation levels, but the fact itself of adopting them and of using them under the same conditions involves the internal reproduction of all the possible levels. The replicating action is quite intentional but it does not involve any selective moment because the selection of a certain material at a certain observation level implies that it will bring with it the complete inheritance of its own nature at all the possible observation levels or, at least, at all those levels which characterised it in the exemplar.

In the end, the replication of technological products is always possible if one often renounces the claim of a truly artificial reproduction, that is to say, of a reproduction that privileges an essential performance, such as the pure and simple exterior appearance or form of a chair built using materials which differ from the original.

Interpreted in this way, a technological system is a closed system which can be completely described in formal terms or as 'design' at a certain observation level, both in terms of structure and process, and this explains why it is replicable.

However, if we do not know the project and the list of the materials, then we shall have no hope of reproducing it at all its observation levels without generating several side effects or sudden events, as is well-known to those who, in the industrial environment, try to replicate some object or some machine ignoring their original projects.

3. Replicating human issues

It is interesting, however, to point out that when the system includes a natural living system, the rigorous replication of the exemplar becomes, at the very least, improbable. Consider the 'replication' of a comedy, a piece of theatrical work, over a hundred evenings. The script will always be identical to itself, as will the stage, the lights, etc. The actors will also be the same, in terms of personal identity, but each evening the comedy will be more or less different.

This will likewise be the same for a concert performance by the same soloist at different times. In these and other analogous circumstances we could say that the human element placed in the system tends to govern it, leaving a wide trace of his ability, which is ineluctable. The human element more or less alters the intensity or even the kind of the performance that he attributes to the same exemplar, be this of text, character or music at different times. That means that when the attempt at replication has to deal with an exemplar that includes a natural living system, its complete description becomes impossible: the human protagonist is unable to define and then replicate himself.

The individual character of the interpretation is also well-known to primitive cultures such as the Hopi, which assign a function similar to that of a personal identity document to a tune, an 'individual song'. This is a song

> known by all people but, in principle, it can be sung only by its 'proprietary'. It isn't necessary that it is an original composition; it is enough that it is executed in a very personal way. A song which reflects in this way the individual behaviour is, in fact, almost inimitable.
>
> (Schneider op. cit., pp. 46-7)

It is plausible to support the idea that, in such cases, the inheritance of factors and of processes which the human element brings with himself, inside the technological system as well, has such a wide and dynamic dimension that it confers onto the system itself a very similar character to that of an open system, which is not completely describable.

The extreme case, in the class of the processes of replication, is certainly represented by logic and by the informational description of reality. In these fields the observation level is formal and the essential performance is implicit (defined *una tantum* by the axioms) in the sense that it coincides with the structure of the exemplar: a certain exemplar can only coincide with a certain performance.

Stating that A is equal to A means to assert that, in a meta-logic sense, all the characteristics of A are to be found in its identical part: what constitutes A coincides with what A could express in terms of its performances. Likewise, in informational terms, a certain pattern of bits can always be exhaustively reproduced (that is to say replicated), as already observed by Searle (cfr. Searle, cit.) in his well-known polemic on artificial intelligence, independently of the physical support that we adopt for the reproduction (flip-flops, bulbs or ninepins).

Information, like the constitutive formal elements of a logical procedure, has its own nature independently of the subject or the energy we adopt for the setting. A closed system, which is consciously settled, and whose components and relations are describable, is reproducible *ad libitum* and, if it is of formal substance, its reproduction will coincide with its replication since, at the information level of observation, there is no possible choice of alternative performances.

4. Possible replication strategies

To conclude, the replication, as a deliberate activity of man, seems to make sense to us in only three circumstances:

1. when we know all the steps and all the components needed to reproduce something, for example, in the case of mass production;
2. when we are able to act as combiners of natural elements which, when they are combined, are necessary and sufficient for producing a complete system, as, for example, in the case of artificial insemination;
3. when the reality to be reproduced is composed or is describable from only one possible level of observation: this is clearly possible only for a reality man has himself created in purely formal or informational terms, as, for example, in the case of replicating a computer program.

A different matter, as we noted above, that is currently diffused and involves the characteristics of a truly artificial reproduction rather than a replication, is the phenomenon of the intentional and, so to speak, impudent imitation of industrial products of various kinds, such as clothes, cars, clocks or even jewellery.

In these cases, for economic or legal reasons, even though the observation level of the original builder is known (and this often includes the materials used and even the particular projects), we tend to resort to a selection of performances (generally the exterior appearance) towards which the completed work of reproduction is addressed. This kind of product succeeds in the market when, and because, the customer assumes the same observation level as that of the counterfeiter and substantially agrees on the essential performance that he (the counterfeiter) aims to achieve.

5. Some regularities of the artificial

In general terms, artificial devices seem to show characteristics and regularities that could be described by the following clauses.

- An artificial is an object, a process or a machine that reproduces some essential performance at a given level of observation of a natural object, process or subsystem taken on as the exemplar.

- We may distinguish between a structure-oriented artificial and a process-oriented one. The former is the result of the attempt to reproduce the essential performance by reproducing the structure of the object, process or sub-system which has been taken on as the exemplar; the latter is the result of the attempt to reproduce the essential performance as such, without reproducing the structure of the object, process or sub-system which has been the exemplar.
- In the artificial object, process or sub-system and in the object, process or sub-system adopted as the exemplar, the number of homologous components is usually reduced (this does not necessarily apply when the exemplar is a conventional machine or an artificial device of a lower order).
- In the artificial object, process or sub-system and in the exemplar the homologous components are, in fact, structurally different: it would be better to define them as analogous.
- In the artificial object, process or sub-system, compared to the exemplar, new components may appear.
- In the artificial object, process or sub-system, compared to the exemplar, some types of internal or external relations are lost.
- In the artificial object, process or sub-system, in comparison to the exemplar, new types of internal or external relations may appear.
- The artificial object, process or sub-system is conceived at a precise level of observation and designed to exhibit some performance which is observable in the exemplar (at the same level). Nevertheless, whatever the 'material' it is made of, the artificial will bring with itself all the inheritance of the levels, known and unknown, involved in those materials, and not only of the particular level selected for accomplishing the performance of the artificial.
- In comparison to the exemplar, the performance of an artificial object, process or sub-system generally covers a different spectrum, which extends beyond the reproduced essential performance. This spectrum is sometimes wider, and sometimes narrower, in both quantitative and in qualitative terms.
- An artificial object, process or sub-system will be sensitive to a typology of environmental dimensions which only partially overlap those the exemplar is sensitive to.
- The set of dimensions to which an artificial object, process or machine is sensitive could be unpredictably neutral or could oppose or facilitate the essential performance that has to be reproduced.
- The research and development of an artificial object, process or sub-system which is of a higher order than the first one consists in the deepening of its characteristics just as an artificial device and this usually weakens the analogy with the latest generations of the device and the object, process or sub-system which was initially assumed to be the exemplar.
- The artificial object, process or sub-system will commonly be accepted as a good reproduction if, and only if, its observable working will show a reliable reproduction of the essential performance of the object, process or sub-system assumed as the exemplar, within a shared judgement.

Some uses of the term artificial

Note 1: As a rule, the several artificials, called automatisms, are excluded.

Note 2: Some of the artificials listed below do not coincide with the definition of 'artificial' introduced in this book: rather, they are the result of the manipulation or the recombination of the same materials as are involved in their exemplars.

Pre-1800

Artificial classification [Linnaeus]
Artificial fires [. . .]
Artificial flower [. . .]
Artificial ice [. . .]
Artificial insemination [L. Spallanzani]
Artificial irrigation [. . .]
Artificial island [. . .]
Artificial lake [. . .]
Artificial propagation (botany, farming)
Artificial rainbow [F. Bacon]
Artificial writing [J. Gutenberg]
Memoria artificiosa [Cosmas Rossellius]
Mutta artificialis [Normans]
Perspectiva artificialis [L.B. Alberti, P. della Francesca]

Post- 1800

Artificial adaptation [J.H. Holland]
Artificial ageing
Artificial arm [W. Kolff]
Artificial bait
Artificial bells [. . .]
Artificial blood [R. Naito]
Artificial bone
Artificial breathing [. . .]
Artificial cavities
Artificial cell [T.M.S. Chang]
Artificial chemical elements
Artificial chromosome
Artificial colourings [A. Baeyer]
Artificial cornea
Artificial diamond
Artificial experts [H.M. Collins]
Artificial extremities
Artificial eye
Artificial fertilizers [J.B. Lawes]
Artificial fibre
Artificial fish [M.S. Triantafyllou]
Artificial flavour
Artificial flower
Artificial granite
Artificial grass
Artificial gravity
Artificial habitat
Artificial hair [. . .]

Artificial heart [W. Kolff, D. Liotta]
Artificial honey
Artificial hip
Artificial jelly
Artificial joint
Artificial horizon [. . .]
Artificial intelligence [M. Minsky, H. Simon, et al.]
Artificial islands
Artificial ivory [H. Scarton, S. Calabrese]
Artificial kidney [W. Kolff]
Artificial landscape
Artificial language
Artificial larynx
Artificial leather
Artificial life [C.G. Langton]
Artificial ligament
Artificial light [T. Edison]
Artificial limb [. . .]
Artificial liver [A. Demetriou]
Artificial lung [J. Mortensen]
Artificial marble
Artificial milk [. . .]
Artificial muscle
Artificial nails
Artificial nest
Artificial oesophagus
Artificial pancreas
Artificial paradises [Ch. Baudelaire]
Artificial pearl [M. Koukichi]
Artificial perfume
Artificial plants
Artificial pond
Artificial proteins
Artificial radioactivity [F. Joliot, I. Curie]
Artificial rain [V. Schaefer]
Artificial reality [M. Krueger]
Artificial reef
Artificial resins
Artificial retina [M.A. Mahowald, C. Mead]
Artificial rock
Artificial rubber [W. Carothers, J. Nieuwland]
Artificial satellite [. . .]
Artificial seashore
Artificial silk [H. de Chardonnet]
Artificial skeleton
Artificial ski slopes
Artificial skin [J. Burke, I. Yannas]
Artificial smell [Sony Corp.]
Artificial snow [Emile Wyss & Cie SA]
Artificial speech
Artificial stones
Artificial sound [. . .]
Artificial taste

Artificial trees
Artificial turf
Artificial twinning
Artificial ultramarine [J. Guimet]
Artificial vessel
Artificial virus

Some examples of conventional technology

(source: G. Rivieccio, Enciclopedia cronologica delle scoperte e delle invenzioni, Rusconi, Milano, 1995)

1602 Medical thermometer [Santorio, Galileo]
1608 Telescope [Lippershey]
1609 Newspaper press [Aviso-Relation oder Zeitung]
1643 Barometer [Torricelli]
1657 Pendulum-clock [Huygens]
1682 Pressure pot [Papin]
1698 Steam motor [Savery]
1733 Flying shuttle for loom [Kay]
1745 Electric condenser [Kleist and Van Musschenbroek]
1769 Motor vehicle [Cugnot]
1775 Tram [Outram]
1775 WC [Cummings]
1781 Centrifugal regulator [Watt]
1800 Electric cell [Volta]
1806 Carbon paper [Wedgwood]
1817 Farrad [Von Drais]
1818 Stethoscope [Laennec]
1818 Steering wheel [Ackermann]
1829 Accordion [Demian]
1831 Electric motor [Henry]
1835 Relay [Henry]
1835 Revolver [Colt]
1837 Screw ship [Ericsson]
1843 Fax [Bain]
1844 Rubber vulcanisation [Goodyear]
1844 Telegraph [Morse]
1846 Nitroglycerin [Sobrero]
1846 Saxophone [Sax]
1851 Gyroscope [Foucault]
1857 Elevator [Otis]
1859 Electric accumulator [Plant]
1860 Linoleum [Walton]
1861 Rotary press [Hoe]
1862 Machine gun [Gatling]
1865 Dynamo [Pacinotti]
1866 Dynamite [Nobel]
1868 Celluloid [Hyatt]
1869 Compressed air brakes [Westinghouse]
1869 Chewing gum [Semple]
1871 Drill [Morrisson]
1871 Telephone [Meucci]
1877 Gramophone record [Cros]

1879 Electric lamp [Edison]
1879 Cash register [Ritty]
1880 Funicular [Olivieri]
1882 Power plant [Edison]
1883 Fountain-pen [Waterman]
1884 Steam turbine [Parsons]
1886 Linotype [Merenthaler]
1886 Aluminium [Hall and Hiroult]
1888 Straw [Stone]
1888 Tyre [Dunlop]
1889 Eiffel tower [Eiffel]
1890 Electric chair [Brown and Kennally]
1890 Electro-magnetic waves detector [Branly]
1892 Thermos [Dewar]
1892 Reinforced concrete [Hennebique]
1892 Moving staircase [Reno]
1893 Zip fastener [Judson]
1894 Sphygmomanometer [Riva Rocci]
1895 Slot machine [Fey]
1899 Magnetic recorder [Poulsen]
1902 Disk brakes [Lanchester]
1905 Diode [Fleming]
1907 Cloche [Esnault-Pelterie]
1908 Vacuum cleaner [Spengler]
1908 Cellophane [Edwin]
1909 Neon tube [Claude]
1909 Cleaner for exhaust [Frenkel]
1910 Radioactivity counter [Geiger]
1913 Petrol pump [. . .]
1914 Traffic lights [. . .]
1914 Brassière [Jacob]
1915 Pyrex dish [Littleton]
1915 Tank [Swinton]
1920 Mass spectrograph [Aston]
1921 Plaster [Dickson]
1924 Electroencephalograph [Berger]
1926 Television [Baird]
1926 Liquid propellent rocket [Goddard]
1927 Radio compass [Busignies]
1930 Helicopter [D'Ascanio]
1934 Nylon [Carothers]
1935 Truth machine [Keeler]
1938 Electroshock [Cerletti]
1938 Soluble coffee [Nestlè]
1938 Photocopier [Carlson]
1939 Spray [Kahn]
1939 Jet aircraft [von Ohain]
1942 Atomic pile [Fermi]
1943 Ball-point pen [Biro]
1945 Atomic bomb [Oppenheimer]
1946 Microwave oven [Spencer]
1946 Radial tyre [Michelin]
1947 Flipper [Mabs]

1948 Transistor [Shockley, Brattain, Bardeen]
1951 Tetra-Pak [Reusing]
1954 Solar cell [Pearson]
1955 Optical fibre [Kapany]
1958 Integrated circuit [Kilby]
1959 Hovercraft [Cockerell]
1960 Laser [Maiman]
1963 Compact cassette [Philips]
1965 Liquid crystal monitor [Heilmeier]
1971 Microprocessor [Faggin, Hoff, Mazer]
1972 TAC [Hounsfield]
1978 Modem [Hayes]
1978 Floppy disk [Apple, Tandy]
1982 Compact disk [Philips, Sony]

6. Social expectations related to the artificial

From a sociological point of view, the cultural transfer of the concept of artificial seems to be significant if one thinks of the kind of originality that it brings with it, compared to that shown by conventional technology. Subsequently, consider the public perception of machines which are very different from each other in terms of origin of ideation, spectrums of latent ability, limits and operational modality.

In fact, these are dimensions upon which several legitimate and illegitimate public expectations depend: it is a matter of expectations that always grow around the diffusion of a new technology. With regard to this it is important to observe that, for example, the use of a conventional machine requires the user to know something about the device. In turn, in an ideal situation, the user of an artificial system should possess familiarity with the exemplar and the essential performances that the machine reproduces and, further, with the machine as such. Thus, the user's expectations

Prof. Willem Kolff, one of the most famous artificialist of our time, with one of his artificial kidneys. In a personal communication, Prof. Kolff predicted that in the 2000 Olympic Games a man equipped with an artificial heart will win the marathon, "but perhaps - Prof. Kolff said - he will be disqualified...". How to perceive and how to live with the artificial, will surely become an important cultural issue in the next century. Source: courtesy of Prof. Kolff.

The heterogeneity of a conventional machine can be so strong , compared to nature, that it has to be disguised by reproducing a natural object. This picture shows the solution for calming down horses in the streets of San Francisco in 1876, who were frightened by the first steam cars. Source: Il secolo delle invenzioni, *Mursia, Milano, 1973.*

should meet the conceptual difference between the conventional and the artificial machine. In using a conventional machine, the user knows that he will obtain certain performances if he uses deliberate commands which conform to technical rules which are formal, or at least heterogeneous, compared to nature.

Conversely, when having to deal with an artificial device, such as an automaton, the user is persuaded to think that the performance will emerge by the simple adoption or appropriation of it. To put this differently, an ideal machine of the artificial should integrate itself directly and immediately in the natural context: by its very nature, it should not need any interface.

Nevertheless, in real cases, the artificial exhibits a relative compatibility with the natural and is often unforeseeable because of the transfiguration which it always implies compared to the exemplar and its performances.

In fact we should not forget that, at the end, all artificial devices are machines since their accomplishment depends closely on conventional technology. This remark opens up a question that we currently cannot answer: will it ever be possible to have a technology of the artificial which is different from the conventional and, if so, what conceptual and material features will it have?

It appears to be evident that the transfer of an exemplar – once it has become an artificial – within a structural context, which differs from the one in which it existed in nature, implies a rather radical change of materials, in the widest sense of 'material'. In the field of activities which have become established (like artificial intelligence), one can speak of artificial matter of the cognitive type, as being more of an entity than metaphoric and yet being constrained to an exclusive symbolic constitution. The diversity of the results in comparison to the exemplars which were the originally assumed targets becomes clear at this point and could be assumed as an intentional aim:

> just because their construction goes through the artificial matter, many constraints of the real matter (natural or synthetic) are removed, freeing universes of ways of being otherwise limited by the physical world.
>
> (Gardin, 1992)

	Concrete artificials (material devices or processes)	**Abstract artificials** (informational devices or processes)
Analytical artificials (reproduction of the structure)	• organs, • cells and tissues, • robots, • Virtual Reality devices connected to the real world • various (e. g.., diamonds, grass, horizon, etc.)	• AI (Artificial Intelligence), • ANN (Artificial Neural Networks), • ALife (Artificial Life), • GA (Genetic Algorhitms), • ...
Aesthetical artificials (reproduction of the appearance)	• sculpture, • architecture, • imitation gadgets, • remakings • ...	• drawings, • maps • figurative arts, • graphic simulators, • descriptive Virtual Reality or Virtual Environment • ...

A classification of artificial objects or processes according to the type of their essential performance (analytical/aesthetical) and of their 'stuff' (concrete/abstract)

One of the most imposing monuments to the artificial: a Japanese dome. *Inside this building, a detailed landscape of a tropical place has been reproduced to include dynamic changes in the temperature, daylight, waves in the sea, etc.*

4. Applying the TA to human phenomena

1. Communication as a self-referential artificial process

As we have already pointed out, communication is one of the more evident, recurrent and functional processes of reproduction that man has invented for survival and closely expressive finalities.

In adopting the language of the TA we could define communication as analogous to a process whereby an actor A attempts to reproduce an exemplar which resides in his own mind at a certain level of observation and to which he attributes a certain essential performance in the mind of an actor B.

In doing so, A has to adopt 'different materials and procedures' from those active in his own mind: thoughts, images, feelings and emotions. These become translated into a language, which hopefully enables their reproduction.

In the case of communication it is also necessary to distinguish two situations which are considerably different from each other. On the one hand, there is daily communication which does not place its trust, or does not solely place its trust, in formal codes strictly governed by syntax, as is the case with the pure and simple exchange of information. In the latter case, the communicative process completely coincides with the replication. Independently of the adopted language, a message of this kind (better characterised, even when it is very complex, as a signal) is always unambiguous, except when it is physical noise, since, as we saw in a preceding section, it is at the pure informational level.

On the other hand, daily communication, which also develops on the basis of syntax and semantics, is governed by the individual personality and by the culture – including the arts – and may be, therefore, rich, personal and profound in a variable measure. When it manipulates information, it goes beyond it and generates ambiguity.

The translation (although it may be more appropriate to speak of a true transduction, from the high energies involved from the daily communication to those which are low and purely informational) of a message consisting of simple and univocal information is at the base of a lot of crucial situations. For example, the effort a detective makes in questioning a witness, and later, the judge in a court, consists precisely in the attempt to isolate the information component from the global communication. In terms of TA we could say that a judge, in listening to a witness, tries to grasp the mental information exemplar that the witness possesses in his mind by eliminating the essential performances which the witness fatally selects and reproduces, despite the continuous calls to answer with only a yes or no.

The contribution of the TA to the study of communication does not push for a general resetting of it. Rather, the TA underlines the internal vocation of the communicative process to generate something which is different from the object that it aims to transfer, just because of the artificialistic structure that such a process cannot but assume. The problem of meaning, or of co-signification (Ogden and Richards, 1922; De Sola Pool and Schramm, 1973; Schultz and Luckerman, 1973) assumes a special turn here. In fact, people share signs and symbols and not meanings. Since it is not possible for something to resemble a 'clearing house' of meanings, they can only be self-referential or subjective.

Communication combines and recombines signs and shared symbols in order to depict mental exemplars and essential performances whose whole nature will remain inside the individual. Symbols have rightly been defined as the reproduction of real objects. However we should not forget that in every attempt at reproduction, they incorporate either, or largely, the essential selected performance into the object, or one constructed by the subject or by his culture, and not the object's conclusive wholeness.

In a dictionary, the definition of 'sadness' will refer to a feeling connected to something disagreeable and gloomy. The definition of the term 'feeling' will also refer to some example, such as sadness. Here the root of the meaning lies not in objective references but in the connection that the actor finds between the linguistic sign or symbol and his own collection of mental states. All that can be said is that, statistically and operatively, people converge, i.e. they agree in the facts, on some of these correlations, but a complete overlap between their mental states and, therefore, subjective and linguistic terms, is highly improbable.

Thus a linguistic message is, from every point of view, a transcript or, to be exact, a reproduction by means of 'different materials and procedures', of some mental states which remain different and intact in their natural state within the mind. We may even say that the exemplar and the subjective essential performance transduced into language, far from being purely and easily 'supported' by words, symbols or art works, become a truly new reality – namely the message – as always happens in the generation of the artificial.

Something of this new reality will certainly intrinsically overlap with the exemplar and the essential performance (human beings, as we said, are in some measure able to understand each other). However, a relevant part of the message will consist in the words *per se*, i.e. in the words and in their interactions rather than in their meaning. Also to paraphrase McLuhan, the medium, or the 'technology', of language becomes the true message. Language, in other words, just like technology, possesses its own characteristics that transfigure the content that it carries, or that instantiates it, thereby transforming it into something (the message) that is an objective linguistic event and, so to speak, at the disposal of whoever captures it from whatever semantic context he starts.

The arts themselves exist thanks to this characteristic of communication. This is exactly the same as the one Socrates contrasted in the technique of writing because it claims to reproduce outside the human mind things which clearly belong to it.

The forms that art takes are made possible because of the technology of communication, be it oral, written, painting, etc. These give form and body to autonomous realities which take the exemplar and the essential performance as simple starting points. The pain expressed in lyrics by Leopardi, the 'Pity' by Michelangelo or 'Joy' by Beethoven are essential performances of common experience, which, thanks to the brilliant use of linguistic, sculptural and musical technologies, become something else, with its own life. This makes the feeling just an ideational hint, which is immediately transfigured (this is also true for other languages) by the artistic form which becoms a substance in itself.

2. The inheritance principle in communication

In the case of oral and written communication, the side effects of linguistic technology are more manifest than ever. Just think of the ease with which the linguistic components of a message can trigger different mental associations to those expected by whomever issued it. Likewise, the expressive use of some 'instruments', for example the use of adjectives or synonyms, could generate effects which are far from what the issuer desired. In this sense the communication that takes place in daily life, when we aim to express ourselves, could be interpreted as a sort of minor art, in which we all try to reproduce in the best possible way some of our exemplars and essential performances, forcing ourselves to combine the signs and symbols in a more effective way.

Nevertheless, the result will always be a transfiguration of the exemplar and of the essential performance, often in a way which is functional in some cultural dimensions, as is clear from the following anecdote:

> Walter Ong describes how, in modern Zaire, a bard who, when asked to narrate all the stories of a local hero, Mwindo, was amazed; no-one had ever performed them all in sequence before. Pressed to do so, he eventually narrated all the stories, partly in prose, partly in verse with occasional choral accompaniment. It took him twelve exhausting days whilst three scribes took down his words. But once written, Mwindo had become transformed. He no longer existed as a continued, remembered recreation of past stories. Instead he had become fixed in the linear memory form demanded by modern cultures.
>
> (Rose, 1993)

Significantly, the judgement that we often make of someone's style of presenting himself, for example how he gives a lecture, is made on the basis of the person's ability to express himself effectively and that often goes beyond the content of the message. The difficulty in communicating lies in the poverty of the language the person possesses and in the ability to use it effectively, that is, to maximise the probability of imprinting it in the mind of the interlocutor with possibly something similar to what one desires to share.

We also need to take account that certain psychiatric pathologies that reveal themselves through self exclusion from the world, such as in autism or in aphasia, could be understood as closely related to the effect of fear generated by the increasing complexity of linguistic technology and of the system of communications. The combination of these complexities with their inexorable semantic avarice, compares sharply with the communicative demands by subjects who particularly need to place themselves in nets of social relations which they can apprehend as being meaningful. As it has been remarked,

> If the risk doesn't frighten, one may say that the unbridgeable gap between the changing, rich fullness of existence and the poor repeatedness of the human word always appeared to the philosophical mind.
>
> (De Mauro, 1994)

Similarly, the great Italian poet Dante says,

> Oh speech
> How feeble and how faint art thou, to give
> Conception birth! Yet this to what I saw
> Is less than little.

(Dante, La Divina Commedia, Paradiso, XXX III, 121-2)
Translanted by H. F. Cary, Project Gutenberg's Etext

The statement 'I have no words. . .' describes clearly the relation between the dimension or the relevance of the mental state and the 'technology' available to reproduce it. This relation is always asymmetric since in following the interpretative lines of the TA, the actor who decides to communicate something inside himself necessarily abdicates from the wholeness of the reproduction. He will therefore select an observation level, an exemplar and an essential performance. It is a matter of a funnel that, in some cases, could discourage us and induce us to be silent.

3. The utopia to reproduce subjective exemplars and essential performances

A decides to tell B about a personal event (we often say that A wishes to acquaint B with the event). This is always to be conceived as a total fact or, in any case, offers an extreme complexity of potential levels. The actor A will select one observation level and, from this, he will select the specific exemplar and then he will decide which is its essential performance.

Thus, from the complete event in which, let us suppose, he suffered betrayal by a friend, for example the theft of an object of value, A will select a central event at an ethical level of observation in trying to communicate to B the deep sorrow he feels. The actor A will exclude, in this way, other levels of observation, such as the financial one, in which the exemplar and the essential performance would appear as completely different.

He will then strive with the best technology of language to maximise the reproduction of the exemplar and of its essential performance in the mind of B. The result of the process will depend largely on A's ability. However, the chain of selections operated by A, when combined with the precariousness of B's ability to decode the message, makes the success of the enterprise unpredictable.

If B never experienced what A reports to him, B's decoding will be (like in a fable for children) solely affected by the linguistic product. B will live it based on the few subjectively known elements for generating something meaningful in his own mind, such as when we are told about a place we know nothing about, causing us to construct an arbitrary image. Conversely, if B has in the past had an experience that sounds analogous, then he will set up a permanent parallel connection between the progress of A's story and that experience, filtering even this through the wholeness of the mental state related to his own experience, re-triggered by the linguistic contents proposed by A.

At the end communication, particularly daily communication, is an expedient which is used for sharing some remarkable elements of experience without any guarantee of success, because not only does it lack a criterion of objective measurement, but also, and above all, there is an internal asymmetry between the exemplars and the subjective performances on the one hand and the heterogeneity of the reproductive media on the other. As Pirandello states,

> Once the transfer from one spirit to another has taken place, the changes are unavoidable.
> (Pirandello, 1908)

and, in the same manner, very infrequently it happens that

> writers are happy that their own work remains the same, or nearly the same, for a reviewer or a reader, as they expressed it, and has not become a different work, badly re-thought and arbitrarily reproduced.
> (Pirandello, ibidem)

Just as concrete artificial objects are generated in terms of machines, in the communication process replication is prevented from making multiple selections and adopting devices, such as language, which is evolved and learned, which are heterogeneous and conventional, compared to mental states.

The replication of a mental state would in fact have to rely on the replication of the experience but also on the complete life history of A into B. The adoption of heterogeneous devices or technologies redefines the message as an artificial product and not as a replicated one. Being an artificial object, the message soon ends in living its own life by incorporating endless latent observation levels and generating unforeseeable, collateral, new phenomenologies. The exemplar, 'eradicated' from the whole context established in the mind of A, becomes as crystallized and objectified as any 'technological' product, at the disposal of the mental context of B.

This also applies to the arts where the critics, and more than ever the interpretation in executive arts such as in music or the theatre, live for just this exchange between author and interpreter or author and the public. From this exchange, thanks to the selections of the author, to the technology used, and to the selections of the interpreter (or of the critics, or the public), the exemplar becomes renewed and endowed with an autonomy and reality of its own.

This reality is, in turn, freed from its purely reproductive ambition and sets itself up as an objective phenomenon, which is simultaneously distant from nature from which it took its ideational hint and from the technology that made it possible.

4. Artificial memory

We will also observe that the memory of an event is only analogous to the generation of the artificial – it is more similar to a representation – but at a low level, without the technological intentional tools of 'interpretation': it is a fact of natural self-reproduction which is regulated by its own laws that are connected to the psychic environment, like the form of an object on the sand compared to its own environment.

Also when memory has re-dimensioned an event, in various orders of relations and in a more compatible measure with the nature of the human mind, this becomes constituted by infinite possible levels of observation, of analysis and of association. Historically in the field of memory one can also distinguish the development of both conventional technology and technology of the artificial. The former bases itself on various conceptions or theories of natural memory – or, more exactly, of the representation we have of it – and has tried to enhance this mental resource for practical aims. Some examples converging on the concept of mnemotechnics can be found in the writings of several authors, going back to Cicero in his *De Oratore*.

A different matter is the attempt at reproducing reality by means of graphical expedients and then through genuinely artificial strategies (which were largely successful after the invention of printing and other modern or contemporary technologies of memory). In some of these attempts, although not those based on writing techniques, the target of the reproduction is twofold since, as it has been maintained (Bertasio, 1994), certain graphical and painted representations assume, as a target, both the communication of the content as such and the formal structure of natural memory. This is partially analogous to what happens in contemporary hypertexts. Examples of this kind can be found in several works from the time of the Renaissance, in the *Thesaurus Artificiosae Memoriae* (1579) by Cosmas Rossellius, in the *Congestorium Artificiosae Memoriae* (1533) by Johannes Romberch (Rose, 1993) and in the *Phoenix seu artificiosa memoria* (1491) by Pietro da Ravenna.

5. Some further sociological remarks

The relevance of the concept of artificial (as in the TA) to our way of seeing lies in its ability to give an account of the genesis of a wide class of social actions, especially those destined to generate cultural models.

To state that something is artificial means to state that it is the result of a reproduction process of multiple selections; of an observation level, of an exemplar and, finally, of an essential performance which is attributed to that exemplar.

Human behaviour, in turn, shows latent uniformities that may be analysed according to strategies which always end, sooner or later, by having to face the theme, both methodological and substantial, of the selections that social action requires for its development and in which it consists.

The theme is methodological since, as for every other science, sociology has to necessarily select the variables which it, in turn, aims at assuming are essential, in the attempt to formulate explanations. We may refer here to two classical examples: that of Marx's selection of the economic variable, which is most remarkable 'in the last analysis', or of the religious one in Weber. But the theme is also substantial since the object of sociology coincides with the net of selections that social and cultural actors continually set up, alter or restore. The complexity that characterises the nets of selections is the fundamental subject that social institutions try to order: social systems, according to Luhmann (1982), exist for just this reason, that is, to reduce complexity in a manner which is self-referential, and always do so by making arbitrary selections. On another level, Berger and Luckmann (1966) attribute a power of permanent initiative to social actors through which they propose their own subjectivity, as a basis of new interactions or, if you prefer,

> differently from the actors of Goffman that seem to recite scripts written by other people, they improvise and create their own scripts.
>
> (Wallace, Wolf, 1991)

The social systems, and the systems of social interaction, both micro and macrosociological, are therefore characterised by the attempt to reduce latent complexity on the basis of individual initiatives or on some institutional actor. Since actors' initiatives determine their own destiny from the moment of their exteriorisation, as Berger and Luckmann would say we can deduce that the success of the initiative depends largely on the success of the phase of subjective selection of the 'script': in other words, of the value, of the 'point of view' or of the cognitive dimension which is assumed as a possible base for the desired interaction.

The 'social construction' that one sets up in this way is only one of the possibilities but, in whichever way it presents itself, it reduces complexity since it allows for collective polarisation: it acts as a selective filter, set up by a selection which has been previously established.

The theory of the artificial underlines the functional and unavoidable character of this attributive selection but also its illusory nature in the field in which the selection, or the attribution of an essential performance to an exemplar plays a key role. In fact, whatever the attempt at reducing complexity in the field of artificialism, such as in scientific research or in daily life, carried on through polarising selections, if it succeeds it certainly generates an ordered and tranquillising framework, but the richness of the exemplar which was thrown out of the door always comes back in through the window.

We could insist all we want on the essentiality, on the fundamental relevance of our selections, and they can also work well. For instance, an artificial social situation – e. g. needed for some emergency case – can reasonably replace a 'natural' one in the systemic conditions in which the selection of its features has been operated. But, sooner or later, some changes in the initial conditions or in the systemic context or in the guest environment will make the delusory essentiality of those selections clear.

This is well-known, of course, to scientists as well as to epistemologists. Nevertheless, according to the TA it is important to place great emphasis upon the principle of inheritance: cultural models, in this sense, only apparently reduce the latent complexity that we would have to face without the active intervention of the system. In fact, since every model is a construction, and we would prefer to say a 'linguistically persuading convention', it characterises the reality in a manner which is compatible with man but without in any way reducing the actual richness, the variety, and the heterogeneity of reality: all these characteristics, including those with latent modalities, will be inherited by the systemic reality that is set up and which the model aims to control.

This is why between the artificial reproduction of an exemplar and the scientific explanation of a natural phenomenon, a perfect homology could be found. Both are, in fact, attempts to establish privileged properties or connections within total phenomenologies in which everything is linked to everything else. It is not a matter, necessarily, of an inextricable solid situation: rather, we have to deal with an endless intersection of latent observation levels among which some are, locally, usefully isolable from others for explanatory and predictive purposes. One sociologist, Gurvitch (1963), argued for this situation with reference to 'social total facts', albeit he emphasised the 'irreducible holistic and inseparable' character of the planes and of the levels that constitute them, whilst, in our case, we only underline the heuristic and pragmatic reducibility of nature.

Gurvitch is right, however, in his insistence on the concurrent presence in every social fact of all the planes and levels that constitute it in depth. Hence, when a social balance is transformed in a structure, thanks to the hierarchic arrangement of its levels, and it becomes easier to point out the essential levels, it could be inferred that the interplay between these levels and the remainder do not stop to act. In fact, it is plausible to assert that it is just from the dynamics of the neglected or secondary levels, however inherited and subsequently enacted, that there is structural change in the balance.

Every cultural model, being an organisation of individual and collective representations, in its turn possesses a simplified structure that tries to dominate other more complex structures. Its crisis always comes from the sudden or gradual 'discovery' of something we were unable to fully reduce and control assuming simplifications. In some cases the crisis is due to the interactions of the internal components of the model but, more often, it is the result of the 'strength of things': that is to say, of the force of some real neglected level whose unavoidable inheritance and therefore presence, in the 'things' that the model should organize and control, accumulate energy to emerge sooner or later in the open.

All this has special value if related to epistemological tendencies that confer both the selective and attributive character that we have underlined to the observation (as Berger and Luckmann did), and also the activity of autonomous construction by the mind (as Maturana, Von Glaserfeld or Von Foerster did).

The greatest danger of a constructivism that emphasises too much the autonomous role of the mind or of the culture in setting up a general understanding of science and technology (Mukerji, 1994) consists in the fact that it does not grant a symmetric autonomy to nature. It is a position that always ends in revealing not only sceptical or even idealistic attitudes (Johnson, 1993), but also, so to speak, 'aristocratic' attitudes with respect to the empirical world and without care for its independent phenomenologies. For example, it is quite right that defining an earthquake as a concept born of individual and collective representations is very interesting, especially within the frame of so-called mass emergency research. Nevertheless, the scientific conceptualisation of an earthquake, albeit always arbitrary and provisional, upholds the empirical and independent nature of the phenomenon.

The proposal for a relativistic-objective conception, which was introduced in this work, has exactly the finality of re-balancing the relation between the observer and the external world, likening one to the other in the parity of rights *a priori*. It should be recognised though that, *a posteriori*, man could not answer for the wholeness of the facts (including those that concern the self), but works through selections, which are always provisional but effective, that transcend them.

6. The 'laws of imitation'

The Italian linguists Devoto and Oli (1981) rightly characterise the artificial as an object achieved with expedients or technical procedures that imitate or replace the appearance, the product or the natural phenomenon. On the other hand, they define the imitative component as the ability to accomplish or pursue, according to some criterion, a more or less exact or adequate likeness. The circular character of the matter emerges in the definition 'feigned', an adjective which according to Devoto and Oli, consists of any product obtained *artificially* as *imitation*.

Certainly human beings, and also many animals, are familiar with the art of fiction and imitation (and would never accept the idea of 'feigned intelligence'?) but the semantic weight of these connotations, especially of the former, for the concept of artificial is probably excessive.

The production of artificial and imitative processes do in some measure overlap, but there is an important discriminating point. Bearing in mind the definitions which have been introduced here, pure imitation and the process of arriving at the artificial share the necessary condition that they draw their inspiration from something that exists. But they diverge in the materials and procedures they adopt. Indeed, we propose to define imitation as the attempt to reproduce the essential performance of an exemplar by adopting the same materials and procedures without aiming at producing a replica.

The presence of an exemplar is certainly shared by the artificial and by imitation. The same could be said for the essential performance but the imitation, especially in the case of the imitation of human behaviour, does not adopt different materials and procedures. The simple repetition of gestures, expressions and postures, as in the case of mime and as observed in many primates, does not consist in resorting to devices different from those adopted by the person who is assumed as the exemplar. One has to speak of pure imitation. The same occurs when we try to reproduce a painting using the same tools adopted by the original painter. Conversely, we should speak of the artificial in the case of those mimes, today fairly diffused, that try to reproduce the 'digital' movements of robots by means of their own body, evidently different from the hardware structure of the exemplar.

In conclusion, the concepts of artificial and of imitation delimit two sufficiently different classes of human disposition. In general terms, the disposition to imitate is characterised by the absence of a model or a theory of the exemplar and, thus, it shows a smaller complexity when compared to the generation of the artificial. Furthermore, since it avoids adopting different materials and procedures, the imitation is more conservative than the artificial which is intrinsically destined to develop new systems, starting from the ones which have been assumed as exemplars.

The imitation presumably has an adaptive function and does not necessitate any particular theorising by the imitator since it lacks the problem of conferring onto two systems, the exemplar and the product of the imitation, something which is structurally common. Often, however, the imitation bears the characteristics of utilitarian behaviour, distinguishable from creative fiction and innovative, as the sociologist Tarde, has maintained:

> Socially everything consists of inventions and imitations and the latter are the rivers of which the former are the fountains.
>
> (Tarde, 1890)

This argument crosses, through a clear analogy, that of the typology proposed by Riesman (1952) when he speaks of hetero-directed men compared to self-directed ones; these being two ideal types of human beings who differ in their emergent disposition to imitate, more or less deeply and frequently, common styles of life, particularly of so-called 'peer groups' and the mass media.

The imitation, in other words, could be defined as the archetipical matrix from which the artificialistic disposition will develop, thanks to the effort of reproducing something that exists by accepting the internal challenge of using materials and procedures which are different from those of the exemplars.

It is fairly clear that in daily praxis, and in the evolution of the species and of individuals, imitation and the artificial frequently intersect.

Likewise it is clear that the truly artificialistic disposition, which man excels in, always requires some degree of awareness, of intentionality: a child who 'imitates' for fun by using his own bodily resources, the movement of an automobile, its noise and the 'essential' manoeuvres of a driver, are much closer to generating the artificial than a butterfly which camouflages its own appearance to defend itself from the predator.

The same argument applies, to use again an anthropological example, to the primitive function of the Duala magicians as singers. Schneider remarks that,

> A good magician should not be a good singer. That doesn't mean that he should not have a wonderful voice; he should be a resonator drain from the sacrifice, able to reproduce all the sounds of nature.
>
> (Schneider, cit., p.72)

Instead, a true imitation, has to adopt the same tools as the exemplars: within music, for example, certain European jazz groups use the same instruments to imitate the North American dixieland style of the twenties, having been inspired by its success.

Although the artificialistic disposition possesses a strong and evident imitative content, it is not limited to inducing behaviours in which modules previously experienced are repeated, to use an expression by Tarde, in a sort of 'sleep-walking' state. The artificialist, in communication as in the case of imitation, almost always openly argues that he, in his own attempt at reproduction, adopted different materials and procedures from the original. This implies re-definition, reduction and transfiguration of the exemplar. In the end, whilst there is no artificial that does not imply imitation, the latter, like the replication, does not imply the former at all.

It should then be observed that the laws of imitation alone do not account for the origin of innovations, which, according to Tarde, would result from particular intersections and special contaminations amongst imitative processes.

In the most primitive instruments and in the most sophisticated contemporaneous devices, the artificial always implies, although to different degrees, some abstraction from the particular case, and then a theorisation which is closely based upon the intensity of the adopted conventional technology. Let us consider an illiterate man who, in having to survive in a community that is linguistically different from his, tries to adapt himself to it by establishing correspondences between the sounds or words and the concrete actions issued by members of the guest community. This is in order to achieve the capability to react adequately to environmental events, in a similar manner as Searle's 'chinese room'. He will build, for his own adaptive use, a semantics based on correlations with the imitative experience, which will also be able to evolve towards richer and more complex stages. Nevertheless a human being in these conditions will almost always remain below the threshold that separates the closely pragmatic use of a tongue from the learned use of it, with all the mental and cultural functions associated with it.

Both in the evolution of species and individuals there is, in fact, a stage in which imitation is transformed in the process of generating the artificial through the abstraction and ensuing classification and generalisation of the forms. These are semantic but above all grammatical and syntactic. Just as

> to think freely is always more tiring than thinking through others.
>
> (Tarde, ibid.)

The imitation constitutes one of the many elementary processes of adaptation and, as such, is static and conservative. Conversely, the artificial, though it is generated by the effort to reproduce something which already exists in nature, yet it always evolves, at least potentially, towards richer and more innovative stages of knowledge, thanks to the conventional technologies and the multiple selections it comes from. These are based on abstraction, generalisation and heterogeneity compared to the exemplar and generate always its transfiguration.

7. Falsehoods and imitation

The falsehoods that appear in the world of painting pose a special problem: are they an imitative fact, a replication or a case of the artificial?

The first question that the observation level presents is: "Which dimension, appearance or 'profile' of the original object should I reproduce with maximum accuracy?" The answer to this question is that it depends on the particular observation level chosen.

If the counterfeiter (who in this case is not one) decides, as it were, to give 'only the idea' of the Gioconda by Leonardo, then he would set himself in the area of the artificial particularly if he adopted materials different from those of Leonardo. He would, in fact, not consider it necessary to reproduce all the observation levels which are implicit in the structure of the original, such as the image in its dimensions, in all its appearances and details, the colours and their chemical nature, types of cloth, etc. He will also fail to use the same materials and procedures; he could actually only generate one sketch using a pencil and arbitrary dimensions. We may say that the same is clear for a graphic representation accomplished by means of a computer, or for the Middle-Age-like constructions of De Andrade.

Nevertheless, the ambitions of a high-level counterfeiter are a much stronger. He wants to pass a true Turing test: his product and the original must be indistinguishable by a person who is an art specialist. Such a desire coincides with the desire to recreate the exemplar *in toto*, that is to say, to generate a true replica. Since, as we have seen, a replication is only possible if one has accurate knowledge of the materials adopted and the details of the 'design' of an exemplar at the same observation level assumed by its original author, the final work of the counterfeiter could be considered a replication when the two conditions outlined above are completely satisfied. These conditions would otherwise be overlooked by a simple imitation: in fact, such an imitation would consist of a reproduction using materials of the same class but only similar to the original, and of a 'design' which is not identical in the details.

The interesting conclusion is that, on the one hand, there is confirmation that there is a conceptual difference between a replication (i.e. a reproduction at all the observation levels implicit in the exemplar) and the artificial, which is the result of deliberately selecting only one observation level and using different materials and procedures. On the other hand, the difference between the replication of a technological product and the replication of human behaviour is underlined – in our case the painting behaviour – which cannot be completely formalised and, then, cannot be achieved merely at the informational level.

In other words, a technological product of which the project or design and the adopted materials and procedures are known can always be replicated because we need nothing else. The activity in accomplishing it, if the procedures are carefully followed, will not in any way affect the final result. In an extreme case, the same will occur for a computer image, where we have knowledge of both the algorithm and the hardware on which it is implemented.

But, in the case of a painting, will acquaintance with the materials, the procedures and the design be sufficient? As a rule the answer is negative, since, in this case, the activity accomplished is not secondary or purely 'executive'. Even if a counterfeiter takes great care of his brush strokes, and assuming that he knows many, if not all, of the painting techniques of the artist, he will nonetheless end up interpreting them: that is to say, he will end by attributing to his own work personal essential performances which are additional or a partial substitution for those attributed to the original artist.

This is why a counterfeiter can never replicate a painting, just as a violinist cannot replicate the performance of a colleague, the execution of which he may try hard to follow in detail. In order to succeed, both must abdicate their personality. Fake works of art are high level cases of imitation and, strictly speaking, are not replica or artificial products. Rather we could speak of them as attempted or naïve replications. It has been correctly pointed out that,

> A high level counterfeiter is certainly not just a simple imitator or copyist or mechanic reproducer of images produced by someone else. . .and it will not even be refuted that his products, although by derivation, have an own artistic value and even show a certain degree of invention and of originality.
>
> (Chinol, 1986)

Albeit a counterfeiter knows the materials used by of the original author and adopts them, the procedure of accomplishing the task, above all in terms of style, will necessarily exhibit, to some degree, his own individuality. Despite the greatest passive openness of the counterfeiter to the authors selections, all that can emerge is some form and degree of transfiguration of personal selection or attribution of performance.

By the way, this aspect of the problem introduces in a new light the old question of the translation of poetry, theatre and literary texts into languages different from the original. A problem which is only apparently captious could be: 'Why is it possible to have fakes of paintings and sculptures, which seems senseless, and yet impossible to have fakes in compositions of poetry, music, or theatre?'

The most correct answer to the above question probably resides in the internal difference between the two groups of art, of which only the second necessitates, in order to be complete, an accomplished performance. The musical score, the poetic text or the theatrical one are, in fact, informational structures waiting to become sensible. In other words, they transform themselves into actual communication. As far as their informational structure is concerned, they could then be, and actually are, easily replicated, because beyond the informational level, a musical score as such does not exhibit other levels.

A computer, which becomes a device that is only able to elaborate information, will easily 'execute' a musical theme of which it is given the score, but it does so without interpretation. The result will be aseptic and impossible to listen to at all, though a project of artificial intelligence has begun to try to reproduce a human interpretation (see Baggi, 1992).

Human execution constitutes the final artificial object in which actual life is given to the mental exemplar of the composer and to his essential performance, interpreted by the performer: a concert is a complete bodily product, rich in levels and, as such, is no more replicable than is a painting. The 'faithful' reproduction by violinist A of a concert performed by violinist B would in fact present the same difficulty as producing a fake painting. Music and the theatre are, in the end, activities of generating the artificial which are achieved by two pairs of hands, those of the composer and those of the performer, whereas a painting, as an artificial object, is definitively generated by its artist. All this makes the performing arts particularly complex, since the selections of the author, above all those of the essential performances and of the exemplar, intersect, more or less easily or organically, with those of the performer. As observed by Pirandello,

> Always, unfortunately, between the dramatic author and his creature, within the materiality of the representation, there is the necessary intervention of a third unavoidable element: the actor. . . But, even when we find a great actor who succeeds in silencing his personality in order to enter that of the character he has to represent, the full and perfect incarnation is often hindered by irreparable causes due to certain facts: for example, the actors' figure. This drawback can be corrected, at least partially, by means of makeup. But we always get an adaptation, a mask, rather than a true incarnation.
>
> (Pirandello, cit. p.97)

We can therefore consider the imitation as a process which belongs to two fundamental classes: low level imitation and high level imitation. The former includes all the phenomena of imitation and those of conscious or unconscious mimicry which show, as a main finality, adaptation and survival. The latter includes, in its turn, activities that are definitely conscious; that tend to replicate the exemplar through an intense and refined study, though usually not scientific, of its characteristics. The two classes of imitation share the incapability to rationally select anything from the exemplar or to use technological materials and procedures. Both, in conclusion, are processes in which the performer shows a strong – or in the case of animal imitation, it is as if they show a strong – disposition to stay in the world rather than to alter it or to reproduce it as an intellectual challenge open to the discovery of new worlds. For both, finally, are a prelude to the artificial, from an evolutionary point of view as well, it is plausible to assert that they precede it.

The artificial, in fact, will begin at the exact moment at which one has the opportunity, or the necessity, to use the knowledge and the building strategies of conventional technology to implement the appearances, functions and features of the exemplar, the imitation of which is revealed as being impossible.

8. Artificial and cultural evolution

The machines of conventional technology and those of the artificial delimit not only classes of projects and lines of research which are different from each other, but also historic periods and phases of cultural development and mental dispositions which are likewise different.

The intensity of the production of concrete artificial objects through history can be described taking the form of a parabola with its concave top. Since primitive civilisations lacked scientific theory and a developed, generalised and shared technology, they founded their elementary techniques (Mc Carthy, 1992) almost exclusively upon the macroscopic imitation of nature, assuming natural exemplars and their related essential performances as being the pragmatic aim of reproduction.

Furthermore, the history of technology and also the history of primitive and non-primitive art demonstrates that we must be aware of the fact that the dimensions and constraints of the natural environment always act on human perception as sources of ideation for building objects (Negrotti, 1993). In this sense we can speak of intentionality or un-intentionality behind the selection of exemplars.

The rise of scientific knowledge and of technology based upon science since the Renaissance reduces the production of the artificial, which has been replaced by intrinsically creative and original inventions, that is, without any natural exemplar. Since rationally based technology aims to dominate and control nature and not to reproduce it, it sets up, in its turn, a new cultural area.

Finally, the further advancements that conventional technology have currently brought persuades us that the reproduction of natural exemplars has again become a realistic capability in exploiting technically available attainments.

The great interest that contemporary artificialists attract testifies, on the other hand, to the existence of a very deep rooted human disposition towards the ancient ideal or ambition of reproducing themselves or other natural phenomenona. More particularly, it is presumed that the human disposition to build the artificial relates to the fact that the human mind, in many activities, and in communication, is permanently committed to a work of 'reproduction' of its own representations or, as we said earlier, of its own exemplars and essential subjective performances. It is a matter of an enduring activity governed by selective unavoidable constraints that, as such, force the mind in every situation to take decisions about alternative observation levels, even those which are in competition with each other and, on this basis, to decide what is and what is not essential.

In doing so, the main purpose is the reproduction of something external or internal but processed by our mind in order to transfer to the outside the characteristics held as essential at a certain observation level. This is a process which, as in every other production of the artificial, implies a selection and a reduction of the exemplar as a whole and, then, a more or less deliberate and broad transfiguration of its structure and performances. This transfiguration (which is the best and most powerful characteristic of the artificial) is furthermore amplified by the unavoidable adoption of 'technologies', both of a hard and soft type, such as language, logics, communication tools and so on.

After the initial ideational moment, in which both man as such and the artificialist are completely absorbed in nature and in isolating a fragment of it, the concrete accomplishment has some hope in only adopting or converting the available conventional technologies. This is why, as we have already stated, the artificial soon moves some distance from the exemplar; a distance that is destined to increase in the subsequent generations and which, in fact, will only be possible through further introductions of conventional technology. We are speaking about a tendency which is defintely typical and verifiable, although often, as in the anecdote that follows, the effect seems to depend on the quality of the research.

> The smoke detector in the new public library Mary works in turned out to be so sensitive that when the employees of the library lit a cigarette in the offices, whole fire departments had to be mobilised. Some sense organs which are artificially created by man respond to a signal of danger with better reliability than the senses we are born with.
>
> (Arnheim, 1989)

Actually, the transfiguration of exemplars and of the essential performances is a general rule in the evolution of the artificial.

At the level of communication, for instance when a history is handed down orally over the passage of time, it loses or transforms its content, often, because of the use of new lexicons or tools of communication. This likewise happens in art, for example in music, when a simple popular feeling and some event related to it are transfigured in a more complex system by the creativity of a great composer. For example, Peter Ilich Tchaikovsky built up various of his compositions starting from popular hints, and

> To hear a Tchaikovsky tune is to want to hear it again and again. But studying Tchaikovsky's music closely reveals that it is often a good deal more cerebral and skilfully constructed than it may appear on the surface.
>
> (Garden, 1989)

The same applies, of course, to musical compositions which are deliberately intended to reproduce natural phenomena, such as several works by François Couperin or Antonio Vivaldi. The type of complexity present in the above works of music is always very different and intrinsically heterogeneous compared to that characterising the exemplars (popular songs or natural phenomena).

The artificial is destined to generate performances and quantitative and qualitative features different from those exhibited by the exemplar. The consequences of side effects in many cases, as in the arts, become the central features and accompany the reproduction of every natural performance: *a priori*, we could not say anything about their positive or negative character.

The side effects introduced by the unavoidable adoption of conventional technology are of great relevance for our understanding of the artificial and how it is always, despite intentions, something original compared to the natural exemplar but also to a conventional machine.

The new reality set up by the artificial should not be misunderstood, as has already happened to conventional technology and the new reality that it has developed, either in the sense of reducing it to pure instrumentality or in the sense of imagining it as a replication of nature: this would mean, in both cases, to ignore the particular characteristics of the artificial.

This implies, incidentally, the great difficulties and responsibilities designers have to build of interfaces between users and the artificial devices.

The machines of the artificial increase the variety both of the natural environment and of the cultural one – while conventional machines only increase the variety of the latter – and then create new possibilities of knowledge and of action inside nature. In fact, the abstract nature of conventional technology sets up realities which often cannot be assimilated by the environment: in a sense, they are 'islands' of specific and local order that are quite, so to speak, unrecognisable when not definitely opposed to the natural structure of the world. Their destiny is to conclude their own life-cycle through material decay, when entropy brings them back to the natural context, although not necessarily through paths compatible with it.

However, the degree of the match between an artificial device and the environment, whether natural or social and cultural, will depend, of course, on its intrinsic approximation to the exemplar and its critical performances in the various contexts. Since, as the TA maintains, this capacity is, as a rule, very low or, at least, limited to the areas of behaviour specifically designed by the artificialists, in the long run the destiny of conventional and artificial technologies would also converge from this point of view.

As a consequence, one of the most pressing problems in the use of artificial things, is and will be that of discriminating, at every moment, what is really compatible in the machines of the artificial – or how it interacts in some congruent measure – with natural systems. In other words, we have to keep in mind that pure conventional technology is only able to act on or affect nature and that the technology of the artificial itself is largely possible only through the conventional one.

For this reason the presence and development of the artificial in our culture, in this new historic phase in which real or virtual but always complex machines take the place

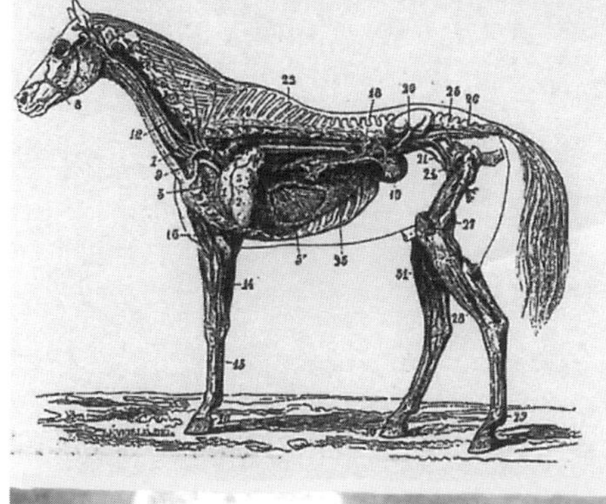

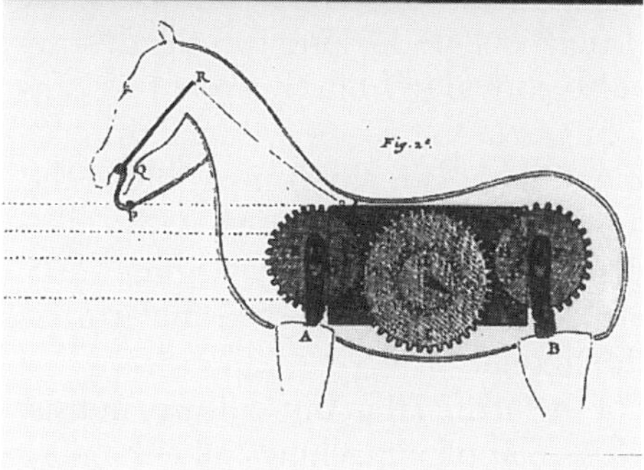

An example depicting four main ways of conceiving a nature object. From top to bottom: the horse is seen at the regular human observation level (level of nature); the horse is seen as an object of analysis (level of science); the horse is seen as a source of energy (level of technology); the horse is an exemplar whose movements are to be reproduced as its essential performance (level of the artificial). M. G. Losano, Storie di automi, *Einaudi, Torino, 1990; L. Gianoli,* Il cavallo e l'uomo, *Longanesi, Milano, 1967.*

of the ancient reproductive dreams of man, could not be perceived in the same weak and nebulous style that has concerned traditional technology. The status of the artificial demonstrates ample elements to define its crucial nature to affect or co-evolve with important areas and cultural functions, such as the role of knowledge, law, human – machine relations and the idea of nature itself as a conceptual and ethical system of reference.

Recently, Jonas remarked, though with too peremptory an attitude, that

> The difference between artificial and natural has disappeared. The natural is absorbed into the sphere of the artificial and at the same time the totality of the artifacts, the works of man that act on him and through him, generates its own 'nature', i.e. a necessity which human freedom has to face in quite a new way.
>
> (Jonas, 1991)

It seems clear that, assuming a perspective like the one pointed out here, the differences between natural, artificial and technological are, in this order, narrower than the large gap that we commonly perceive between the first term and the second two.

Furthermore, in the second part of this essay we have tried to support the idea that several human activities show, in their own nature, an artificialistic orientation. The generation of the artificial is, then, a

Natural forces may sometimes produce realities which look as if they have been made by man, that is, with a typical regularity of form which characterises human projects. Likewise, sometimes man, unaware of doing so, designs and builds objects which already exist in nature.Source: Questa meravigliosa Europa*, Selezione del reader digest, Milano, 1977.*

fundamental anthropological disposition and the production of machines is only a special case, though, to appreciate its value we need to adjust our backward conceptions of technology and of man himself.

Especially on the themes of the responsibility and of the image man has of himself and of nature, for doing only two examples, the problems announce themselves, in the same time, interesting and pressing. In fact, the ability of the artificial to absorb fragments of nature and then to transcend them, thanks to the multiple selections it implies and their unavoidable use in the development of conventional technology, demonstrates enough elements to establish a wide-ranging discussion on machines and, more generally, on the human processes oriented to the reproduction of creation.

The artificial does not necessarily reproduce exemplars and essential performances which belong to the empirical world (in the picture, Coppo di Marcovaldo, L'inferno, *Florence baptistry). Actually, as no reproduction refers directly to the object but only to our mental or cultural representation of it, we could even reproduce something that does not exist as an empiricial object.*

This means that the limits men encounter when they try to reproduce something that exists in nature, or something they believe exists, are not necessarily a constraint: rather, they are natural rules for human development.

5. Case study I: the musical observation level and the artificiality of music

> . . . and in the same way it happens with the mysterious
> stream which flows in the depth of the human soul:
> the word enumerates, names and describes
> the transformations of this stream,
> adopting a material which is extraneous to it;
> on the contrary, music makes running
> on our eyes the stream itself.
>
> W. H. Wackenroder, 1799

1. Premise

There are many possible case studies of the artificial that one could undertake as a way to understand human phenomena. We have chosen two of them, namely music and painting, owing to their crucial communicative roles throughout history and today.

As we shall see, if one adopts the TA for describing and explaining both music and painting, then one gains a wider and much more unifying perspective compared to strategies which only account for the peculiarity of these two arts, avoiding their inclusion in a higher class, i.e. that of the communication process and, therefore, of the artificial. Music and painting are primarily considered to be communication processes, which will reveal their own specificity in a very illuminating way: they will even inspire some possible innovative knowledge on the nature of communication itself and on some aspects of the way in which human beings interact with the world.

2. Musical communication

As we have maintained in previous chapters, communication is a process which generates artificial objects and it is self-referential. In fact, the reproduction of mental status kept, by definition, inside the ego of the subject, cannot rely on the commonly shared observation or representation of the exemplar and of its essential performance. This happens more easily in the area of hard natural exemplars and performances and their related technological objects or machines.

For instance, when we wish to communicate, that is to say to reproduce, our happiness, we cannot indicate the status we refer to in a space and time system: it is very clear to us but quite impossible to observe, in itself, from outside. What is common and observable from the outside is that human beings are sometimes happy and openly manifest this feeling, but the subjective nature of it remains something we cannot grasp directly.

We have to declare our intention to reproduce our happiness, giving it the only reality it can assume outside us, whether this is a linguistic utterance, gestural or of any other expressive nature, in which we inexorably have to transform it.

In this sense we can define such a transformation of the message as a true *transduction* process rather than a translation from one language into another: in fact, once it is transformed in whatever linguistic terms, happiness as a mental status no longer exists. It takes form and substance from, or in, the 'material' we adopt, through the conventional technology we shall use to communicate.

Artistic phenomenology arises from the adoption of conventional technologies and becomes a kind of exercise in using them, just as, in some sense, the medium becomes the message in McLuhan's well-known thesis. Artistic languages are not, therefore, a kind of tool with which the artist gains a special enhancement of his faculties for reproducing his subjective exemplars and essential performances. The artist is also a prisoner of his own ego.

Rather, the self-referential nature of the artistic process will consist in the search for the best composition techniques and improving them until the artist is persuaded that he has reached the maximum of formal completeness, according to his own criteria and not necessarily according to some already shared expressive rule. This is not only true of the great innovators and masters but is also valid for their students. Igor Stravinsky once pointed out that:

> To realise [music] the only and indispensable requirement is the construction. Once the construction is achieved, the order is established, and there is nothing else to say. It would be useless to seek or to expect anything else from it. It is precisely this construction, this gotten order, that produces in us a unique emotion, which has nothing in common with our ordinary sensations and with our responses themselves to the impressions of daily life. We cannot better define the sensation generated by music than stating that it is identical to the one which comes from contemplation of interplay of the architectural forms. Goethe had well understood this when he defined architecture as petrified music.
>
> (Stravinsky, 1936)

The *Gloria* in *Re maggiore* by Vivaldi, and many other classical compositions including the fugues by Johann Sebastian Bach, may offer exactly this sensation of isomorphism with the architectural environment within which they had to be executed.

Any kind of art is possible thanks to the fact that communication technology, be it oral, written, pictorial, etc., imposes and, at the same time, allows realities – which are autonomous from the simple exemplar and from the simple essential performance – to gain form and substance in themselves. The essential performances of the artist are transfigured through the special use of the technologies he adopts.

The result of the transfiguration is an entity, an object or a process which is complete in itself and exceeds the subjective exemplars and essential performances.

In truth, the artist cannot communicate what no man could communicate: however, he is much more able than other people to build up something new, within which his feelings and ideas are encapsulated and soon transfigured in a form that becomes the sole substance we can appreciate.

Thus, the ambiguity that accompanies the work of art, instead of generating misunderstandings and frustration, as happens in day-to-day communication, produces beauty, that is to say, a specific aesthetic gratification.

By the way, all this seems to also be valid for theatre. We shall limit ourself to quote again the view of Pirandello, which is quite close to the theses we maintain here, particularly when he underlines the transfiguration of the character of recitation which is one of the 'technologies' adopted by the dramatist. This is a process which not only involves the scene but a reflection upon communication itself, when he observes:

> How many writers are disappointed when they see what their work becomes through the spirit of this or that reader, who perhaps congratulate him for some effect which he never planned to produce.
>
> (Pirandello, ibid.)

The conclusion is that, in all cases, human communication poses various kinds of problems and is not always a simple affair, particularly when the matter involved is very deeply rooted in the subjectivity of the person. Furthermore, as far as language is concerned, that is to say the main technology we have developed to communicate, the problem of its efficiency and effectiveness in allowing the transfer of 'personal knowledge' arises.

In fact, the human mind continuously produces representations, images, intuitions and so on, while communication can only concern a very limited part of each of them. The communication process is always, therefore, a process which starts and develops through selections of both the mental exemplars and essential performances and of the most suitable linguistic materials to reproduce them.

It is also clear that, in quantitative terms, we think much more than we can externalise through language. Therefore, every language acts as a filter, always creating some kind of bottle-neck in our capacity to reproduce our mental exemplars and their subjective essential performances.

3. Language as technology

For the above reasons to put the case of music into the frame of the artificial, we need an opening remark on the problem of language in general.

In earlier sections of this book we maintained that, analogous with what happens in the field of the technological artificial – made of concrete objects or machines – communication is a reproduction process which then directly relates to the nature of the artificial. Within it, he who communicates attempts to reproduce his own exemplar and essential performance into the listener's or reader's mind at some observation level that he seeks to share with his interlocutor.

Furthermore, we added that such a process necessarily has to rely on a shared linguistic technology whose nature is different from the mental states to be reproduced, that are pre-linguistic in their own bio-psychological, cognitive and emotional specificity.

Nevertheless, in this situation, it is a fact that oral or written language can be understood, at least in its roots, as being an unusual case of a true technology of the artificial rather than as a conventional technology which is intentionally forced to reproduce something, as happens in all the cases of concrete technological artificials.

Actually, what is a language used for, if not to communicate? In other words, with language we are dealing with a technology devised just for, and only for, reproduction aims and not for deliberately generating new entities, as, in our case, linguistic stuff, independent of the given reality we wish to communicate.

A phrase has 'sense' if and only if it communicates something, i.e. if it tries to reproduce some cognitive or, more generally, some mental state. Rather, we could underline that the development of language during cultural evolution has undergone so many structural and functional differentiations, semantic, syntactic, stylistic, that, in the end, it has really become something very different from that set of immediate tools for communicating which it consisted of in primitive cultures.

Thus, the onomatopeism, envisaged by Giovan Battista Vico (1668-1744), which characterised the expression of psycho-physical status in primitive cultures, fear, pain, happiness, etc., has been gradually replaced by sequential structures that are remarkably more complex, and to some extent abstract and based on formal rules. They really make the developed language something which is more similar to a conventional technology than to a technique capable of generating a reproduction that is immediately expressive and recognisable.

For this reason the artificial object which is generated by modernised and learned communication is likely to be much more ambiguous and constitutes a much deeper transfiguration of the exemplars and of the essential performances than the artificial generated in the communication processes within primitive tribes. Actually, language is a case of an artificial technique which has dramatically developed towards a conventional state.

This evolution probably involved, at least as far as the standardisation and rise of formal rules is concerned, music itself, after the introduction of musical notation in the sixteenth and seventeenth centuries (Sinding-Larsen, 1990).

If musical notation, on the one hand, has allowed enormous developments in this art, it has perhaps also made the externalisation of mental states, which were reproducible by means of the immediately previous primitive techniques, almost impossible. The latter was based, by the way, on the materialisation of strongly shared mythical representations and on that modulation of human natural sounds which gradually became music.

It is clear that a language should guarantee, in order to be such, a more or less illusory sort of concord between the mental states of communicating people and, more importantly, it should allow the interlocutors to establish such a concord with their own internal states. These states, therefore, have to develop before they can become an utterable message.

Perhaps the thesis that thought consists of linguistic events is reliable in some measure, particularly in cultures in which the use of language is central and permanent. Nevertheless, it is probable that the forming of representations, images, hints, intuitions and feelings leaves out any linguistic issue and that, therefore, their expression waits for the transduction we spoke about.

The difficulty that man often encounters when he tries to 'explain with words' some particularly complex state – which is a difficulty also for himself in purely linguistic terms – suggests that the original, mental 'material' is something different from the linguistic one.

Therefore, the transduction of mental states into communication messages implies the use of different materials and of a suitable conventional technology for generating them as artificial objects. Actually, when we are communicating, we do not exchange feelings or opinions, images or representations, but artificial constructs, signs, symbols and complete messages, to which we entrust those mental states, hoping that they could reproduce their content in the listener's mind. What really happens is that the artificial objects which we set up by the communication process, and which have a strong and clear 'meaning' for the person who generated them, tend to become autonomous entities whose nature depends much more on the linguistic technology they are made of than on the mental exemplars and essential performances they want to reproduce.

4. The meaning of music

This premise aims at approaching the theme of music with a different 'profile' compared to the usual way of dealing with its problematic linguistic character.

Many classical and contemporary composers or thinkers have placed themselves on opposite sides regarding the 'expressive' and, therefore, linguistic character of music. For instance, in contrast to Frédéric Chopin who maintained that he could conceive a music that did not express anything, we have Stravinsky's famous view that the expression has never been an important property of music; whereas Richard Strauss refused to believe in abstract music, Eduard Hanslick strongly maintained that music does not mean anything in itself. The contemporary composer Aaron Copland, in his turn, confessed that he believed in the existence of meanings in music but that he was unable to indicate what they were.

Nor can we ignore the work of Ernst T. A. Hoffmann, who has contributed in such a remarkable way to the destruction of the idea of imitation, that is, of something extra-musical, although his argument does not completely converge, as we shall see, with our thesis on the specificity of music.

The debate has, of course, involved historians and theorists of music as well; from musicologists to psychologists. A very good review of this debate can be found in Collisani's work (1988) in which he tries, interestingly, to establish a meta-symbolic understanding of music.

Among the psychologists, the cognitivists have tried to discover, as have other researchers, the meanings of music, that is to say, its universal semantics. In doing so, however, they produced very poor results, limited to higlighting particular associations between mental states or feelings and some typical musical intervals (Sloboda, 1985; Stefani et. al., 1990; Cooke, 1959). Or they proposed sociological or philosophical theses on the supposedly intimate, universal and fundamental nature of music or on some of its basic structure (Blacking, 1973; Schenker, 1935).

Other scholars, on the other hand, took different directions, denying not the expressive nature of music as such but the possibility to reconduct it to precise semantics, thus rejecting the possibility of establishing any analogy with any referential language: the one in which every term indicates or refers to, though in a standardised way, some particular object or concept.

Lèvi-Strauss, for example, denies the possibility of reducing musical meaning to any particular linguistic entity.

He assigns to music a strong freedom from the senses, in its materialisation into sound, while the myth is free from the sound and enslaved to the sense (Lèvi-Strauss, 1974). De Schloezer even more clearly maintains that in music,

> the meaning is immanent to its significance, the content to the form to such an extent that, rigorously speaking, the music has no sense but it is a sense.
>
> (Fubini, 1995)

Furthermore, concerning the uncertain symbolic nature of music, it has been maintained that

> Its life is the articulation though it never asserts anything, its characteristic is the expressiveness but not the expression.
>
> (Fubini, ibid.)

The ethnomusicologist Blacking brings us to a most useful ground for the analysis we wish to develop when he states, referring to the Ninth and the Tenth symphonies of Mahler,

> I shall not attempt to express with words what I feel when I listen to this music (Mahler explicitly said that it was necessary for him to express himself through music when 'undefinable emotions emerged' and that, if they were expressible in words he would do so). I wish to say that, for me, the above symphonies express something about life, death and man's struggle for self-fulfilment and spiritual peace. . . Now I ask myself if I have experienced the same feelings that induced Mahler to compose those scores or have I re-interpreted them on the basis of my own experience?
>
> (Blacking, 1973)

This is a question which everyone ask themselves at least once just after listening to a musical composition and, above all, one which has caused something well defined within us.

Nevertheless, the fact that in other cases music 'says nothing' to us does not imply that we are justified in our belief that this was the intention of the composer. Actually, rejecting some music as being difficult to understand is a much more radical fact than being unable to understand an ordinary communication or a poem: if music were a language, as poetry surely is, then the fact of being unable to understand it implies a sort of illiteracy either of ourselves or of the author.

Both these possibilities have some likelihood in themselves, of course, but, at least in the case of the music of the seventeenth and eighteenth centuries, it is much more plausible that what it communicates to us or, rather, what it produces in us, comes from our inner life. When we 'understand' it without faltering, we often assign a meaning to the music, exactly as if it were an oral communication or the contemplation of a landscape, transduced into words. When we 'don't understand it', we seem to be negating its existence just because no extra-musical mental state rises within us and thus, having no possibility to make it 'speak', we neglect its genuine musical nature.

On the contrary, in the case of Romantic music, which forces the listener, within certain limits, to take that 'passive sinking' that Besseler speaks of (Besseler, 1959), our dependence on understanding the author's personality and his music is much more evident: namely, he leads us into the landscape he has chosen. Therefore, not to understand this kind of music means, simply, not to like it.

This may be due to too great a distance or, possibly, to a paralysing resonance between the musical observation level of the author and the one to which we are willing to accede.

5. Musical observation level

If communication is the non-material analogy of the reproduction of concrete exemplars and essential performances by means of language, which is understood, particularly in the case of learned language, as conventional technology, and if the music does not have linguistic meanings, or only possesses them in a *sui generis* nature, then we have only two possible cases before us.

The first one is to maintain that music is not communication and, as a result, it does not consist of anything artificial: it would be an original reality and proposed as such. The second case is to consider music as an activity that is able to generate artificial realities in which some kind of transfiguration is present, typical of whatever form of artificial it is, whether of communication or of art.

Making the provisional analogy with language on the one side, whether spoken or written, and with music on the other, according to the theoretical perspective introduced here, may be useful for initially classifying music itself within the artificialistic activities. We can now present some elements which apparently support the above analogy.

Art and music, and most human interactions, possess an intrinsic teleology which is dominated by the desire to share exemplars and essential performances starting from given observation levels, selected by the person who decides to communicate.

Both language and music presumably have their origin in the onomatopoeticity made possible by the physiological emission of sounds by means of the vocal chords. That primitive phase was characterised by a very slow development, and many clear fragments of it appear in some of today's communication forms, particularly in children's expressions or in some less learned basic expressions. It was also a phase in which the sound and the word belonged to the same class – there was no real difference between them – and generated symbols of various kinds and power. They were and are artificial entities which, in terms of expressive content, are very close to their exemplars and essential performances, without particular modulation or style differences.

Both language and music have developed towards more and more articulated forms. The former surely must have developed its own functional differentiation long before the latter. When the musical notation system appeared at the beginning of the seventeenth century, language, written and oral, had already reached a well-established maturity and facilitated the generation of poetical and literary traditions of a very high level of complexity.

When they reached their own technical maturity with their own syntactic and grammatical rules, both language and music generated semantics which were further from the immediate exemplars and essential performances and more conceptual. They became increasingly generalised, unable to individualise without ambiguity objects events, circumstances, feelings and so on.

Language, in particular, can be described at two different semantic levels: the *pragmatic* level, on which meanings are very much shared since it develops almost only in informational or even quantitative terms; and the *knowledge* level, within which ambiguity dominates, there is uncertainty in permanence, definitions are vague, and it has a strong, intrinsic individualising nature, in other words, subjectivity.

While science, technology and a large part of the functional aspects of daily life are on the first level semantics, all the activities oriented to the reproduction of the subjectivity are on the second, as is the case in poetry and literature but also in some daily life itself.

On the contrary, music develops towards a definitely asemantic configuration, leaving some traces of its strictly communicational function in only very impoverished and narrow domains, as happens when some symbolic arrangements of sounds is strongly finalized: e.g. in the sound of bells or military music, in children's songs or in the less elaborated folk music.

The complex, post-notational music, subsequent to the rise of the conventional 'equable scale', generates forms which are uprooted from any immediately recognisable semantics, even in its version named 'music at program'. Whether it is descriptive or onomatopeic, as we shall see, it becomes an autonomous reality or, rather, a new way to look at the world or construct it. In this way music becomes a mixture of formal rules of substance and ideas that are properly musical, and to make itself understood, it has no need to pass through the generation of extra-musical meanings as a necessary condition.

The notation and temperament of the scale, in other words, assigns a strong and rigorous conventional technology feature to music, which stimulates its autonomous development. This happens, as we know, in all the cases of the development of artificial objects.

We therefore need to get over the linguistic analogy, owing to its incompleteness. If music appears to many as a language this is because both language and music are able to produce mental changes or psychological effects. But the identity of two effects does not imply the identity of their causes.

We propose that music be considered the result of a generation of artificials which, differently from any other artificialist generation, starts from an observation level which is quite autonomous and consistent with the conventional technology that, then, should be adopted. We may speak, therefore, of a special observation level, namely a musical one.

It is not, of course, a physical but a mental level, arising from the evolution of the cultural system. It is made possible by the existence of technological tools, such as the notation, the equable scale and the instruments, that allow it to establish and then reinforce its presence and further development.

Furthermore, it is a matter of a level from which the composer observes or constructs both the external and the internal world, perhaps according to those 'streams of fantasy' which Elias considers to be the basis of geniality if they converge with the 'pulse of consciousness', as in the case of Wolgang Amadeus Mozart (Elias, 1991), but which, in every case, generate formally complete and self-sufficient constructions.

In other words, there are no exemplars in the natural world which are intrinsically musical. Therefore the musical observation level is a cultural outcome. The existence of noise and sounds is only a casual fact which concerns only a small part of the natural events the composer looks at.

The work of the painter starts from the sensible, visual observation and, reproducing what he sees, the painter constantly inteprets and transfigures reality but adopts a language and a technique that are necessarily of a visual nature: sometimes, and always in the case of classical painting, it is a matter of an easily recognisable reproduction.

On the other hand, the music composer does not have this possibility nor this role. Though he is immersed, like every human being, in the sensible world which is internal or external to him, he generates something that, having no extra-musical recognisable exemplar, should be understood as coming from and belonging to his own way to perceive, see and construct reality.

Apart from the cases of a deliberate musical description, in which the composer, in some way, behaves intentionally like a painter, thanks to the available technologies, in every other case he does not reproduce reality through a language: he sees reality as something musically meaningful, even beyond the usual categories of space and time. His exemplars and his subjective essential performances cannot be shared except in terms of concepts and ideas constituted by the musical form and not by means of semantics.

This point is particularly evident, to cite one example, in *Les papillons*, by François Couperin, a piece for the harpsichord: the flight of the butterflies, deliciously erratic, takes a course in the rythm and in heights of sound, in a musical space and not a visual one. The space within which the music moves, in other words, is only observable musically and its translation into ordinary space has no aesthetic significance.

The ability of the composer to reproduce natural phenomena only demonstrates that musical technique, exploiting the tools of conventional technology on which it is founded, can also be used for such secondary aims. Nevertheless, while for almost all the other arts the reproduction of the shared, extra-artistic reality is the main foundation on which art, (i.e. the transfiguration of reality) is possible, for music it is only a side-possibility and not a necessity.

The painter also adopts what we could name a sort of 'painting observation level', but his exemplars should be the same ones that we see all around us. The painter, in the end, cannot do anything but paint, that is to say, reproduce visual aspects of the world according to his own poetics, and communicate them as such because even his transfiguration of the reality should be of a visual nature.

In his turn, the composer cannot do anything but write musical scores, and therefore the world, as we perceive it, disappears and is replaced by musical matter, that is to say, by the composer's special way of perceiving reality.

The fact that every composer belongs to a precise historical situation, the fact that he shares ideals or religious beliefs and possibly refers to some musical tradition, are all relevant elements in assigning a cultural significance to his works. But all this has nothing to do with the intrinsic meaning of his music as such, in the same way that the discovery of differential calculus, although consistent with the general cultural world in which it arose, has nothing to do with the sensible reality but provides a way to look at reality which is already constituted by mathematical entities. It is not surprising then that a musicologist like Deliège (Deliège, 1966) refers to the mental world of the composer as an 'imaginary universe'.

This point of view, which is the same as Poincaré's cited above, seems to us to be significantly similar to that held by the philosopher Sapir, according to whom music has to deal with a:

> level of mental life which is, on the other hand, more difficult and more elusive than the expression iself.
>
> (seen in Treitler, 1991)

It could be interesting to take into consideration the following interpretation, drawn again from Blacking:

> the music is able to create a universe of virtual time that, as maintained Gustav Mahler, can bring 'in another world, in which things are no longer subject to time and space'. Balinese people speak of the 'other mind' as a state of being one can reach by means of dance and music.
>
> (Blacking, cit., p. 70)

6. Noises, sounds and music

From a cultural point of view, the centrality of sound and music has often been underlined in anthropology, and also in relation to the myth of Creation (Schneider, cit., 23-31).

A great variety of sounds exist in nature and their 'music' has certainly accompanied human evolution as an important anthropological and environmental dimension (Murray Schafer, 1977).

Post-notational music, however, is founded on rules and, above all, on sound generators that, although they often originate far back in history, exhibit little similarity with the natural sounds which are, so to speak, readily around us.

The piano, for instance, which is and has been a truely princely instrument for many composers and performers, has often 'told' us about brooks or thunder, storms and birds but all in musical terms and no longer as pure sounds. For this reason the introduction of natural sounds or noises within a composition, for instance by means of the technique of digital sampling or magnetic recording, unless it is justified by educational aims or as an occasional embellishment, removes from the music its power to reveal an autonomous world at least in the domain of complex Western music.

The more the sounds and the noises of nature invade music, the further it is prevented from revealing man's musical ideas; ideas of the composer who has built up a vision of the world without limiting himself, in other words, to imitate it in an objective way. Rather, the composer tries to reproduce his own musical version of the world.

The introduction in *I pini di Roma* by Ottorino Respighi, of the nightingale singing, recorded on a disc, or the opening to the noises of the street introduced by John Cage, do not add anything to the music but seem, rather, to generate a regression, for a few moments or for the whole work, of the reproduction of the composer's ideas to a primitive imitation, to their reduction to a mere daily reality.

Maybe this all corresponds to some respectable poetics but, in our opinion, it vanifies the essence of music, which does not live off the reflection of reality except at the beginning of its transfiguration.

7. The musical construction of the world

Musical thought is a way to see or to construct the world and it tries to project itself as such to the world. What is reproduced, and further, transfigured by the conventional technology of musical order, in terms of notation, instrumentation and performing styles, is what becomes perceptible to the composer's mind from this special observation level.

If, as Mach pointed out, 'the world consists of our sensations', then it remains for us to accept the idea that music or, rather, organised sound, gives to the composer a particular observational sense. A mental module, placing the action of the physiological senses within a system regulated by musicality, allows him, or better, forces him to see the internal and the external world as a melodic, rythmic, tymbric or harmonic phenomenology.

In the sensible world, the one we observe daily and also the one which is studied by the sciences, there is nothing which is immediately musical nor are its images structures bearing musical *a priori* sharable meanings or configurations. While these could exist for painters or poets, this is not so for the composers. Therefore the musical observation level is exactly the sort of category of the mind which, while it is sometimes infuluenced by common observation levels, for instance in descriptive music, always leaves this out in the executed musical transduction of the perceived object. In fact, initially, the exemplars and the essential subjective performances of the composer belong to his mental life and not to the domain of empirically given natural things.

Plato maintained that art is a 'copy of the copy' of the world because it is the reproduction of what we perceive, and what we perceive is only a distorted and partial image of the true reality, that of ideas. For the composer, and this is valid in our opinion for Bach and Debussy, Chopin and Wagner, the world of the ideas resides in the 'purity' of their mental representations of a musical kind and, therefore, the music which they generate has no other worlds below or over them.

As we have seen in the first chapter, even for psychology, the mental representations constitute a field of problems which are very far from solution, and it is just about their configuration or effects (images, morphisms, states, sequence of states, etc.) that the debate is centered (Braga, 1996).

What is clear is that, as a general conceptual basis, we may think of any representation as something which needs some referential object or event, and this is why we defined them as meta-artificial objects. But in the case of music, and more radically in mathematics or logic, representations are self-referential, though stimulated by extra-musical events. The musical self-representation is, therefore, the original reality that shall be reproduced artificially, through not only notation but also through the unavoidable mediation of the performance. The latter, in its turn, will involve concrete instruments and the personality of the performers and the result will be further transfigured thanks to the inheritance principle which governs all artificial objects.

8. Musical observation levels: knowledge and recognition

We have to underline that musical observation allows for the interpretation of the world by generating mental images within the composer's mind which are direct and real but properly musical and not reducible to something else. The technology adopted for the reproduction of such mental images is consistent to the requirements of their expression, and when it is not, some new instrument or rule is created *ex novo*. Thus, Franz Joseph Haydn can say that:

> Musical ideas pursue me to the point of torture. I cannot get rid of them, they stand before me like a wall. If it is an allegro that pursues me, my pulse beats faster, I cannot sleep; if an adagio, I find my pulse beating slowly. My imagination plays upon me as if I were a keyboard.
>
> (Dies, 1810)

More paradoxically, and subtly underlying the self-reference of the reproduction of musical exemplars and essential performances, Bach said:

> There is nothing remarkable about it [the organ]. All you have to do is hit the right notes at the right time, and the instrument plays itself.
>
> (Köhler, 1776)

Our understanding of a musical composition implies, then, an ideally perfect syntony between not only two different entities in a generic psychological sense but between two sensitivities, musically oriented in the same observation direction. Sometimes, repeated listening makes this convergence easier since it allows us to gradually assume the same observation level of the composer, in such a way that:

> The repeated listening of a symphony or of a nocturn is more important than whatever essay or analysis. It is the work of art itself that teaches us the way for understanding it.
>
> (Rosen, 1994)

In any case, we have to consider that between the composer or, rather, his music and the listener there should be some initial elective affinity which is able to induce repeated listening. Otherwise listening will be avoided or it could lead to an appreciation only if the composition is recognised, if it is familiar, perhaps as a signal associated with particular existential events, rather than to musical knowledge in itself.

A direct consequence of this theoretical position is the sharp separation, which does not mean lack of interaction, between the world as it is described from any other observation level (physiological, psychological, social) and the one generated by music.

The sound is the basic matter which developed music organises in self-sufficient systems, that is, compositions, within which it proposes and fulfils itself, in terms of corporeity (Barthes, 1985) but on the basis of its own precise formal structure and matter, rather than in linguistic terms.

The form of music is the bearing structure of the transfiguration, without which the result would be pure expression, which any human being and animal could make. A pure expression would be devoid of any 'construction' worthy of aesthetical contemplation, trivial externalisation of a daily pragmatic 'significance' and not of what can be seen and known from the musical observation level. Thus, one can easily understand the position of Camille Saint-Saëns, according to whom

> What gives Sebastian Bach and Mozart a place apart is that these two great expressive composerss never sacrificed form to expression. As high as their expression may soar, their musical form remains supreme and all-sufficient.
>
> (Saint-Saëns, 1907)

In other cases, which can only superficially be evaluated as being less important, such as of Tchaikovsky musical observation forces an immediate reproduction which, nevertheless, is unimpoverished in terms of structural richness and power. Tchaikovsky himself was aware of his own formal weaknesses and maintained that when a musical idea took him he,

> started trembling and my heart leapt; very improbably I can start with a scheme, when the ideas are pressing on my mind.
>
> (Tchaikovsky, 1956)

In his turn, though he had an ordered and scrupulous character, Haydn confesses,

> I would sit [at the piano], and begin to improvise, whether my spirit were sad or happy, serious or playful. Once I captured an idea, I strove with all my might to develop and sustain it in conformity with the rules of art.
>
> (Haydn, in Griesinger, 1809)

To complete the outline of ambivalences which concern the intimate nature of musical creativity, it is worth recalling a sentence by Jean-Philippe Rameau, who, despite his rigorous studies of technique and therefore the rules, particularly that of harmony, said:

> Whilst composing music, it is not the time to recall the rules which might hold our genius in bondage. We must have recourse to the rules only when our genius and our ear seem to deny what we are seeking.
>
> (Rameau, 1726)

While it is possible to exaggerate some of the above positions, it is clear that composers are really as involved in musical matters as we are involved in the air. In other words, they live in an environment which acts on them and which they can see adopting an *ad hoc* observation level whose main tools are technical rules and their understanding of the musical instruments, with their abilities and constraints.

9. Intrinsic descriptive nature of music

The conclusion we have reached above is that musical observation is the modality through which the composer interacts with the world and which, therefore, poses itself as a *prius* and not as a representation of the world, subsequent to his perception through some other physiological sense.

As we said, all this could be valid for other artists: we could speak of poetical, architectural or painting observation levels. Nevertheless, with this formulation, we would discern a sort of 'double observation': before that of ordinary perception and, then, the one of the poet, the architect or the painter.

The history of the arts, music excluded, testifies that the natural object is the referential basis of the representation which will then be transduced into the final, concrete artificial object (Bertasio, 1996). The 'double observation' of the poet, the architect or the painter implies that the first observational phase, that of ordinary perception common to all human beings, comes *before* the mental representation of any poetical, architectural or painting order. The final product, the artificial or artistic work, will then be the result of a process which, starting from the exemplars and the subjective essential performances of the artist, will lead to a complete object which will reflect just those mental states, though transfiguring them.

In the case of music the initial perceptive sharing – e.g. the one according to which everybody could perceive the Moldava river as it was perceived by Bedrich Smetana as a human being – is only partial. In fact, in the composer's case, there is no transduction of the perception into music, since it is not a fundamentally physiological process but a process that is already widely characterised by the observational sense given to him by the music. In this understanding, music bears more similarity to mathematics and to some sort of philosophical imagination rather than to the other arts: before a beautiful musical phrase is composed, there is nothing at its place.

Expressed differently, the observation of reality through the ordinary senses, sometimes gives the composer only the motivational context for the composition and not its goal.

To some degree Diderot, despite his orientation towards the descriptive nature of art, understood this additional novelty which music bears upon human sensitivity when he wrote, in his *Leçons de Clavecin* of 1771, that:

> the painting is a more natural art while the music is an art more close to the man. . .The composer possesses the great advantage of painting the things which one cannot hear, the art of the composer consists of the ability to replace the sensible image of the object with the movement which its presence induces in the heart of those who contemplate it.
>
> (Diderot, 1771)

Of course, the beauty of a painting or of a sculpture transcends the represented object as an ordinary exemplar: nevertheless, aesthetic appreciation has to take it into consideration, just in the sense that the vision of a painting or of a sculpture cannot separate, isolate the aesthetical essential performances from the exemplar to which they are attributed. As Danila Bertasio will better explain in Case Study II, the exemplar of painting or of sculpture should be recognisable, in some way and measure: to ignore this point results in the solipsistic painting that is so well-known today, and not in the discovery of new observation levels since, at least, they lack any established universal set of rules similar to the ones existing at the base of the musical composer.

In music, on the contrary, not only is it quite possible to leave out the exemplars but, rather, it is the sole operation that the listener can perform, even when the composition has some extra-musical references.

We can say that, *de facto*, one appreciates music as such and the reference fades away: it is eclipsed and assumes a pure background role, until it totally disappears.

Perhaps some evolutionary aspects of painting and sculpture, for example, the concentration on lines, curves and colours, that is to say, on the formal elements separated from any recognizable object, could induce us to think that these arts can also generate, sooner or later, their own 'canonics', something analogous to the shift towards autonomy which music exhibited between the seventeenth and the eighteenth centuries.

Up to now, there is no trace of all this and we see a shattering rather than any signs of growth toward a series of shared rules. Thus, for now, only music possesses a distinctive world in which the exemplars and their essential performances, even when they start from something extra-musical, are observed and constructed in their own terms and are, therefore, autonomous if not intolerant for the external or internal objects as such.

A little bird living in the forest of Iowa gave Antonin Dvorák the idea for the violins in the third movement of his *American Quartet,* and referred to the creature as a 'damned bird'. The sweet 'damnation' of the little bird consisted, perhaps, in the fact that its attractive singing interferred with the composer's inspiration, dictated some musical paraphrases to him and prevented him, though we say this in a non-literal sense, from autonomously seeing and constructing the forest of Spillville as he would have desired. The musical observation, in other words, was 'perturbed' or pre-oriented by homogeneous events. In addition, the singing of the birds is in fact an organised sound which entered into resonance with the musical perception of the composer.

This means that the descriptive nature of the music is a characteristic which is alway present in compositions but it concerns the composer's musical representations and not the representations of natural objects as such.

In any case, musical observation should not be confused with ordinary observation, made possible by the physiological senses, even if, in descriptive music, composers have made and make a wide use of the imitative possibilities offered by instrumental technology.

This is a matter of a fact, frequently in reference to birds, whose resonant contemplation by the composer always seems to start with a sort of praise but invariably becomes a deliberate re-creation.

Ludwig van Beethoven also conceived his music whilst walking in nature but, as a comment on his *Sixth Symphony*, the *Pastoral*, he insisted that it:

> expresses feelings and is not a painting. . .[also because] whatever musical painting there is in the instrumental music, if it is too obvious, it loses its efficacy.
>
> (Il mondo della musica, 1956)

Yet, conceding something to the painter's ability or, perhaps, to the beauty of nature, Beethoven himself, with reference to the Andante of this Symphony, ordered his copyist to:

> write the following words: nightingale, quail and cuckoo on the parts of the first flute, first oboe, first and second clarinet, exactly like they can be found in the score.
>
> (Il mondo della musica, cit., p. 1973)

But, in Beethoven, apart from some aspects of the above Symphony, detachment from the descriptive music of the eighteenth century is already taking advantage of a closer musical poetics or, if one prefers, of a selection of the exemplars and of the essential performances in the 'internal landscape', that is to say in the world of interiority examined and made possible by the musical observation level. In the end we have to recognise that:

> Beethoven, in the years of his deafness, hears his own compositions beyond their actual sound, and knows them outside the space and time within which they are performed, out of the material world; and he can laugh at the fantastic and intuitive incapacity of other men who, in order to listen to music, need to play it on inadequate and limited instruments.
>
> (Collisani, cit., p. 77)

The composer, in other words, always describes himself as a musical entity, that is to say, as an observer of the world which is constructed in its own image, rather than exploiting some kind of referential language in order to depict what we all see.

10. Ordinary sense organs and musical sensitivity

The calls of the composers to the function of the ordinary senses are numerous, but the musical observation or vision exceeds the immediate perception.

Many composers would agree with the position held by Edgar Varese, when he says, 'I love the images as well as I love music'. However, this reference to music as something else compared to visual images explains the existence of another world which can be approached by means of organised sounds and their 'colours' rather than by means of words and drawing.

Dvorák exhibits a great ability to describe the country in his *Fourth Symphony*, the *English* and, as is well-known, Claude Debussy had the gift of transducing in music the visual impressions that entered his imagination, often coming from painting or literature (Cortot, 1930). Significantly, Mallarmé wrote that Debussy's translation in music of his *Prèlude a l'aprés-midi d'un faune,*

> . . . extends the emotion of my poem and defines the scene more passionately than the colour.
>
> (op. cit. Lesure, 1994)

Frédéryck Chopin himself, according to George Sand, sang during his walks, but this cannot be perceived as a reproduction of natural sounds. Rather, if we must adopt some metaphor for music, Chopin's music seems to reflect his musical way of perceiving colours, shadows and light, perspective depths, grace of movement and even perfumes.

Using the concept of observation one should conceive, also on scientific grounds, any interactive modality, even in its constructive versions, of man toward his own environment. Nevertheless, it is very clear that musical observation, based on elaborated or organised sound, surely corroborates what is communicated by all the physiological senses, perhaps with a particular regard for vision.

Alhough this could seem paradoxical, hearing is only assigned a pragmatic role, an unavoidable role of connecting with reality and, above all, a role of verifying execution, as if the sounds that this physiological sense brings to the consciousness were able to generate an impure competition with musical thought, reminding the composer of primordial matter, again ingenuous, from which his art developed.

This is an art which in Bach reaches the greatest detachment from nature, apart from Capriccio on the departure of his brother, where the reproduction of the noise of the horses' hooves and the sound of the mail-coach appears to be a sort of secondary ornament, possible but not essential.

The musical observation level allows, by definition, physical and spiritual visions of the world, but it has purely situational connections with the physiological senses. These connections are perhaps unavoidable and sometimes corroborate the perceptive context, but, though with some differences among themselves, they are secondary issues in the composition.

The fact is that the musical observation constitutes a modality of thought and not a simple filter or a sensory apparatus of a physiological order.

In this understanding, one could maintain that all music is descriptive, programmable or onomatopeic, if one wishes to say that it is always the attempt to reproduce exemplars and subjective essential performances which coincide with the composer's musical thought, by means of a notational, instrumental and interpretative technology irriducible to anything else.

Thus, it is legitimate to attribute meanings to music, for example, the tragic *Requiem in re minore* by Mozart or the joyful faith in the *Ninth Symphony* by Beethoven or, even more, the passions of the *Fantastic Symphony* by Hector Berlioz, who himself, starting the season of music 'at program' of the nineteenth century, defined it as an 'Episode of the life of an artist'.

In fact, the above meanings may be understood as the subjective essential performances the composers attributed to their musical exemplars. What is not legitimate is to attribute to these meanings the communication role which they normally have in day-to-day life or in scientific life, since they are musical facts and not existential or literary.

We have already examined Mahler's argument, who found it necessary to compose when his feelings were undecided and inexpressible. Another great composer, Felix Mendelssohn, took an apparently quite different position, maintaining that

> For me the thoughts that music expresses are not undefinable; rather, they are too definite to describe by words.
>
> (op. cit. Mila, 1956)

The indefinable character of musical ideas, irreducible through different communication codes, is the same as its own nature which becomes clear and definite only in itself. In the end, Mendelssohn also confirms that musical observation possesses its own, precise autonomy which does not need to be supported by anything else.

11. From description to transfiguration: from imitation to the artificial

All this may, perhaps, explain why the descriptive or onomatopeic music, as well as that which draws inspiration from folk or national songs, cannot be easily transformed in complex musical entities like sonatas or symphonies, in which, usually, the reproduction of extra-musical elements is almost always absent or irrelevant.

Actually, in the traditional definition, in the non-onomatopeic compositions, the musical observation level is much more free; it is not conditioned by the perceptive matter which limits and pre-orients and prejudices its development.

Rather, it is easier to find beauty and musical complexity in the variations of a composer on themes originally written by another, exactly as if it were a matter of permanent research or exploration that should be taken up from the point where the first composer provisionally ended his work.

Of course the onomatopeism, conceived as the deliberate imitation of nature and of its events, even of sound, has never prevented great authors from transcending the reproduction effect. In *The Four Seasons* by Antonio Vivaldi, the onomatopeic pieces for harpsichord by Couperin, in *Moldava* by Smetana and in the *Seasons*, in an oratorium form, which Haydn composed without enthusiasm in 1801 – just as Tchaikovsky unenthusiastically did with his twelve pieces for piano, one every month – the music soon overwhelms the imitation.

The fact that, in the history of music, deliberate onomatopeism – though recurrent in some measure – has had a shorter season than in other arts is very meaningful.

The exemplars and the essential performances of the composer are musical from the very beginning and their connection with the ordinary observation levels, though often elegant, is only possible in technical terms, not aesthetically or, rather, they are not as aesthetically relevant as those strictly constituted by ideas sculptured in the musical matter.

There is no doubt that the human being is a unitary entity within which not only the personality but also the interplay among the ordinary senses sets up the context within which musical ideas themselves can grow. In this way, the implicit or explicit reference to natural events, as well as social or historical, is fully justified. The history of music is also beyond the onomatopeic season, often characterised by elements of this kind, that are present in the titles of musical works.

The point is that discription is only the openly declared aspect, evident in *Pierino e il lupo* by Sergey Prokofiev, of a condition that music is always in, if one accepts the idea that, at the moment it is written and even more when it is performed, it does nothing but artificially reproduce the mental states of a man who stays in the world and observes it musically.

For this reason, when it is not onomatopeic or descriptive in the traditional definition, music can be more difficult to 'understand' than the other typologies of artistic reproduction, which can rely on an immediately sharable object, that is to say the exemplar and, often, the subjective essential performances attributed to it by the author.

On the other hand, the possibility to more or less immediately recognise the pictorial object may limit the appreciation of music, preventing the stylistic understanding and the formal beauty which it implies and which is always far removed from immediate pleasantness.

A traditional descriptive music, in some measure, can be subjected to the same process, while, conversely, a musical composition which is uprooted from intentional imitation aims needs to be enjoyed straight away, to facilitate the shift to understanding it as only music and not as the reproduction of shared phenomenologies.

Also the enjoyment of music as such may generate some kind of representation, since feelings and perceptions, memories and impressions are a common issue for human beings and, therefore, also for the composer, even for the less romantic and the more detached listener. Nevertheless, the rise of a recognisable representation, of joy, death, pain, love, myth etc. is not only often a largely subjective fact but it is subsequent to, or independent of, the appreciation of the musical substance in itself.

Concert no.2 op. 21 by Chopin for piano and orchestra may be enjoyed as if it were a portrait of a lake in the light and shade of a winter fog but the composer himself declared to have conceived it while thinking of a woman, the singer Costanza Gladkowska, and when he completed it he dedicated the entire work to another woman, the countess Delfina Potocka.

Variables such as the philological, historical competence and the musical, in a narrow sense, and also some natural disposition to music, must surely influence the judgement of the listener as well as that of the composer.

But what it is important to our aims, is to emphasise that the *ubi consistam*, the core of music does not involve common or daily understood questions that are expressible by words or other codes. Musical understanding consists, rather, in the deepening of its own matter through the execution or, better, the alternate possible executions of the same musical work since, in contrast to a painting or architectural work, a musical idea lives only if it is reproduced in a two stage process: first of all by the author and the transfiguring selections he operates and, secondly, by the interpretation of the performers which further transfigures it. Mila rightly says that

> there is never only one legitimate intepretation of a musical work, a 'unique' intepretation does not exist. We accept the Debussy from Gieseking and that of Cortot, the Chopin from Paderewski and that from Rubinstein, the Beethoven from Furtwängler and that from Toscanini. Thus, what is the reality of the musical work of art in this multiplicity of interpretations, which are certainly different from each other and certainly legitimate?
> (Mila, cit. p. 181)

In answer, Mila, taking a hint from modern physics, refers to the concept of reality as a dynamic and changing relationship, of which the musical work would be 'a pure and perfect example'.

We prefer the unavoidable transfiguration which is intrinsic to any attempt to reproduce reality, both the internal and the external. It would be enough to consider the relevance of musical notation and of the musical instruments which the music cannot, of course, avoid.

12. Musical technology and human performance

Although we are not here concerned with contemporary music and its roaming around to find new timbres and new notational codes, it is worthwhile noting that electronic technology, as well as the informatic one, puts at the composer's disposal a variety of alternatives that have never been experienced in the past. To cite one example, the availability of machines able to generate completely unheard sounds, is far removed from the proposal by Arnold Schönberg to pursue deeper timbrical research.

On the other hand, the fact that a music based on these technologies has not, in our opinion, produced great results, is fundamentally due to the absence or insufficient presence of the human performer. Technically, an informatic machine can perform a piece of music without diverging from the composer's original project but, clearly, the transfiguring presence of the performer, so much discussed and so crucial, is intrinsically necessary for achieving a true musical event.

The traditional composer writes knowing that the performer, to his delight and damnation, is, the sole reference point that is able to process the knowledge, not only the information, on whom he can rely in order to be understood. A new musical revolution on the basis of electronic and informatic instruments will be possible if and when the devices will allow a flexibility in their use, and are intelligent enough to allow for the rise of a new figure of the performer.

The musical idea of the composer and the musical observation level do not necessarily imply, in themselves, an instrument or a group of instruments, though, *ex post*, one could almost always establish a perfect syntony between these two elements. The vast production of transcriptions or reductions from one instrument to another and even from the orchestra to a solo instrument, demonstrates that, before anything, the knowledge content of the music is hidden conceptually in the pentagram, that is to say in the 'document' into which the knowledge work of the composer is initially reproduced. Goldbeck remarked:

> Of works that exist in two versions, for piano and for orchestra – such as Liszt's *Mephisto Waltz* and *Ravel's Alborada del gracioso* – the keyboard alternative is as satisfactory as the orchestral, sometimes more so. And even the Tannhäuser Ouverture – an orchestral Rubens – was hardly ever better performed when played by Busoni in Liszt's piano transcription.
>
> (Goldbeck, 1960)

Already in this reproduction phase the transfiguration intervenes with some relevance: the perfection of notation is nothing more than the measure of its defects of a linguistic nature. There are never enough signs or rules for the reliable reproduction of any musical idea and, therefore, the greatest compositional results that we know do not exhaust the evolutionary possibilities of this art.

The corrections composers themselves made to their own works testify not only the search for a perfect reproduction of the idea as such, but also the need to give as clear and detailed interpretative indications as possible.

Beethoven, who often resorted to such corrections, provides a good example, as reported by Rosen, when he writes to his publisher, concerning the *Scherzo* of the Sonata op. 69:

> In the very first beat it is necessary to take away the ff. Further on. . .it is again necessary to eliminate the ff and place a p on the very first note, and also to the second change of tonality the ff should be eliminated

After five days, Beethoven writes:

> Laugh as you like at my composer's anxieties. . .in the *scherzo molto allegro*, leave the ff at the beginning as it was indicated, and do the same for the remaining occurrences. [a footnote adds: "I wish to say that it is fine where it was before.
>
> (cited in Rosen, cit., p.22)

But one of the most persuading pages on the difficulty and the exhaustion of musical reproduction is perhaps due to Sand, when she describes the creative process in Chopin:

> His creation was spontaneous and miraculous. He found it without seeking it, without foreseeing it. He came to his piano suddenly, complete, sublime, or it sang in his head during a walk, and he was impatient to play it to himself. But then began the most heart-rending labour I ever saw. It was a series of efforts, of irresolutions and of frettings to seize again certain details of the theme he had heard. . .He shut himself up in his room for whole days, weeping, walking, breaking his pens, repeating a bar a hundred times, writing and effacing it as many times, and recommencing the next day with a minute and desperate perseverance.
>
> (Sand, 1854)

The transfer to the instrument of the written, or merely conceived, music, exhibits the highest amount of transfiguration, that is to say of the encounter between the musical idea and the materials and procedures which the artificial needs for achieving itself.

The composer always keeps clear in his mind what he needs and, rather, what he lacks. In a letter of 1774 by Carl Philipp Emmanuel Bach, one of the sons of Johann Sebastian, one can read:

> He [J. S. Bach] understood the construction of the organ in a total measure. When a builder had worked conscientiously but, he made some little mistake, he was able to persuade him to remedy. Nobody understood the art of the pre-setting of the registers as much as he did. Builders was terrified when he seated down to play one of their organs and pushed the registers at his own manner, fearing that the effects weren't good as he planned them; but then they appreciated the marvellous sounds.
>
> (C.P.E. Bach, 1774)

We also know that Beethoven was dissatisfied with his pianos, both before and after the progression of his deafness. What is astonishing, and which well describes the difficulties of the match between the musical idea and the available materials for reproducing it, is the clearness of the request from and the limitation of the instrument. On the one hand, the extreme variety of the pianos of that time and, of course, of ours merely serves to further underline not only the subjective character of the possible interpretations of a work of music. Actually, the interpretations also depend on the preferences for some kind of instrument rather than another although they might belong to the same class.

On the other hand, the relationship between the author and the performer, and such variety on the other, also clarifies the close connection between the musical idea, i.e. the whole of the mental exemplars and of the essential performances which the composer attributes to them, and the instrument with its own material and cultural heritage.

In a letter of 1796, reported by Newman, to the fortepiano builder Streicher, Beethoven writes:

> I would cheat you if don't say that, in my judgement, your fortepiano is to a great extent too good for me. Why? Because it prevents me from creating my own tones. Of course this shouldn't dissuade you from continuing to build your pianos in the same way. Certainly, there are not so many people that think like me
>
> (Beethoven, in Newman, 1988)

The requirement Beethoven refers to, was, of course, precise timbre or dynamic needs which the composer knew were indispensable to reproduce his own musical idea. Since these needs are known to the performer too, even though his do not necessarily overlap those of the composer, when they are known, one can undertstand the extent to which the transfiguration of the original musical exemplars and essential performances is unavoidable and intense.

The performance by the author himself cannot always be a guarantee of a lower transfiguration of the musical content of his work, compared to the beauty another performer could find in it.

In this regard, one may propose an even more radical thesis. Suppose that every composer from the past, of the classical period or any other, had a recording device at his disposal, which could be re-activated by whoever wanted to play it subsequently. The more obvious analogy would be with painting, where a work of art, once composed, is fixed forever as it was conceived by the author.

In such a circumstance, what meaning could the interpretation by different performers have, given that someone were brave enough to attempt such an enterprise? Paintings do not need performers: though, what of the remakers and of their 'fakes'?

If we possessed the 'true' interpretations of these composers could we then define a 'counterfeiter' as an interpreter performing the concerts of Beethoven or Chopin.

If music were in the condition of painting, we would probably accept, as a consequence, the impossibility of hearing versions which, with sublime beauty, have been offered to us by the greatest performers.

In the end, the musical interpreter could perhaps be defined as an imitator – counterfeiter of the composer – performer only if he had the possibility of listening to, say, the 'official' version of a score. In the real situation, at the least because we do not know the execution intended by the author but know only his prescriptions and indications added to the notes, the performer cannot be defined in any other way, that is to say, as someone who completes the artificial generated by the composer, giving reality to a work which was written to be fully achieved through the execution.

If each performer plays differently, this is consistent with the fact upon which we have remarked many times in this book, that the artificial always tends to live a life different from its exemplar and, thus, it offers several new possible realities. The conception of work of art by the composer, at his own observation level, is unavoidably, and, in this case, usefully transfigured not only by a notational and instrumental technology but also by the musically observational personality of the intepreter.

Actually, while the remaker of paintings has to face an artificial that is already completed in all its aspects, the musical performer and the actor in a play must deal with a purely informational artificial product: a sort of codified representation of the knowledge of the exemplars and of the essential performances generated at some musical observational level by the composer.

The playing, which is the same as the performance, has the notable job of once again transforming information into knowledge; the result will not constitute, of course, a replication of the musical mental states of the composer. The musical mental states of the composer, in fact, have already been transduced in the codification phase, and thus the performer will generate a sort of second order artificial which will include his own intentional transfigurations and also the ones coming from his techniques and from the instrumental technologies he will adopt.

The materials and procedures which, in the field of generating concrete artificials are a central cause of the transfiguration of the final object compared to the exemplar, are in the case of music, dominated by that special 'material' which is man, that is to say a performer who bears with himself, according to the inheritance principle, all the richness of his nature.

13. The options of the performer and that of the listener

The syntony, mentioned above, between the listener and the composer, must be based on the musical observation level of the performer, with his stylistic and instrumental selections. A total and stable syntony among these factors is quite improbable and the sole constant reference is the score, the notational reproduction of the original musical idea. Though this is a reduction, in some measure already transfigured, of the musical exemplar and of the essential performance attributed to it by the composer, it is, however, the more certain trace of them, but only in conceptual, or, informational terms.

If one reads a musical score, then one has to orient himself, so to speak, towards the same observation level adopted by the composer, and try to join him at some mid-way point: the one in which the composer decided to place the reproduction, accepting, or, rather, looking for its transfiguration as an aesthetical fact but also as a limit owing to the purely informational nature of the technology of musical notation. Collisani says that

> really, the sole, true listener who is able to understand a musical work in all its full value as a work of art is the artist himself.
>
> (Collisani, cit., p. 77)

This means that the informational reduction of the musical idea is actually a reproduction – as are all artificial objects – (or the first phase of it, in anticipation of the real performance) which tries to make the musical exemplar and its essential performance by means of different materials understandable.

Nevertheless, since information is not knowledge, no reader of musical scores, and, by the same token, no composer, determines his level only in this way. Both know that notational material refers back to, as well as coming from, the sound, to create form which has to make musical substance, and, thus, the sound again assumes its critical role in the working of the musical observation or construction level. Here the process shuts in on itself, proposing again the transfiguration dimensions cited above.

We cannot but accept the thesis that music is thought, the thought of organised sounds which generate in the composer's mind a special way to observe and to construct his internal and external world, but which, in constrast to day-to-day communication and from scientifically based knowledge, does not aim at achieving any objectivity.

The only objective aspect of music is, in fact, the score: but it is a matter of an informational objectivity and not of an objective knowledge. The music actually performed can only invite us to approach a reality which, on the basis of given ideas, is constantly open to interpretative variation according to several possible points of view at the same observation level.

14. Conclusions

Our theoretical attempt to explain the genesis and features of the technological reproduction of natural objects seems to us to provide an encouraging enough result to extend its application to other phenomena, such as music, which, both in their genesis and in their technical dynamics, seem to exhibit a noteworthy compatibility with the generation of artificial objects. All this surely does not solve the problem of the intimate nature of this art but, perhaps, it can go some way towards highlighting some aspects which it has in common, at least for analogy, with other reproduction processes.

A musical composition is the artificial product of the composer's attempt to reproduce exemplars and essential performances at his own musical observation level, through materials and procedures given by the notational tradition and by the instrumental one, which are later reproduced by another human being, namely the performer.

The musical observation level, which is potentially present in all of us but is certainly much more accessible to the composer, can be configured as a result of the cultural evolution and, though it is connected to the ordinary sense organs, does not reduce itself to them and in some measure, in fact, even clashes with them.

Every art, during the cultural evolution, involved the development of some particular sensitivity at some special observation level. Nevertheless, only music, being increasingly void of immediately recognisable meanings, will meet the problem of reproducing its own ideas without the comfort – or the constraint – of an initial, public sharing of the exemplars and the essential performances.

In other words, the composer, observing the world from his musical level, ends with a radical construction of it and, therefore, what he sees is already of a musical nature rather than visual, tactile, or even purely sonorous. This is why the public expectation cannot easily be satisfied by the final work, both because it has been generated at a level which is impossible to experience in daily life and because it is the result of a further transfiguration, introduced by the need to reduce the exemplars and the subjective essential performances to the requirements of the musical notation, of the materiality of the instruments and to that, both intellectual and cultural, of the performers.

Even in the more or less intense and recurrent onomatopeic, descriptive or 'at program' traditions, the autonomy of the musical form, substance in itself, always prevails over recognisable effects, that is to say, on the invasion of daily nature into the purely musical world the composer wishes to lead us into.

The beauty of a descriptive composition cannot often be separated from its evocative or just imitative capacity, like the artificial cannot be easily separated, at least in its early stages, from its exemplar. Nevertheless, the separation of the musical form from the sharable effects is an intellectual operation without which we would attribute a didactic or even pedagogical nature to the music that it does not at all have. The *Pastoral* by Beethoven and the *Four Seasons* by Vivaldi clearly show that this separation can and should be done, particularly if one refers to the soloist parts (cfr. Baroni, 1988).

In this art, what constitutes a permanent compositional aim, is the formal solution to formal problems which becomes musical substance when executed. This is true both in the case of some aspects of the Vivaldian style, such as thematic integration which is reappropriated by Bach, and of so called expressivity, conceived as the melodic and intense use of the available technologies, that always seems, with Vivaldi, to introduce the Romanticism (cfr. Talbot, 1984).

We do not refer, necessarily, to a dogmatically formalistic vision of art and of music in particular, but only to its special interpretation of the world through which it differentiates itself from all the other arts.

For this reason, the insistence on the so called content of art, if one assumes it as the substance of art itself, would imply the,

> "consequence that, and we paraphrase the remarks of a student of Focillon, George Kubler, since the meaning of a thing becomes more important than what that thing is, the meaning relegates the style to a rather secundary background."
>
> (Abbate, 1995)

On the same level, but here we need different cautions, there is the question of musical rhetoric and of the convergence of the music with the text. Tough in these cases, - we may refer to the thousands of symbolisms included in the *Missa solemnis* by Beethoven - the composer does not observe generically the world but the work done by some literary author or even a sacred work, like in the case of the *Missa*.

Even here, despite the exegesis highlighting facts, or producing interpretations and hypotheses on the descriptive or symbolical roles of Beethoven's choices (Kirkendale, 1988), the music certainly prevails over the text and on the religious finality connected to it.

The interaction between word and music can also be explained within the TA. In fact, if our thesis on the impossibility of synthesizing two or more observation levels is true, then whatever interaction might be tried in a work of art, some of the interacting component will unavoidably prevail over the other. One of the major early theorists, Gioseffo Zarlino (1517-1590), has already maintained, for example, that music could have a 'preparatory' role for better understanding the texts. But the contrary could also be true, of course.

In trying to synthesize two observation levels, we could get a third level and, therefore, in the field of the arts, the resulting artificial would become a sort of *Gesamtkunstwerk* whose features would be no longer those of a musical composition but those of a literary text or a continuous shifting from one level to the other, as happens in almost all the lyric operas of the nineteenth century.

The subordination of music to the word, as one of the possible outcomes of the above interaction. Berlioz indicates this, with some exaggeration, in 'Wagner's crime', where the musical form only exists as a 'humble slave of the word', while the composer is always looking for a type of music that is,

> free and proud and sovereign and conquering. I want it to grasp everything, to assimilate everything. . .How to be expressive and true without ceasing to be a musician. . .this is the problem
>
> (Berlioz, 1856)

A quite different matter, in our opinion, is the discourse on the psychological or even social effects of music, above all as they are related to its capacity to reproduce the composer's views of the world, like the magnificent two *Suites* by Georg Friedrich Handel, or of the history and of ideas, as in Wagner's case, either with or without any reference to the texts.

Actually, to understand music means to be able to accept, at an observation level as near as possible to the composer's, the effects which the artificial generates, that is to say, the effects of the transfigurations of the exemplars and of the essential performances it relates to, including texts.

In the same way, to listen to a descriptive piece of music, in fact to any kind of music, and believe that we are really interacting with the exemplar and essential performance the composer drew inspiration from, would be the same as trying to interact with an artificial intelligence program as if it were human intelligence. In both cases we lose their true reality, power and beauty.

Often, when we listen music we instinctively close our eyes, driven, perhaps, by an awareness that to attempt to observe the world in the way the composer suggests requires that we eliminate, put into parentheses, the ordinary sense of reality and, in general, everything that is extra-musical.

In fact, there is evidence that listening to music often generates deep and legitimate 'visions' which differ from each other, since the listener, and not only the author, contributes to the transfiguration of the musical work in his own mind. Further, the above remark explains why, for instance, religiously inspired music can be easily enjoyed by non-believers.

As we have maintained in this book, the artificial, in all its instances – objects, machines, communication messages or artistical entities – always begins from some existing thing in the domain of sensible experience or in the visions man has of himself or of the world.

The destiny of any artificial is still that of developing towards its own realities, far away from its exemplar though its reference object, in some measure, is recognisable. The ambiguity, the unforeseeability and also the fascination of the artificial consists of just this destiny, that is to say, of this *novum*, compared to the original.

If musical compositions are the result of a process oriented to generate something artificial, then they do not escape from this rule and their beauty cannot be limited to their capacity to induce effects which are similar to those generated by the natural exemplars from which the composer drew his inspiration.

Furthermore, a peculiarity of the artificiality of music is that the true exemplars of the composer are constituted by his internal musical representations, and come to us after a complex transfiguration process due to the unavoidable inheritances of the notational reduction, of the materiality of the instruments and of the performer's interpretation.

The enjoyment of a work of music, therefore, involves the ability to grasp and to hold firmly onto the main musical idea, that is, the exemplar and its subjective essential performance, in their previously established musical nature which is fixed in the score in informational terms, and, then, to discover the knowledge content of the executed transfiguration of that idea.

In the end, the only fundamental unity of the arts consists of the fact that every art accomplishes the effort to externalise mental states, included those which derive from drawing exemplars which are external to the mind, inventing different means than those available in daily communication.

Thus, music exhibits, by its very nature, the specificity, genetically relevant, to generate and to consist of musical mental states without coming or passing through the mediation of the other senses. For this reason what it externalises is surely a complex whole of data and of events, since even in the musician's mind all things are interconnected.

Nevertheless, the final result, the one we can enjoy is through our senses, expressed in a language no different from the one the composer had in his mind from the beginning. Rather, the musical transfiguration process, which in language-based communication is due to the heterogeneity of languages compared to the mental reality, arises through the need to give concreteness to the musical imagination. This occurs through various steps, from the informational transduction to the performance, conceived as technologies which give life to ideas that are otherwise made possible by the special observation level which the technologies themselves have set up throughout the evolution of culture.

References

ABBATE, F. (1995), 'Introduzione' a M. SCHAPIRO, Lo stile, Donzelli Editore, Roma.

ALEXANDER, J. (1988), Introduction: Durkeimian sociology and culturel studies today. In J. Alexander (ed.), Durkheimian Sociology: culturel studies, Cambridge, UK: Cambridge University Press.

AMIS, J; ROSE, M. (1989), Words about Music, Faber and Faber, London.

ANCARANI, V. (1996), La scienza decostruita, teorie sociologiche della conoscenza scientifica, Franco Angeli, Milano, p. 138.

ANCESCHI, G. (1988), Monogrammi e figure, teorie e storie della progettazione di artefatti comunicativi, La Casa Husher, Firenze.

ARNHEIM, R. (1989) Parables of the Sun Light, tr. it. Parabole della luce solare, Roma, Editori Riuniti, 1992, p.53.

ARNHEIM, R. (1989), Entropy and Art. An Essay On Disorder and Order, University of California, tr. it., Entropia e arte, Einaudi, Torino,.

BAGGI, D. (ed), Readings in Computer Generated Music, IEEE, Los Alamitos, Ca.

BARONI, M. (1988), 'La musica barocca tra Sei e Settecento', in M. BARONI, E. FUBINI, P. PETAZZI, P. SANTI, G. VINAY, Storia della musica, Einaudi, Torino.

BARTHES, R. (1985), L'ovvio e l'ottuso, Einaudi, Torino.

BATESON, G. (1972), Steps to an Ecology of Mind, Chandler, San Francisco p. 250 .

BERGER, P. LUCKMANN,T., (1966), The Social Construction of Reality, Doubleday, New York, tr. it. La realtà come costruzione sociale, Il Mulino, Bologna, 1974.

BERLIOZ, H., Lettera del 12 Agosto, 1856, in 'Briefe von Hector Berlioz an die Fürstin Carolyne Sayn-Wittgenstein', La Mara, Breitkopf & Härtel, Leipzig, 1903.
BERTASIO, D. (1992), Ars ex machina, Quattroventi, Urbino.
BERTASIO, D. (1994), The Tree: from Symbol to Sign, IMES-WP, Urbino.
BERTASIO, D. (1996), Studi di sociologia dell'arte, Franco Angeli, Milano.
BESSELER, H. (1959), Das musikalische Hàren der Neuzeit, Akademie-Vorlag, tr. it., L'ascolto musicale nell'età moderna, Il Mulino, Bologna, 1993 pp. 85-7, .
BLACKING, J. (1986), How musical is man? University of Washington Press, Seattle-London, 1973, Come è musicale l'uomo?, Ricordi, Milano, p. 79.
BLASIS, C. (1844), Studi sulle arti imitatrici, Chiusi, Milano, pp. 1-2.
BLAUKOPF, K. (1972), Musiksoziologie, Arthur Niggli, Niederteufen, tr. it., Sociologia della musica, CEMSM, Trento.
BOAS, F. (1927), Primitive Art, Instituttet for sammenlignende kulturforskning, Oslo, tr. it., Arte primitiva, Boringhieri, Torino, 1981, p.174.
BOWLER, A. (1994), Methodological Dilemmas in the Sociology of Art, in Crane, Diana, ed., 1994: Sociology of Culture, Cambridge Mass., Blackwell.
BRAGA, F. (1996), La rappresentazione come problema in intelligenza naturale e artificiale, 'Metis', I, Febbraio, 1996, pp. 7-50.
BREDEKAMP, H. (1993), Antikensehnsucht und Maschinenglauben, Klaus Wagenbach, Berlin, tr. it. Nostalgia dell'antico e fascino della macchina, Il Saggiatore, Milano, 1996, p.112.
CESERANI, G.P. (1969), I falsi Adami, Feltrinelli, Milano.
CHINOL, E. (1986), I falsi nell'arte, Laterza, Roma-Bari, 1986, pp. 127-128.
CHURCHMAN, C.W. (1979), The artificiality of science: Review of Herbert A. Simon's book 'The Sciences of the Artificial', "Contemporary Psychology", 15, 6, June, p. 385-86.
CIAIKOWSKI, P.I., Letter to Nadejda von Meck, in Il mondo della musica, Garzanti, Milano, 1956, p. 567.
COLLINS, H.M. (1990), Artificial Experts: Social Knowledge and Intelligent Machines, The MIT Press, Cambridge, Mass.
COLLISANI, A., (1988), Musica e simboli, Sellerio, Palermo.
COOKE, D. (1959), The Language of Music, Oxford University Press, Oxford,.
CORDESCHI, R. (1991), The discovery of the artificial. Some protocybernetic developments 1930 – 1940, 'Artificial intelligence & Society', London.
CORTOT, A. (1930), in Il mondo della musica, Garzanti, Milano, 1956, p. 706.
CRANE, D., ed. (1994), Sociology of Culture, Cambridge, Mass., Blackwell.
DE MAURO, T. (1994) Capire le parole, Laterza, Bari, p. 6.
DE SOLA POOL, I.; SCHRAMM, W., et. al. (1973), Handbook of Communication, Chicago.
DEL GROSSO DESTRERI, L. (1988), La sociologia, la musica e le musiche, Unicopli, Milano.
DELIEGE, C. (1966), Approche d'une sèmantique de la musique, 'Revue Belge de Musicologie', XX, pp. 21-42, in Collisani, A., Musica e simboli, Sellerio, Palermo, 1988, p. 159.
DENIS, M. (1989), Image and cognition, Presses Universitaires de France, Paris.
DEVOTO, G., OLI, G.C. (1981), Vocabolario illustrato della lingua italiana, Le Monnier, Milano.
DIDEROT, D. (1876), 'Leçons de clavecin et principes d'harmonie par M. Bemetzrieder', in Oeuvres completes, Assezat, Paris, XII p. 490.
DIES, A.C. (1810), Biographische Nachrichten von Joseph Haydn, quoted in Arthur Jacobs, Music Lover's Anthology, Winchester Publications, London, 1948, in AMIS, J.; Rose, M., Words about Music, Faber and Faber, London, 1989, p. 78.
DREYFUS, H.L., DREYFUS, S.E., (1991), Making a Mind Versus Modelling the Brain: Artificial Intelligence Back at the Branchpoint, in M. Negrotti (ed.), Understanding the Artificial, Springer-Verlag, London.
ELIAS, N. (1991), Mozart. Zur Soziologie eines Genies, Suhrkamp Verlag, Frankfurt, tr. it. Mozart. Sociologia di un genio, Il Mulino, Bologna, 1991.
ETZKORN, K.P. (1989), 'Introduction', in HONIGSHEIM, P., Sociologists and Music, Transaction Publishers, New Brunswick, 1989.
FAENZA, R. (1985), Computerland, Sugarco, Milano.

FODOR, J.A. (1987), Psychosemantics. The problem of Meaning in the Philosophy of Mind, MIT Press, Cambridge Mass., tr. it. Psicosemantica, il problema del significato nella filosofia della mente, Il Mulino, Bologna, 1990, p. 45.
FUBINI, E. (1995), Estetica della musica, Il Mulino, Bologna, p. 114.
GALLONI, M., 'Microscopie e microscopie, dalle origini al XIX secolo', Quaderni di storia della tecnologia, 3, 1993, Levrotto & Bella.
GAMBARDELLA, L.M.; CATTANEO, P. (1990), Vita artificiale, 'Technical reportó', IDSIA, 9, Lugano, p. 2.
GARDEN, N. (1989), Bloomsbury Good Music Guide, Bloomsbury, London, pp. 201-2.
GARDIN, F. (1992), Materia artificiale, 'Sistemi intelligenti', IV,2, p. 329.
GIDDENS, A. (1987), Structuralism, post-structuralism, and the production of culture. In Anthony Giddens and Ralph Turner (eds.), Social Theory Today, Stanford, CA: University of Stanford Press.
GLASERFELD von, E. (1993), Response to D.K. Johnson's Response, 'Cybernetics & Human Knowing', 2, 2, p. 55.
GOLDBECK, F. (1960), The Perfect Conductor, Dennis Dobson, London. Visto in Amis, J, Rose, M. (1989), Words about Music, Faber and Faber, London.
GRIESINGER, G.A. (1956), 'Biographische Notizen ber Joseph Haydn', in Mor genstern, S., Composers on Music, Pantheon, New York.
GURVITCH, G. (1963), La vocation actuelle de la sociologie, Parigi, La vocazione attuale della sociologia, Il Mulino, Bologna, 1967.
HENSHEL, R.H. (1976), On the Future of Social Prediction, Bobbs-Merrip Comp., Indianapolis, p. 76.
HOFFMAN, W. (1995), Forging New Bonds, in Inventing Tomorrow, University of Minnesota Institute of Technology, Spring.
HONIGSHEIM, P. (1989), Sociologists and Music, Transaction Publishers, New Brunswick.
HULL, C.L.; BAERNSTEIN, H.D. (1929), A Mechanical Parallel to the Conditioned Reflex, 'Science', 70.
Il mondo della musica, (1956), Garzanti, Milano, p. 1972.
JOHNSON, D.K. (1993), The Metaphysics of Constructivism, 'Cybernetics & Human Knowing', 1,4.
JONAS, H. (1991), Un nuovo principio etico per il futuro del'uomo, 'Il Mulino', P. 176.
KARLQVIST, A.; SVEDIN, U. (1993), Introduction, in Haken, H:, Karlqvist, A., Svedin, U. (eds.), The Machine as Metaphor and Tool, Springer Verlag, Berlin Heidelberg, p. 7.
KEAVENY, T. (1996), Presentation page for the Berkeley Orthopaedic Biomechanics Research Web site in Internet, http: / / biomech2.me.berkeley.edu / prosthesis.html.
KIRKENDALE, W. (1988), 'La Missa solemnis di Beethoven e la tradizione retorica', in G. Pestelli (a cura di), Beethoven, Il Mulino, Bologna.
KÖHLER, J.F. (1776), Historia Scholarum Lipsiensium, quoted in David, H. T. and Mendel, A., The Bach Reader, Dent, London, 1946, in AMIS, J., Rose, M., Words about Music, Faber and Faber, London, (1989), p. 186.
KUHN, T. (1970), The Structure of Scientific Revolutions, Chicago University Press, Chicago.
LANDOW, G.P. (1992), Hypertext: The Convergence of Contemporary Critical Theory and Technology, Johns Hopkins University Press, London, p. 170.
LANGTON, C.G. (1992), Vita artificiale, 'Sistemi Intelligenti', IV, 2, 1992, pp. 189-246.
LATOUR, B.; WOOLGAR, S. (1979), Laboratory life. The construction of scientific facts, Princeton University Press, Princeton.
LEISER, D.; CELLERIER, G.; DUCRET, J.J. (1976), 'Une ètude de la fonction representative', Archive de Psychologie, XLIV, 171.
LEROI-GOURHAN, A. (1964), Il gesto e la parola,
LESURE, F. (1994), Debussy, gli anni del simbolismo, E.D.T., Torino, p.118.
LEVI-STRAUSS, C. (1974), L'uomo nudo, Il Saggiatore, Milano.
LOSANO, M. (1990), Storie di automi, Einaudi, Torino, 91.
LUHMANN, N. (1975), Macht, Ferdinand Enke Verlag, Stuttgart, tr. it, Potere e complessitá sociale, Il Saggiatore, Milano, 1979.
LUHMANN, N. (1988), 'Wie ist Bewusstsein an Kommunikation beteiligt?', in: Gumbrecht H.V., and Pfeiffer, K.L. (eds.): Materialitaet der Kommunikation, Suhrkamp Verlag, Frankfurt A.M.
LUHMANN, N. (1982), The Differentiation of Society, Columbia University Press, New York.

MAHOWALD, M.A.; MEAD, C. (1991), 'La retina di silicio', Le Scienze-Scientific American, 275.
MATURANA, H., and VARELA, F. (1986), The Tree of Knowledge: Biological Roots of Human Understanding, Shambhala Publishers, London.
McCARTHY, E. (1992), Culture and Technology, draft, IV workshop on Human Centred Systems and the Culture of the Artificial, IMES-LCA, Urbino.
MERTON, R.K. (1981), La sociologia della scienza, Franco Angeli, Milano.
MEYER, L.B. (1984), Emotion and Meaning in Music, University of Chicago Press, Chicago and London, tr. it., Emozione e significato nella musica, Il Mulino, Bologna, 1992, p. 105.
MEYER, L.B. (1991), 'Semplicitá grammaticale e ricchezza di relazioni: il Trio della sinfonia in sol minore, k550', in Durante, S., Mozart, Il Mulino, Bologna.
MIKOS, A.G.; BIZIOS, R.; WU, K.K.; YASZEMSKI, M.J. (1996), Cell Transplantation, The Rice Institute of Biosciences and Bioengineering, Web site in Internet http://www.bioc.rice.edu/Institute/area6.html.
MILA, M. (1956), L'esperienza musicale e l'estetica, Einaudi, Torino, 20.
MINSKY, M. (1991), 'Logical Versus Analogical or Symbolic Versus Connectionist or Neat Versus Scruffy', Artificial Intelligence magazine, 12, Summer, AAAI, Menlo Park, pp. 34-51.
MONOD, J. (1972), Le Hasard et la Necéssité, tr. it. Il caso e la necessit‡, Est Mondadori, p. 18.
MORIN, E. (1977), La methode. I. La nature de la nature, Editions du seuil, Paris, Tr. it., Il metodo, ordine, disordine, organizzazione, Feltrinelli, Milano, 1983-94.
MUKERJI, C. (1994), Toward a Sociology of Material Culture: Science Studies, Cultural Studies and Meanings of Things, in Crane, D. (ed.), The Sociology of Culture, Blackwell, Oxford.
MURRAY SCHAFER, R. (1985), The Tuning of the World, McClelland & Stewart, Toronto, tr. it., Il paesaggio sonoro, Unicopli-Ricordi, Milano.
NEGROPONTE, N. (1995), Being Digital, tr. it. Essere digitali, Sperling & Kupfer, Milano, 1995, p. 123.
NEGROTTI, M. (1995), 'Verso una teoria dell'artificiale' in Negrotti, M. (ed.), Artificialia, Clueb, Bologna, 1995, p. 70.
NEGROTTI, M. (ed.) (1991), Understanding the Artificial, Springer Verlag, London, 1991, tr. it., Capire l'artificiale, Bollati-Boringhieri, Torino, 1990, 1993.
NEGROTTI, M. (1993), Per una teoria dell'artificiale, Prometheus series, Franco Angeli, Milano.
NEGROTTI, M. (1996), L'osservazione musicale: l'artificiale fra soggetto e oggetto, Franco Angeli, MIlano.
NEWMAN, W.S. (1988), 'I pianoforti di Beethoven e i suoi ideali di pianoforte', in G. Pestelli (a cura di), Beethoven, Il Mulino, Bologna, p. 301.
OGDEN, RICHARDS (1922), The Meaning of Meaning. A Study of the Influence of Language upon Thought and of the Science of Symbolism, Routledge & Kegan, London.
PEREIRA, M. (1995), 'L'elixir alchemico fra natura e artificium', in Negrotti, M. (ed.), Artificialia, Clueb, Bologna, 1995.
PIAGET, J. (1972), L'èpistèmologie gènètique, Gonthier, Paris, p. 5.
PIRANDELLO, L. (1908), Arte e scienza, Mondadori, Milano, 1994, p. 106.
POINCARE', H. (1952), Mathematical Creation, in B. Ghiselin (ed.), The Creative Process, Univ. of California Press, Los Angeles, p. 33.
POLANYI, M. (1966), The Tacit Dimension, Doubleday, New York.
POPPER, K.R. (1968), The Logic of Scientific Discovery, tr. it. Logica della scoperta scientifica, Einaudi, Torino, 1970.
POSNER, R. (1989), What is culture ? Toward a semiotic explication of anthropological concepts, in W. A. Koch (ed.), The Nature of Culture, Brockmeyer, Bochum, pp. 240-95.
QVORTRUP, L. (1995), 'Sistemi naturali, sociali e artificiali: verso una tassonomia dell'artificial', in NEGROTTI, M. (ed.), Artificialia, Clueb, Bologna, 1995.
RAMEAU, J-P. (1726), Le nouveau systéme de musique thèorique, Paris.
REGGE, T. (1994), Infinito, viaggio ai limiti dell'universo, Mondadori, Milano, p. 142.
RIESMAN, D.; DENNEY, R.; GLAZER, N. (1950), The Lonely Crowd, Yale University Press, New Haven, tr. it., La folla solitaria, Il Mulino, Bologna, 1956.
ROSE, S. (1993), The Making of Memory, Bantam Books, London, p. 61.
ROSEN, C. (1994), The Frontiers of Meaning, tr. it. Il pensiero musicale, Garzanti, Milano, 1995.

ROSEN, R. (1993), 'Bionics Revisited', in Haken, H.; Karlqvist, A.; Svedin, U. (eds.), The Machine as Metaphor and Tool, Springer Verlag, Berlin Heidelberg, pp. 94-5.
SAINT-SA»NS, C. (1771), Letter to C. Bellaigue, in Morgenstern, S., Composers on Music, Pantheon, New York, 1956.
SAND, G. (1965), Histoire de ma vie, in Gal, H., The Musician's World, Thames & Hudson, London.
SANES, K. (1998), Internet Site: http://www.transparencynow.com/zoos2.htm
SCHANK, R.C. (1991), Where's the AI ?, 'AI Magazine', Winter, 12, AAAI, Menlo Park, pp. 38-47.
SCHENKER, H. (1935), Der Freie Satz, Longman, New York.
SCHNEIDER, M. (1960), Le rÙle de la musique dans la mythologie et les rites des civilisations non europénnes, éditions Gallimard, Paris, tr. it., La musica primitiva, Adelphi Edizioni, Milano, 1992, p. 35.
SCHUTZ, A.; LUCKMANN, T., The Structure of the Life-World, Chicago, 1973.
SEARLE, J. (1984), Minds, Brains and Science, Harvard University Press, Cambridge, Mass.
SHWEDER, R.A. (1991), Thinking Through Cultures: expeditions in cultural psychology, Harvard University Press, Cambridge, Ma., p. 156, in S. Derné, Cultural Conceptions of Human Motivation, in D. Crane (ed.), The Sociology of Culture, Blackwell, Oxford, p. 269.
SILVERS, S. (ed.) (1989), Rerepresentation, readings in the philosophy of mental represenation, Kluwer Academic Publishers, Dordrecht.
SIMON, H.A. (1969), The Sciences of the Artificial, MIT Press, Cambridge Mass., tr. it. Le scienze dell'artificiale, ISEDI, Milano, 1970, pp. 18-19.
SIMONS, V.G. (1983), Are Computers Alive? Birkhaser–Boston, Thetford, 1983.
SINDING-LARSEN, H. (1990), Computers, Musical Notation and the externalization of Knowledge, in NEGROTTI, M. (ed.), Understanding the Artificial, Springer Verlag, London, 1991, tr. it, Capire l'artificial, Bollati-Boringhieri, Torino, 1990, 1993.
SLOBODA, J.A. (1985), The Musical Mind. The Cognitive Psychology of Music, Oxford University Press, Oxford.
SMELSER, N.J. (1992), Culture: coherent or incoherent. In M nch, R. and Smelser , N.J. (eds), Theory of Culture, Berkeley: University of California Press.
SOMENZI, V. (1996), Naturale e artificiale, Proceedings, LXIII meeting, SIPS, Urbino.
STEFANI, G.; MARCONI, L.; FERRARI, F. (1990): Gli intervalli musicali, Bompiani, Milano.
STRAVINSKY, I. (1936), An Autobiography, Simon & Schuster, New York, in Amis & Rose, cit., p. 16.
TALBOT, M. (1984), Antonio Vivaldi, in Arnold, D.; Newcomb, A.; Walker, T.; Talbot, M.; Grout, D.J.; Sheveloff, J., Italian Baroque Masters, W.W.Norton & Company, New York.
TARDE, G. (1890), Les lois de l'imitation, Paris, tr. it. Le leggi dell'imitazione, UTET, Torino, 1976, p. 45.
THE WHITAKER FOUNDATION (1995), Annual report: Tissue Engineering. Web site in Internet http://fairway.ecn.purdue.edu/bme/whitaker/95_annual_report/tissue95.html.
TREITLER, L. (1991), 'Mozart e l'idea di musica assoluta', in Durante, S., Mozart, Il Mulino, Bologna, p. 193.
TRIANTAFYLLOU, M.S.; TRIANTAFYLLOU, G.S. (1995), Un robot che simula il nuoto dei pesci, 'Le Scienze-Scientific American', 321.
WALLACE, R.A.; WOLF, A. (1991), Contemporary Sociological Theory: Continuing the Classical Tradition, Prentice Hall, Englewood Cliffs, tr. it., La teoria sociologica contemporanea, Il Mulino, Bologna, 1994, p. 339.
WEBER, M. (1904), Il metodo delle scienze storico sociali, Einaudi, Torino, pp. 92-4.
WIENER, N. (1993), The Care and Feeding of Idea, MIT Press, Cambridge, tr. it., L'invenzione, come nascono e si sviluppano le idee, Bollati-Boringhieri, 1994, p. 45.
WILDE, O. (1901), Aforismi, tr. it., Newton Compton, Roma, 1992.
WOOLGAR, S. (1991), The turn to technology in social studies of science, 'Science, Technology & Human Values', 16, pp. 20-50.
WOOLLEY, B. (1992), Virtual Worlds. A Journey in Hype and Hyperreality, Blackwell, Oxford, p. 70.
YOUNG, J.Z. (1964), A Model of the Brain, Oxford University Press, Oxford, tr. it., Un modello del cervello, Einaudi, Torino, 1974, p. 278.

6. Case Study II: Artistic communication and the artificial (by Danila Bertasio)

1. Artistic language: between representation and reality

Artistic language tends to integrate itself into a cultural reality, that is, to make itself compatible with a socially shared reality. Thus, the artist is one who, in showing his ability to understand the profound meaning of his *ego* and of his experience, is capable of transforming it and of proposing it as a symbol of a 'truth' that he wishes to communicate.

This process is made possible by the language of expression adopted: if the language is more mature, and thus culturally established, the mind of the observer, listener or reader will be more capable of *reconstructing* a fragment of the reality that will be equally convincing *per se*.

If integration between the author and the public is to take place, it is necessary that the one who gives the message takes into account certain variables, or rules, that are, as such, the constituents of every communication process and, therefore, also of the artistic process.

Let us assume that an artist A wishes to transfer a mental representation to the public B. In order to do so, A must prepare a message. The message must be capable of being cast in a context that B can share, and the message will be expressed in a code at least partially common to both. Finally, A will chose a *medium* or, according to Jakobson's definition, a 'physical channel' (Jakobson, 1958) which is capable of setting up and maintaining the communication.

However, the idea that art can be regarded as a form of communication has not always been accepted unanimously. For example, the linguist Mounin (1968, 1981) and the aesthetologist Passeron (1962, 1969) both denied *a priori* that the function of painting could be communication. In fact, according to them, the art of painting is a strictly self-referential expression, i.e. the external proposition of an internal subjective representation. However, beginning from an attempt to define the essence of painting, Passeron realised that a mental representation cannot be transferred to another's mind unless it goes through a communication process.

However appreciable the difference (proposed by Passeron, 1969) may be between communication induced by the expressive language of the figurative arts and that induced by verbal language (which has surely to be more rigorous since it refers to clear-cut syntaxes), we believe that it is not meaningless to define artistic language, in general terms, as a medium that becomes totally identical to the message it conveys.

On the one hand, it is true that language permits the public to have access to the artist's subjective experience. On the other, as language becomes poetics and style, it resolves in itself and transfigures the message as a pure specimen, i.e. the real object both internal and external to the artist's mind that the author wishes to communicate, 'putting in common'.

If we use the terms proposed by the TA, it becomes possible to affirm that both the exemplar and the subjective essential performance conveyed by language are not simply 'committed' to the word, the symbol, the object of art as a 'support' of something that will travel more or less unchanged with them. Instead, they become a new reality, as is always the case in the generation of the artificial. Of course, the transformation, or transduction, does not permit a total superimposition upon the mental representation of the artist, nor *a fortiori* upon the representation of the observer.

But, following Pierce (1989), the *icon*, by virtue of its internal nature, maintains the essential characters of the object and allows the artist to communicate his mental representation.

The problem of the relation between iconism and object has also been widely explored, first by Morris (1938, 1939) who proposed the concept of scales of iconicity, providing several levels of similarity between the icon and the object; later by Moles (1958) and more recently by Maldonaldo (1974). The latter, for example, maintains that there is a substantial difference between sign and signal and emphasises that communication among people is only possible through a symbolic–semantic link.

Morris's theory enjoyed a great success amongst those scholars who thought that art is a language of communication; the term icon is often repeated and has contributed to the definition of a particular attitude of American aesthetics.

Wimsatt (1954), a supporter of Morris's theory, maintains that the term was used by semiologists to refer to a verbal sign which shares the properties of, or is similar to, the objects it denotes. Equally, Read (1953, 1954), certainly influenced by Morris, in a lecture given at Harvard emphasised that in a work of art there is inevitably a priority of the icon over the idea.

Of course, our assertions are not to be taken as a strict support of the 'theory of pure visibility', founded by Fiedler (1987), studied more deeply by Riegl (1901) and Wölfflin (1991), and more recently criticised by Brandi (1966), for whom:

> the theory has failed, since it claimed to transfer an essentially synchronic method (that is to say a method related to the internal organisation of the objects independently of their temporal evolution) to a very closed conception of history and of its developments.
>
> (in Calabrese, 1989)

However, leaving aside the methodological questions that are still the object of a strong debate among students of semiology, our point of view, e.g. concerning painting, is that artistic language inevitably represents the visibility of the world in a painting, since its final aim can only be the culturally, and, hopefully, artistically perfect configuration of an optical phenomenon.

For example, medieval art, and in general any form of religious art, which proposes a voluntary decline in interest in the reality around us in favour of an assumed transcendental and fantastic reality does not destroy the possibility of recognising the forms. Rather, it modifies and surrounds them with a new meaning.

During the Counter-Reformation, the Church dictated that artists should free themselves from the imitation of natural reality and give up the values in which humanists had believed but it could not avoid the representation of the supernatural becoming visible in the representation of sensorial experience. Once again, just as in Middle Ages, the figures became longer and the colours sharper, thus stimulating reason rather than sentiment.

However, because it was realised that it is not possible to represent, in the sense of reproducing, something that is beyond human experience, artistic representation of a transcendent reality continued to make reference to the experience of the immanent: God, angels and saints maintained their human features and were eventually purified of profane traits.

Religious art, which tends to represent an empirically unexplorable reality, clearly demonstrates, perhaps more than any other form of art in the course of art history, that in order to communicate something, it is inevitable that a compromise to make reference to an acceptable reality be reached.

Thus, the natural object becomes a pretext for generating the artificial, not as a trivial imitation, or copy, of natural reality (which would not persuade anyone of the existence of a hypothetical transcendent reality), but in the full conscience that it is only possible to render plausible to the eyes the characters intellectually attributed to the immanent reality, and to the trascendent, through the artificial.

Although the rigid rules imposed by the Church may seem to have restrained the artists' creativity, the use of natural models permitted the expression of an extraordinary imagination, that is to say of the transfiguration which always comes along with any artificial.

Through artistic creativity, natural objects and known places could become a fairy garden, as it were, populated by fantastic beings, where the problem of the contrast between true and false was meaningless.

The pictorial invention of the devil is only one among the many examples that we could cite. If we look at a particular feature of the *Giudizio Universale* in the Baptistry of Florence, the mosaic by Coppo di Marcovaldo, *L'inferno* (about 1270), the devil is represented as a grotesque and dramatic figure. But his figure is modelled on, and inspired, by man.

The devil is sitting on a throne-like seat and is surrounded by the convulsive figures of the damned. The contour of the devil, with horns, is traced hard, and along the sides of his dreadful face and hips there are snakes holding the motionless bodies of the sinners in their sharp teeth. Thus, this work gives us the opportunity to note how only by starting from the sensible world is it possible to reach a sort of 'realism' that can be defined as 'radically something else', since the object that is being artistically represented is justified *in se*, rather than through a comparison with the model.

In other words, religious symbolism which is artistically expressed has filled the gap between spirit and sensible world, because immanence did not replace, nor deny, transcendence. Instead, religious symbolism permitted and made possible the intellectual and formal creation of transcendence starting from the immanent.

At this point, we may think that medieval art, and religious art in general, appears to be more artificially concrete than, say, the art of the Renaissance. If the latter remains linked to nature, as the ground-chained statues of the Greek sculptor Daedalus, the former shows how man does use his right to abstract from the appearance of the model and to freely create, following his own laws.

Man expresses his freedom by uniting what appears as divided in nature, and by separating what nature keeps united. He forgets the rules of common sense and of the obvious so that he may reveal the possibility of different rules of 'seeing' (rules that are not in contrast with natural rules, but allow him to express, concretely and incisively, the essence of his art).

Thus, the process of 'transducing' a subjective mental vision into a language does not represent some kind of compromise imposed by culture on the artist, to make himself understood. Rather, this process represents the very thing that makes art possible.

In artistic communication, as in everyday communication, what is being communicated is not a total replication (in any case impossible) of a subjective representation, because the subjective representation must necessarily transform itself into a recognisable language of expression. On the other hand, because language is intrinsically heterogeneous in comparison with any real pattern, it will entail a reduction of the complexity of the model, but it will also permit the expression of aesthetic values deriving from the artist's ability to use it.

Thus the public, when confronted with a work of art, will perceive the value represented by the chosen language, without necessarily making reference to the other values that it might represent in reality. It is only possible to set up a realistic, culturally shareable, reference between the real object and the artist's mental representation of it, through a more or less skilful use of a language.

2. Artistic communication: a case of generating the artificial

A language, as we have tried to show, is always to be regarded as the conventional technology that the artist–artificialist must use to reproduce his mental states. Since any technology intrinsically represents something heterogeneous with respect to the 'matter' constituting the exemplar and its performance, the resulting artificial object, which in our case is the work of art, will be more persuasive the more the author shows his ability to generate something fine, beyond the sheer effort to communicate / reproduce mental states.

This effort is hopeless, in itself. On the other hand, it can be carried out for non-aesthetic aims, through many different and well-established daily pragmatic procedures.

On the other hand, the referential nature of the work of art is not rigid but consists of different *degrees of modularity* or *scales of iconicity*. These permit the artist to not only represent an object or exemplar on one established observation level but also to make a subjective choice among many observation levels. Here, concerning the unavoidable fact that the artist must inevitably build a relation between intuition and expression, i.e. between his own mental representation and its semiotic reproduction, it is interesting to quote Croce, an important Italian idealistic philosopher:

> An unexpressed image, that does not become word, song, drawing, painting, architecture, or at least a word whispered within oneself, a song echoed through one's heart, design and colour as seen in one's imagination and colouring one's whole soul and organism, does not

exist. We can assert that it exists, but we cannot prove it, because the only document of our assertion could be that the image has taken shape and body, and has been expressed.

(Croce as viewed by Vattimo, 1977)

In fact, internal reality, even when best expressed in the most sublime style, shall remain enclosed within itself or at least a significant part of it will remain unexpressed, not replicated and not replicable.

But artistic form/substance will indeed be concrete and definitively set into being as a finished work. To exist as a cultural object, a mental representation must become tangible reality. As we have tried to show, the use of a language makes it impossible for the representation to retain its original nature. To transfer this original nature, an artist has to use a language.

The transfer of a mental representation into a work of art does not permit a replica of it and this clearly points out a condition in the human being. However, the transfer will certainly permit the artist to enrich, and to make visible, the existence of additional performances which the artist will attribute to an exemplar (in the naturalistic and metaphysical or psychological senses).

An exemplar in art is not something that we can define once and for all. Instead, it becomes an inexhaustible reservoir of defining features, physical, dimensional or symbolic (depending on the observer's ideative and expressive preferences).

Let us suppose that an artist decides to represent, on a psychological level, grief in man. This choice implies:

1 that the artist excludes the representation of feelings that are different from and opposed to the one he has selected, i.e. human grief;
2 that the artist possesses, or creates, a language that is suitable, in his judgement, for representing this mood.

The psychological observation level chosen by the artist will permit him to approach at least one exemplar in which grief can be easily singled out as an essential performance and easily shared. The artist's work will be recognised as a work having universal value if the essential performance has highly persuasive contents, both semantic and aesthetic. Furthermore, in spite of the obvious and unavoidable reduction of ideative possibilities deriving from the obligation to choose only one observation level, and only one type of exemplar, the performance will not create, in the public, any radically extraneousness feeling. In other words, the artist, through the language chosen, must prime, to some degree, a cognitive process which justifies and makes his choice acceptable.

The artist proposes an essential performance which, at times, will eventually affirm itself as a possible, conventional and undisputed manner of observing that type or class of exemplars. An example of the universality that artistic expression sometimes attains is suggested, in the case of grief, by Winkelmann's description of the Laocoön:

The grief that one perceives in every muscle and in every tendon of the body, that is felt just by looking at that stomach painfully contracted, not to mention the face or the other parts that grieve, I say, does not express itself in the anger in his face or in his whole

> posture. He does not give any dreadful scream – as Virgil sings of in his Laocoön: the opening of the mouth does not permit him to do so; it is, instead, a murmuring full of anguish and repressed, as in Sadoleto's description. The pain in the body and the greatness of the soul are equally distributed over the whole composition of the figure and, in a manner of speaking, balance one another. Laocoön does suffer, but his grief is not like in Sophocles' Phyloctetes: his ruin penetrates our soul but we wish that we would be able to endure it like this great man does.
>
> (Winkelmann, 1992)

Representing grief does imply the exclusion of all other possible psychological types and does not exhaust *per se* all the possibilities of representation offered by the universe of man's inwardness. This clear-cut process of restriction in some way reminds us of N. Luhmann's 'transfer of reduced complexity' in communication (Luhmann, 1975).

However, any choice is required, by its own definition, to be arbitrary. Once arbitrariness has been used, the perceptible spectrum of options always appears to be infinite; at the outset, the reduction in complexity is only apparent/illusory.

It is pragmatically effective only after the artist has made reality compatible with the limits of man but it becomes an illusion as soon as reality overwhelms the simplification and re-introduces, from the window, once and for all, the alternatives, options and characters that had been laboriously put out through the door. This characteristic pertains not only to art but even to science and, of course, to artificialism, according to the inheritance principle explained earlier in this book.

According to this principle, every real action always carries within itself the whole inheritance of the realities involved, whether known or unknown, independently of any reductive intention and rational selection by the actor. Thus, the artist cannot but impose on the observer a clearly defined perceptual process and try to give it, through the use of a language, an efficient autonomy or protection from all the other possibilities that must be kept at bay.

The author's freedom of interpretation permits him to autonomously select the essential performance of a certain exemplar on one level of representation, in accordance with his vision of the world, and to represent it with his ability to use a technology (language) characteristic of his specific art.

To appreciate the artist's work, the public must reconstruct the essential performance of the exemplar, and it is sufficient that they appreciate a mental configuration or mood by comprehending the form of expression. To this end, the artist must make radical mental selections and propose a culturally involving observation level.

Once the essential performance has taken on a culturally legitimate form, it becomes part of the common way of thinking, seeing or listening and, as a result, it takes on a symbolic function proportional to the intrinsic greatness of style. The symbolic function is the fundamental function of a work of art. In fact,

> symbol, in the fine Greek tradition, is the *tessera hospitalis*, the pottery that is divided in two parts, one of which remains with the friend's host who stays behind, whilst the other part is given to the friend taking his leave. Thus, between the two of them, a link shall remain, over distance, and a hope that they will meet again.
>
> (Rosati, 1992)

It becomes ever more evident that the language used by the artist is not simply a tool to transfer a subjective mental image to the external world. Instead, it may have a more general cultural function. Saxl (1990) discusses the activity of Venetian miniaturists of the fourteenth century who reproduced both Greek and Latin classical models. He stresses how their imitations were greatly influenced by the culture they belonged to. At the same time they did not strengthen but destroyed the cultural distance between the classical culture and Venetian culture of the fourteenth century. To demonstrate this point, Saxl gives us the example of a manuscript from the first Decade of Livius, executed in Venice in 1372, and comments on a story illustrated in the drawings that illuminated the manuscript:

> Here we can see Marco Fabio's daughters; in the lower part of the page there is a typical Venetian well near the door of the house, and on this door the leaf. At the front of the house there is a wide window through which one can see the daughters in animated discussion. It

depicts a typical Venetian scene of that time, which has none of what we could call the magnificent style of Livius. But one may understand in this way the pleasure with which a fourteenth century Venetian used to read his Livius, and why these illustrations were so sought-after. They are indeed the graphical translation of the ancient Latin text into the Venetian current style.

(Saxl, 1990)

The relation created between an artistic representation and the norms, or conventional values, defining a culture prevent us from believing that culture may be considered only as the result of a sort of 'innocent' or pure perception of reality, to use Ruskin's words (1856). Indeed, if the language and the form used are sublime, the public will recognise in a reproduced image, for example, not what they see but what they know.

Artistic reproduction is not a simple representation of an object or of a sentiment, as seen at a given observation level: it is, on the contrary, a never-ending process of 'proposing'.

The painter, like any other artificialist, does not chose to reproduce an exemplar as such but his representation will be strongly influenced by the representational rules imposed by the culture he belongs to, and sometimes by his own new rules and by what he wants to communicate by choosing that exemplar, *vis à vis* the performance that is essential for him, in that moment.

Let us take, as an example, *Gelosia* (Jealousy), a lythography by Edward Munch as seen through Arnheim's eyes:

The rhombus face of the husband, whose hunchbacked body is just visible, appears hanging around the central horizontal axis in a non-structured darkness. The axis is not drawn explicitly, but it cuts the painting at eye level with the man, like a spit on the fire. His interest has focused, as seen in his eyes, to the semi-sections of the guilty couple. Nevertheless the communication bridge is broken down by the central vertical division, and the difference between the two worlds is fundamental. The white face of the man is open, while the man and the woman on the right are closed in their talk. They are also shifted up to reach the freedom of the right quadrant on the high part of the painting space, and are surrounded by a savagely active environment. There is a symmetric correspondence between the two worlds. The observer, while he enters the painting from the left, identifies himself with the intense and compact face of the jealous man; and it is from the perspective of this basis that he perceives the adultery scene.

(Arnheim, 1984)

A further confirmation of how much the mental representation of the artist is influenced by typical elements of the culture to which he belongs (and thus of how much these elements play in the expressive choices of the artist) is given by a description of jealous people found in *L'orso e il bacio*, a short story by the Scandinavian writer Isak Dinesen, a countryman of Munch:

when they remain sitting down to watch somebody. . .like a cat facing the hole of a mouse, they hold their breath, to such an extent that it is difficult to stir: and they become so stiff that their eyes have no life in them

(Arnheim, cit., p. 119)

Because the term *imago* comes from the Latin *imitor*, it means that an image is never completely the result of an arbitrary creation. Rather, it is the result of a continual imitation, reproduction and reactualisation of cultural models.

Art in all its greatness reveals, against all the constraints imposed by one's culture, the artist's effort to aim towards an intuition, the essence of things, at ever increasing levels. Then art takes on particular connotations and, so to speak, becomes the form of communication *par excellence*. On this point Gadamer writes:

> The language of the work of art is defined by the fact that the single work is able to concentrate and express that symbolic character which, from the hermeneutic point of view, belongs to every being (*essente*). Differently from all the other linguistic and non-linguistic traditions, it is, for every present, absolute presence and preserves in the same time, and in an enigmatic way, the upsetting and the collapse of all that is usual.
>
> (Gadamer, 1986)

In daily communication, when we want to transfer a sentiment or an experience of ours, we must often use analogies or trivial descriptions because we believe that, if a sentiment or a sensation is taken back to some elements of everyday language, our message will be easier to comprehend. The point here is that even when our listener gives a coherent answer, and confirms his understanding, we are the first to realise that in using our particular language we have only transferred a small part of what we wanted to communicate.

Even the artist commits his most intimate and profound feelings of his soul to a language. But, in contrast, his technical, or artificialistic, capabilities give him the possibility to express his mental representations with greater ability, that is to say, with a more powerful effect.

In other words, the artist is the one who, compared to other human beings, can communicate his specific aesthetic message with the best results. This means he not only has the capacity to transfer exemplars and performances which are less reduced or less impoverished than ones we might transfer, but that he is able to give them back enriched with artistic form, to the point that they will become elements of universal knowledge. Arnheim observes this in the thoughts of Lucien Freud, then a young and promising English painter:

> A moment of whole happiness never can be found in a work of art. We can see the promise in the creation act, but it disappears when the work is approaching its end. In that moment, indeed, the painter realises that he almost dared to hope that the figure could jump out alive.
>
> (Gombrich, 1965)

For this reason, a work of art, especially when it is great, is a celebration of the desperate effort of man trying with his entire soul (but differently from the common man, and possessing better tools) to abate the wall of incommunicability, transparent and enigmatic. Perhaps art is the demonstration, and the celebration as well, of the most stringent profound solitude that impregnates the existence of every human being and keeps him in a never-ending wait for a part that may complete him; that solitude which was most extraordinarily expressed, and not by chance, in the poetry of Quasimodo's poem *Ed é subito sera*.

If, on the one hand, artistic communication reveals man's illusion that he can duplicate an exemplar, it is, on the other, the very presence of such a limit, that holds art in common with other human activities which aim at reproduction, to induce and favour the research into new styles of expression. In fact, every discovery in art, as in science, will always announce or reveal the probable existence of new proposals, new observation levels, and new representations of essential performances that will be possible within a reality that always maintains its character of being infinite.

On this basis, new artistic languages and new styles emerge, to try once again, perhaps for the last time, to bridge the gap between the artist and the world. In brief, they attempt to reconstruct the link (bringing us back to a story recounted in Plato's *Symposium*), like the one that unites man and woman: both would be only one half of the primeval androgynous whom Zeus in his arrogance had punished by cutting in two parts, leaving both to live in the constant hope of being rejoined.

3. When artistic language is sublime

No one could contest that the idea of beauty expressed by Tiziano in the *Venere di Urbino* was dictated by one of his personal mental representations. However, the greatness of the artist does not only lie in the choice of the model, or in its posture: his success lies in having recombined technically the form and content in his imagination in such a complex way that he realises a work that could reflect not only his subjective vision of beauty, but also enclose within itself an unsuspected variety of possible representations of beauty, so as to propose itself as a universal cognitive event.

It is not coincidence that Freedberg (Freedberg, 1993), when he comments on the effectiveness and power of the images in referring to the *Venus* of Tiziano, points out that such representation is open to complex iconographic interpretations. Here, undoubtedly, the essential performance that the artist imposes on the public is *feminine* beauty. But the transduction of it into a work of art, as a reproduced reality, is open to a variety of different interpretative *modulations*.

Thus, in the end, Tiziano's representation appears as an abstraction distilled from the entire surface of the different conceptions of beauty.

The possible different readings, even after the inevitable selection of a single observation level, make it possible for us to infer that the artist was perfectly conscious that it is not possible to determine, once and for all, the constituting element of beauty; because, as Stendhal says, there are many kinds of beauty, at least as many as the usual ways to look for happiness. For example, to some people, the beauty Tiziano represents is above all a bursting sexuality; to others, the beauty is physical perfection, *tout court*; to others the representation does not suggest any of these. Instead, the type of beauty that the exemplar suggests is still one that celebrates the values of matrimonial fidelity.

Maybe Tiziano wanted to exhalt one of these features, or maybe all of them; maybe he intended to represent the idea of beauty he had taken from the mythological tradition. However, his most extraordinary style of representation permits the observer, through different historical periods, to recognise this essential performance without completely giving up his personal representation of feminine beauty. And this is because:

> a good painting, loyal like the dream that generates it, has to be produced like a universe. Like the creation, in the reality surrounding us, it is the result of several creations, where the ones that come after are able to complete the previous ones, in the same way a painting, harmonically drawn, consists of a set of overlapped paintings, where every new layer gives the dream a new reality, raising it a degree towards perfection.
>
> (Baudelaire, 1992)

This result, expressed so magnificently by Baudelaire, was certainly attained by Tiziano, since his representation of Venus is recognised by the observer as an expression of a sharable experience. Because of the rationality intrinsic to the 'rules' of composition present in artistic language, this expression can become an intellectual experience, where emotion and reason reach their maximum equilibrium or synthesis.

Clearly, this idea is opposite to the widespread view that art should only accomplish an emotive function. Without further deepening the problem, although it is of great scientific interest, this view brings us back, as Goodman justly observes,

> to the dispotic dichotomy between the cognitive and the emotive.
>
> (Goodman, 1976)

Further,

> in aesthetic experience emotions function at a cognitive level.
>
> (Goodman, ibid.)

In fact, always, according to Goodman:

> the cognitive, while opposed to the practical and to the passive, doesn't exclude the sensorial and the emotive; what we know through art, is felt in our bones, nerves and muscles, and is grasped by our mind, since all the sensitiveness and response capacity of the organism take part in the invention and in the interpretation of symbols.
>
> (Goodman, cit., p. 256)

Goodman's interpretation is one of the most widely accepted scientific positions on mental behaviour. Of course, we must cite the recent debate on artificial intelligence that has made valuable contributions to the interaction among these important mental dimensions.

However, at a merely artistic level, in order to comprehend how the interaction between reason and emotion may act on behaviour, one may refer to the case of religious artistic representations. It is interesting, for example, to quote the words of Giovanni Dominici, in 1403, on the relation between art and education. He was so convinced that artistic images could represent an effective tool in the learning of correct educative rules that he did not hesitate to suggest that in bedrooms there should be:

paintings, in the house, of saints or young virgins. . .The Virgin Mary with the baby in her arms and the little bird or the pomegranate in her hand is acceptable. Also acceptable is the nusrsing Jesus, the sleeping Jesus in the lap of the Mother.

(Dominici, 1403)

This applies not only to painting but to any type of artistic expression, to music as well as poetry or sculpture. Hence, the representation will be the result of a rational selection, of a personal choice of subjectively emphasised elements, that will exhalt some expressive possibilities and hamper others in favour of the elements chosen.

The unity of artistic representation with culturally shared systems of significance is warranted by the language, which builds:

> the fixing of the intuition-expression in an object which we shall name material or physical, as metaphors, though is not actually a matter of a material or physical nature, but of spiritual work.
>
> (Croce, in Vattimo, cit., p. 204)

4. Language and subjective reproduction

A work of art tends to generate a communicative reality and this happens when, as we have tried to show, the language that has made it possible for the artist to transduce a personal mental representation is culturally comprehended.

This correspondence between the artist and the user entails a requirement that the content carried over by the language be considered, in a sense, as already experienced through personal vicissitudes that have already been experienced. Maldonado writes:

> There is no doubt that to recognise something, the subject must know what is represented. In other words, the subject must have had previous perceptive experiences of the object.
>
> (Maldonado, 1992)

Indeed, the observer intuits the existence of a cultural affinity between himself and the artist at the very moment that he evaluates the work of art. Through the recognition enabled by the realistic reference that unites the image with the thing represented, the observer is induced to assume the same observation level and evidently the same exemplar.

In reality, even the most naïve observer/spectator is not limited to enjoying the work of art. Instead, even if he does not give a complete account, he evaluates and interprets it in the light of his own mental reference models. That is, to have access to a work of art means that the user, when observing a painting or a sculpture, reading a text, or listening to music, carries with him a set of prejudices, his historical reality.

Rather than being a hindrance, these prejudices are the means for comprehending and interpreting the work. This, in turn, does not mean that the person who interprets must of necessity enclose himself within his subjective world, thus allowing his prejudices to prevail. Instead, the observer, on the basis of his prejudices, will appreciate the alternatives apparent in the artistic representation. To use Gadamer's words, the artist should be sensible to the alternative, since it

> does not presuppose either objective neutrality or oblivion of self, but requires a precise consciousness of one's pre-suppositions and of one's prejudices. One must be conscious of his preventions, if the text must present itself in its alterity and possesses concretely the possibility of affirming its content of truth in comparison with the presuppositions of the interpreter.
>
> (Gadamer, 1994)

However, even if a work of art is great, it is possible that the formal language conveys a subjective representation that is not accepted by the interpreter. To quote Gadamer once again, this depends on a closure or a pretext for manifesting one's own personal conceptions or ideas. In fact, it is possible that at the start, the observer is open to confrontation, but that later, when confronted with the essential performance represented in the work of art, he does not find the observation level chosen for that specific representation to be sufficiently plausible or legitimate. Thus, the observer is confronted with the problem that he must doubt the validity of his own precognitions or prejudices.

Generally, the observer will interrupt the communication process, look away or stop reading or listening. Consequently the relation with the work of art cannot transform itself into an experience intellectually and culturally relevant. This may happen for two reasons:

1 one understands and realises that one's acceptance means that eventually one must discuss the plausibility of other personal mental representations;
2 the language used is so innovative that it does not permit the possibility of even a minimal semantic linking between the subjective representation of the artist and the representation that is cuturally accepted.

The first case has been commented on by Swinburne and Twain in reference to the Venus of Tiziano. Swinburne uncovers a subtle sexual tension that causes him to consider both the content and the form of artistic ideation as banal; Mark Twain describes an enclosure towards the representation, causing him to be scornfully hostile.

It is likely that for these two authors to have accepted the plausibility of Tiziano's representation, they would have had to critically revise other personal representations, for instance, their vision of feminine pudicity. After a visit to the *Uffizi*, Swinburne ironically writes to a friend of his:

> As far as the Venus by Tiziano is concerned – Saffo and Anattoria in a sole figure – four odious fingers buried *dans les fleurs de son jardin* – as if any creature in a range of thirty square miles could keep herself virtuous, exceeds my understanding capability. I think that Tannhause would never be bored with her, even until the end of the world: but who knows?

Mark Twain's comment is equally severe:

> It isn't that she is nude and lying on the bed, no, it is the attitude of one of her arms and of the hand. If I would venture on a description of that attitude, there would be great disdain and shouting – but look there, the Venus lying in such a way so that all can devour her with their eyes at their pleasure – and she has the right to stay there, since she is a work of art and, of course, art has its own privileges.
>
> (Freedberg, cit., p. 510)

The *Venere di Urbino* is only one of the many examples that testify to how the use of a language opens interpretative scenarios which were possibly unforeseen even by the author, who has been completely absorbed in his conception of beauty.

These scenarios go beyond the most intimate personal intuitions and motives of the author and, in the case of great pictures, can, as in the cases of Swinburne and Twain, even be rejected. To tell the truth, the history of art abounds in sensational examples that bear witness to the possibility of such incomprehension. Among these is that which involved the work of Caravaggio. We refer in particular to *San Matteo e l'angelo* (1597 - 8).

The painter was commissioned to represent the life of Saint Matthew by the priests of San Louis of France, probably through the intercession of his protector, Cardinal Dal Monte. His typical painting which is antimanierist, anti-idealist and anti-conformist led him to paint a saint who, as Bellori suggests (1992), did not look like a saint, having neither decorum nor a devout attitude. It was vulgar, showing in the foreground his legs crossed, and large naked feet. He seemed like a rough and illiterate old man whose hand had to be guided by an angel so that he might write the gospel.

The painting was destined for the altar of Cappella Contarelli but was not accepted by the priests of Saint Louis. The artist was required to produce a different representation of the Saint, which is certainly much less spontaneous than the first one. The original work was later sold to the Friedrick Museum of Berlin and destroyed in 1945, during the battle for the German capital.

However, in the case of great art, such instances of art being rejected owing to a lack of appreciation of the work of the artist on the part of the user are rare. They represent normal statistical clusters around a majority clustering of attitudes of acceptance. The fact that a work of art is considered to be great, beyond any mere temporal question, means, therefore, that most often common sense has prevailed over rejection, since the work suceeded in showing that it belongs to systems of stably interiorised meaning. That is, acceptance by the public requires that the work have the capacity to reflect some nucleus of anthropological elements, presumably universal, in line with the evolving general cultural system.

A second reason why there might be a disruption in communication between the artist and the user is because the language used is so innovative that it does not allow the possibility of even a minimal semantic link between the subjective representation of the artist and the experience of the user. As in the situation we have previously described, the observer does not understand the language used; therefore he must, more or less rationally, reject it.

This is the case, for example, with certain modern and contemporary art that uses a language generating forms that apparently have no empirical meaning. Because abstract language is an expression of the artist's refusal of the object, of a tangible reality, it cannot, by definition, rely on consolidated semantical and syntactical canons.

This phenomenon could not happen through the language adopted in the figurative arts: it is understood that there is a sort of total balance between form and content in non-figurative art which, as such, tends to annihilate the object, and does not permit the observer to recognise the essential performance of an exemplar represented in the work. This inevitably prevents the necessary psychological connection between what is represented in the work and the receiver; therefore the latter cannot decipher and learn the form, the expressive style, into which the exemplar and the performance are transduced.

Even the most abstract ideations can become accepted – and this applies also to the most revolutionary undertakings – provided that the artist, at the very moment that he expresses his rejection of the object, invents and makes accessible the new criteria or 'rules of reading', without recourse to captions or exegeses taken from artistic communication as such (the only acceptable exception to this is the title).

In other words, for this type of language to become accepted, new criteria, canons or languages must be invented, proposed or imposed by the artist, at the very moment of his rejection of the object. If this is not done, the artist ends up in a very delicate relationship with a minimal nucleus of anthropological elements, the lack of which may trigger a desolant solipsistic process. In this process art will end up dramatically losing its essence at the very moment that it frees itself from the envelope of the things represented.

This position is somewhat analogous with the view of objective relativism (brought forward in TA), but emphasises the subjective component of relativism as an ideative primacy of the ego, a primacy that pretends, at the moment it claims to become art, to generate shareable, objective worlds.

However, since acceptability cannot rely upon consolidated symbolic canons, it must find its realisation through new criteria, canons and languages that the artist will generate and communicate in some way. Indeed, some artists have tried to do just this: consider Klee or Kandisky. Nevertheless, as Gehelen rightly remarks (Gehelen, 1989), their effort resulted in a language only for themselves, since it did not make any reference to any nucleus, even minimal, of culturally recognisable values. Of course, their terminological efforts were insufficient, since they were difficult to extend beyond their own ideations. In fact, the lack of consolidated languages, canons and symbolisms favours only a sort of communicative detachment, of *attente*.

The work and its author, in the name of a 'truth' that is only interior, appear to close in on themselves, denying to art the possibility of exerting an immediate communicative function, in the hope, often illusory, of eliminating any common and 'external' meaning and of replacing it with the same number of internal elements that will be imposed only by virtue of their own expressive power.

And then, as in the paradoxical comedies of Ionesco, dialogue is replaced by monologue. Facing the work of art, each person continues to follow his own train of thought and sees in the case of painting, or hears in the case of music, what he wants to see or hear but cannot explain what he really sees or hears.

To give some examples, in the white paintings of Malevic, in the cuts of Fontana, and in Pollock as well, memory seems to disappear, giving way to the deep and tormented sea of being. In Kandisky, whose art is intended as a a research of interiority and is not objectified, the work is dictated by a profound necessity to make transparent the convinction that this choice is the only possible one, so that art may be regarded as the expressive result of 'real' tensions, although exclusively spiritual origin, or at least only subjective.

This objective, by definition, cannot depend on there being well-defined rules, even in the micro-world of the artist. But fortunately it ends – perhaps only for the great artists – in a useless act of rebellion whose representation is in any case evident, and therefore recognisable in the same way and for the same reason that the tragic meaning of existence emerges from the tormented figures of Michelangelo.

If we leave out the schools and the exasperated movements, for which the loss of the object entails also an obstinate refusal of the real, the research of 'pure' forms, of a specific and irreductible expressivity as compared to the one that has been denied, must tend, perhaps even more directly than other, to more realistic styles, towards the discovery of deeper and more real mechanisms, both subjective and objective. This means that, in the best cases, this results not only in the discovery of other realities, but also in the revelation of unknown aspects, perhaps of some internal realities, new perspectives, be they at different observation levels of the unique reality of which we are a part.

It is an illusion to believe that art can invent radically different realities from typically artistic realities and, in any case, the artist's *ego* never runs the risk of being overwhelmed by the real – as many contemporary artists fear – since his subjective and innovative contribution, from the choice of one observation level to the formal transduction of the essential performance, is not only possible, but unavoidable.

5. Art as communication

Art, as has been emphasised above, is artificial because it reproduces something that exists with materials and procedures different from those which give birth to the exemplar. Art is then an original construction of accepted significations which, by nature, are deeply rooted in a known reality. Thus art permits the user to restore the necessary and customary connections between reality as lived and reality as represented. This is a necessary, though not a sufficient, condition to define the communicative function of art.

To propose a specific theory of aesthetics is beyond the scope of sociology. Yet we must remark that in some contemporary art, the presumed 'discovery' of other realities, radically opposed to the naturally given reality, necessarily determines the fall of the communicative function which is traditionally attributed to art.

The representation of fragments of the idea of a reality, that the authors themselves often hesitate to realise when confronted with the choice of their semantic tool, cannot any longer be regarded as a vehicle of aesthetic experience, hence as a culturally shared product. In other words, the loss of the object presupposes that the observer owns a type of preparation which can be realised only through a complete immersion in the artist's subjectivity. Because of this loss, for instance in many contemporary works that do not respect even a minimal nucleus of shared elements, it is not possible (as Proust affirms in his *Recherche* when he comments on the representations of his friend Elastir):

> to perceive the charm of each of them consisted in a sort of metamorphosis in the things represented, analogous to metaphor in poetry; and that if God the Father had created things by naming them, Elastir re-created things by unnaming them or by giving them a new name.
>
> (Proust, 1981)

The representational argument is thus totally compatible with the limits and attitudes of human nature and with the cultural function proper to art as a form of communication.

However, 'to represent' does not mean, in this sense, 'to reproduce only the visible part', but it means, above all, to show what may not be observed in the visible portion (including the internal states of the artist's *ego*). This does not mean, of course, that a hypothetical internal reality of the subject is made visible: on the contrary. It does mean that, starting from fragments of a shareable reality, the fragments are modulated and subjective models of what is possible are built. What is possible, in any case, does not imply a removal from the real: it originates from the real and only in this sense does it become a instigator of new projects.

Contrary to Malevic's view of new art, the content of art, as a cultural product, cannot be art itself. An art that founds itself on art is a nonsense, because any human expression, if it is to be revealed, can only appeal to the domain of sensible phenomena.

When Malevic choses the square as a form not pertaining to an object, we find ourselves enquiring into the reason for his choice; for, in Western logic, the perception of the 'non-object' is impossible (Menna, 1983).

Malevic himself realises that this logical solution is impossible (even if he realises it indirectly, and unfortunately not to find a remedy but to further emphasise the non-objective nature of his art). He writes:

> When, in 1913, in the course of my desperate efforts to set art free from the ballast of objectivity, I took refuge in the form of a square and I exhibited a painting representing only a black square on a white background, the critics and the public started to complain: 'All we have loved has been lost. We are in a desert. Only a black square on a white background is before us!' And they would start looking for 'overwhelming' words, to remove the symbol of the desert, and to find again, in the 'dead square' the favoured image of 'reality', 'the true objectivity' and 'the moral sensibility'.
>
> (in de Michelis, 1989)

In short, when the artist wishes to communicate his personal mental representation, he follows a clear praxis:

1 he always *assumes*, on one observation level, the exemplar that he will reproduce as a real referent (perhaps only an internal referent);
2 he *selects*, or *attributes* to the exemplar he has chosen some essential performances, depending on his personality and the culture of his time;
3 he actually *imitates* the exemplar, but in many ways he does not reproduce the full reality of it;
4 he transduces the exemplar and its performances into only one subject and language and, therefore, he *transfigures*, reduces or exalts them.

In a sense, this pattern is the prerequisite condition for linking the figurative and non-figurative arts. If the latter is to continue to be art, and not something different, the artist must be able to give a recognisable consistency and language to formal expression. In the same time, he will thus avoid that formal expression, in its effort to free itself from the imitation of nature, and will, once again, fall into a kind of naturalistic illusion.

Indeed, the languages used in modern and contemporary art do not often make transparent the content that the form intends to represent. Hence languages give origin to a circular process which, in Jauss's view, goes from the experience of the work to the experience of oneself, and does not open to the experience of others (Jauss, 1985).

On the communicative level, the problem posed by some abstract art is not the introduction of forms which contradict the ordinary relations between reality and representation of reality. The problem is rather the claim that the observer may be able to recognise the meaning of what is being represented *independently* of possessing a knowledge derived from experience and a mental representation of at least some of the sensorially perceived forms. In other words, the argument that art can stand as a self-justifiable philosophical system is illusory. This, perhaps, could be acceptable for music, owing to its lack of necessary external reference, as has been clearly maintained in this book by Negrotti, but the other arts, and particularly painting, cannot avoid the connection with the sensible world since they depend on it.

The view which says that the reference object may be ignored is the more illusory, when the presuppositions of art lie in the refusal of significance and in the acceptance of the semantic ambiguity of sign. Here the point is not only that the world of things and men would suddenly become devoid of meaning and would have to be forgotten; nor that it would become a refusal of naturalistic myths and beauty. Rather, art, to answer itself, must explore man and the world around him. What this adds up to, then, is that a work of art clearly cannot escape from its true nature: it is a message from the artist to the audience and, as such, must, in the first instance, follow the rules of information theory (Moles, 1960). If perception of the message is to be transformed into aesthetic appreciation, the artist and the observer at least must have some symbolic elements in common ('common' because these have been generated within one's culture).

Only thus does, *au fond*, perception become a helpful tool in comprehending the innermost significance of reality; it becomes invention and creation.

Things would not improve if a communication structure were to become crystallized with time. However, this process is not only impossible but undesirable. Like other forms of communication, artistic language inevitably possesses a relatively unstable structure and, like ideas, it is bound to transform itself, or to fuse, with other languages, in relation to changing significance systems and expressive techniques. Only by starting from an assured, if even minimally, semantic acceptability, will art originate new and culturally meaningful realities.

References – Case Study II

ARNHEIM, R. (1984), Il potere del centro, Einaudi, Torino, 1984, p. 120.

BAUDEALAIRE, C. (1992), Scritti sull'arte, Einaudi, Torino, p. 228.

BELLORI, P. (1672), Le vite dÀ Pittori, Scultori et Architetti moderni, Roma, in Panofsky, Nuova Italia, Firenze, 1989.

BRANDI, C. (1966), Le due vie, Laterza, Bari.

CALABRESE, O. (1989), Il linguaggio dell'arte, Bompiani, Milano pp. 8-9.

DE MICHELIS, (1989), Le avanguardie artistiche del novecento, Feltrinelli, Milano, p. 269.

DOMINICI, G. (1860), Regole del governo di cura familiare, Firenze, seen in Fiedler, K., 1876, Uber die Beurteilung von Werken der Bildenden Kunst, Leipzig, Teubner, tr. it. L'attivitá artistica, Venezia, 1963, p. 131-2.

FREEDBERG, D. (1993), Il potere delle immagini, Einaudi, Torino, pp. 34-8.

GADAMER, H. (1960), Verita' e metodo. Principi di una ermeneutica filosofica, in Tassinari, S. (1994), Storia della filosofia, vol. 3. Bulgarini, Firenze, p. 306.
GADAMER, H. (1986), L'attualita' del bello, Marietti, Genova.
GEHLEN, A. (1989), Quadri d'epoca, Guida Editori, Napoli, p. 196.
GOMBRICH, E.H. (1965), Arte e illusione, Einaudi, Torino, p. 116.
GOMBRICH, E.H. (1989), La storia dell'arte raccontata da E.H.Gombrich, Einaudi, Torino.
GOODMMAN, N. (1976), I linguaggi dell'arte, Milano.
JAKOBSON, R. (1958), Closing statements: linguistics and poetics, in Th. A. Sebeok, Style in language, New York – London, 1960, pp. 350-77.
JAUSS, H.R. (1972), Apologia dell'esperienza estetica, Einaudi, Torino, pp. 34-5.
LUHMANN, N. (1975), Macht, Ferdinand Enke Verlag, Stuttgart, tr. it, Potere e complessitá sociale, Il Saggiatore, Milano, 1979.
MALDONADO, T. (1992), Reale e Virtuale, Feltrinelli, Milano, p. 34.
MENNA, F., Profezie di una società estetica, Officina Edizioni, Roma, pp. 66-7.
MOLES, A. (1960), Creation artistique et mecanisme de l'esprit, in Ring des arts, Parigi, p. 380.
MORRIS, C. (1938), Foundations of the Theory of Signs, Encyclopedia of Unified Sciences, (trad. it. lineamenti di una teoria dei segni, Paravia, Torino, 1954).
MORRIS, C. (1939), Aesthetics and the Theory of Signs, in Journal of Unifiied Science, 8.
MOUNIN, C. (1968), Introduction à la sèmiologie, Minuit, Paris.
NEGROTTI, M. (1993), 'Towards a Theory of the Artificial', Cybernetics & Human Knowing, Brier, Odense, 2,2.
NEGROTTI, M. (1994), 'L'artificiale, questo sconosciuto', Sistemi e Impresa, XXXX, 7, sett., Milano.
NEGROTTI, M. (1995), Verso una teoria dell'artificiale, in M. Negrotti (ed.) Artificialia, Clueb, Bologna, 1995, p. 70.
PASSERON, R. (1962), L'oeuvre d'art et les fonctions de l'apparence, Plon, Paris.
PASSERON, R. Clefs pour la peinture, Seghers, Paris.
PIERCE, C.S. (1980), Semeiotica. I fondamenti della semeiotica cognitiva, Einaudi, Torino.
PROUST, M., La Recherche, vol. 1, 1981, p. 902.
READ, H. (1955), Icon and Idea. The Function of Art in the Development of Human Consciousness, Faber and Faber, London.
RIEGL, A. (1901), Spätrömisches Kunstindutrie, Siemens, Berlin, tr. it. Industria artistica tardoromana, Einaudi, Torino, 1853.
RIESMAN, D., The Lonely Crowd, Yale University Press, New Haven, tr. it., La folla solitaria, Il Mulino, Bologna, 1956.
ROSATI, M.P. (1992), La funzione trascendente, in °topon, annoII, vol.II, 1-2, Istituto Mythos, Roma, 1993, p. 92.
RUSKIN, J. (1896), Elementi del disegno e della pittura, Bocca, Torino, p. 4 nota 1., cfr. E. Gombrich, Arte e illusione, Einaudi, Torino, 1965, p. 359.
SAXL, F. (1990), La storia delle immagini, Laterza, Roma-Bari, p. 81.
VATTIMO, G. (1977) (a cura di), Estetica moderna, Il Mulino, Bologna, p. 203.
WIMSATT, W.K., The verbal icon, University of Kentucky Press, 1954.
WINCKELMANN, J.J. (1992), Pensieri sull'imitazione, Aesthetica, Palermo, p. 43.
WöLFFLIN, H. (1915), Kunst Geshtliche Kunstbegriffe, Basel, Schwabe & Co, tr. it. I concetti fondamentali di storia dell'arte, Milano, Minuziano, 1946.